Migrants of Identity

BERG

Ethnicity and Identity

SERIES

ISSN: 1354-3628

General Editors:
Shirley Ardener, **Founding Director, Centre for Cross-Cultural Research on Women, University of Oxford**

Tamara Dragadze, **School of Slavonic and East European Studies, University of London**

Jonathan Webber, **Institute of Social and Cultural Anthropology, University of Oxford**

Books previously published in the Series

Sharon Macdonald (ed.), *Inside European Identities: Ethnography in Western Europe*

Joanne Eicher (ed.), *Dress and Ethnicity*

Martin Stokes (ed.), *Ethnicity, Identity and Music: The Musical Construction of Place*

Jeremy MacClancy (ed.), *Sport, Identity and Ethnicity*

Simone Abram, Jackie Waldren and Donald Macleod (eds), *Tourists and Tourism: Identifying with People and Places*

Jeremy MacClancey (ed.), *Contesting Art: Art, Politics and Identity in the Modern World*

Sharon Macdonald, *Reimaging Culture: Histories, Identities and the Gaelic Renaissance*

Migrants of Identity

Perceptions of Home in a World of Movement

EDITED BY

Nigel Rapport and Andrew Dawson

Oxford • New York

First published in 1998 by
Berg
Editorial offices:
150 Cowley Road, Oxford, OX4 1JJ, UK
70 Washington Square South, New York, NY 10012, USA

Berg is the imprint of Oxford International Publishers Ltd.

Library of Congress Cataloging-in-Publication Data

A catalogue record for this book is available from the Library of Congress.

British Library Cataloguing-in-Publication Data

A catalogue record for this book is available from the British Library.

ISBN   1 85973 994 6 (Cloth)
       1 85973 999 7 (Paper)

Typeset by JS Typesetting, Wellingborough, Northants.

[I]t becomes ever more urgent to develop a framework of thinking that makes the migrant central, not ancillary, to historical process. We need to disarm the genealogical rhetoric of blood, property and frontiers and substitute for it a lateral account of social relations . . . An authentically migrant perspective would, perhaps, be based on an intuition that the opposition between here and there is itself a cultural construction, a consequence of thinking in terms of fixed entities and defining them oppositionally. It might begin by regarding movement, not as an awkward interval between fixed points of departure and arrival, but as a mode of being in the world.

Paul Carter: *Living in a New Country*

Contents

Acknowledgements

In drawing up this volume, many debts have been incurred. In particular, the editors would like to thank Robert Paine for his critique of an earlier gathering of papers and speakers in a workshop ('At Home (or Homeless) in Europe?') at the 1994 Association of American Anthropologists conference in Atlanta. The Universities of Hull and St Andrews were also generous in providing grants for conference travel and administration.

Further debts are owed to the following for their constructive commentaries at various stages of the project's becoming: Michael Anderson, Aleksander Boskovic, Peter Collins, Eve Darian-Smith, Judith Doyle, Milyan Hills, Julia Holdsworth, Tamara Kohn, Stuart Mclean, Caroline Oliver, Nerys Roberts, Jonathan Skinner, Deborah Wickering and Thomas Wilson. At Berg Publishers, Kathryn Earle has remained a most supportive editor. Finally, we are grateful to Andrew Strathern for nominating an alternative title for our theme: 'On the dialectic between motion and emotion'.

As the project was being undertaken, two overwhelmingly sad deaths occurred: that of Robert Paine's wife, Lisa Gilad, in a car accident in Canada; and that of Ladislav Holy, from cancer, shortly after the writing of his chapter had been completed (with the help of Kate Mortimer). We miss them both, and it is to their memories, with respect and love, that this volume is dedicated.

NJR and AD
St Andrews and Hull 1998

Part I
Opening a Debate

The Topic and the Book

Nigel Rapport and Andrew Dawson

'**M**igrants of identity' was the phrase that Theodore Schwartz used in the mid-1970s to describe the continual search by American youth for an identity that they found 'acceptable and authentic' (1975:130). Individual identity was always and everywhere dynamic, Schwartz suggested, always something 'problematic', something calling for a resolution that was never wholly acquired, because it was through the search that the individual *per se* came to be defined. However, what he felt was particular to the search of contemporary Americans was the location of that search in time as well as space; individuals increasingly used time as an anchor for their identity, as a means of bounding and expressing their membership of groups, so that cultural difference became synonymous with generational difference. Certainly, as global travel and communications made distinctive identities set up purely in terms of place and geographical difference (geophysical criteria alone) less viable and attractive, Schwartz concluded (1976:217–21), so 'authentically different identities' encompassed other, new kinds of difference.

Since Schwartz wrote, much ink has been spilled in anthropology concerning 'modern cultural identity'. Schwartz was not the first to consider space–time co-ordinates, or to hypothesize a play-off between time and space in the constitution of modern identities (*vide* Innes, McLuhan); but his ideas certainly resonate with what has become of major anthropological import: an appreciation of the practices of identity-formation in a world (modern, late-capitalist, postmodern, *fin-de-siècle*, supermodern) where processes of globalization (creolization, compression, hybridity, synchronicity) have made traditional conceptions of individuals as members of fixed and separate societies and cultures redundant.

3

This is a book about contemporary identity; it is a book where identity is treated as a search, either physical or cognitive, and is conceived of in terms of fluidities – of time and space, time or space. It is also a book that explores the implications of such fluidity for anthropological theory. More precisely, in place of traditional anthropological classifications of identity, we discuss and analyse the search for identity in terms of conceptualizations of 'home'.

Comprising eight substantive chapters, plus a polemical introductory essay and a concluding critique, the book intends to offer a new slant on questions of identity in the modern world in two main ways. First, identity is treated in relation to, even as inextricably tied to, fluidity or movement across time and space. Second, the book is animated by the claim that traditional anthropological classifications of identity fail to convey this movement. Hence, the book calls for the anthropological appreciation of 'home' as a useful analytical construct: as a means of encapsulating, linking and also transcending traditional classifications.

Furthermore, the dual approach of examining contemporary identity in terms of home and of movement enables the book to treat migrancy both physically and cognitively. 'A world of movement' can be understood in terms of actual physical motion around the globe and also as an imagination: an awareness of movement as a potentiality and a vicarious knowledge of movement as a phenomenon of overriding impingement.

In short, this volume explores physical and cognitive movement within and between homes, and the relations between the two; in treating analytically a contemporary 'migrancy of identity', the book examines individuals and groups in movement within and between conceptions of home.

A World of Movement

A traditional concern of anthropological description and analysis has been the identification of socio-cultural 'places': fixities of social relations and cultural routines localized in time and space. Societies were identified with cultures conceived as complete wholes; here were localized universes of meaning, with individuals and groups as their transparent components, their representative expressions.

Of late, this localizing image of separate and self-sufficient worlds (of relations, culture, identity and history) has come in for much criticism, from perspectives professional, epistemological and political. At the root of this criticism is the claim that the image may never have been more than a useful ideology that served the interests of (some) local people, and a provisional myth that was animated by the practices of (some) anthropologists. For example, at one level, the image has been compounded by claiming fieldwork – in its traditional sense of going to a place, undergoing a process of acculturation, and returning from that place – as a professional rite of passage. The point is that the transition metaphor becomes meaningless if cultures are not seen as separate entities that can be entered and exited.

At another level, the image is compounded by anthropology's traditionally authoritative, realist and objectivist style of writing (cf. James *et al.* 1996:1). The separate socio-cultural place, usually expressed as the 'field', has its uses as a trope of authority. It is represented variously as the locus of a panoptical gaze, as a part through which one can represent the cultural whole, and, evoking the authoritative tones of natural science, as a pseudo-laboratory (cf. Clifford 1992:98–9). In this respect, too, the narratives of entry and exit that the idea of separateness facilitates are crucial, for it is distance that is seen to enable objectivity (cf. Pratt 1986).

At another level still, and somewhat paradoxically (given that the anthropological construction of separate socio-cultural places as coherent universes of meaning grew out of an entirely laudable concern to challenge the implicit ethnocentrism of Western modes of understanding), the image resonates with a series of politically reactionary discourses: from the idea of primitive cultures perfectly attuned to their usually remote and marginal environments (cf. Ellen 1986), to hegemonic discourses of sedentarism, and modern-day and exclusionary nationalist ideologies (cf. Foster 1991:91; Kapferer 1988:88).

Finally, the image is reinforced by anthropology's own exclusionary practices. In an era characterized by challenges to its territory from other disciplines, anthropology appears often torn. On the one hand, there is a recognition of the need to develop methodological practices that come to terms with the global interconnectedness of societies and cultures (e.g. Marcus 1995). On the other hand, anthropology engages in a defensive strategy whereby its distinctiveness is defined ever more in terms of a methodological commitment to spending an appreciable time in one local setting (cf. Gupta and Ferguson 1997:4).

Having said this, our interest here, however, is the substantive critique: the image of socio-cultural 'places' rests on a conceptualization of time and space that, it is widely held, contemporary movement in the world now overwhelms and relativizes. As John Berger phrased it (1984:55), market forces, ideological conflicts and environmental change now uproot such a number of people that migration can more and more be portrayed as 'the quintessential experience' of the age. At the least, mass media of communication, a global economy (of individual entrepreneurship), global politics, ease of travel, global tastes, fashions, texts and entertainments – in a word, a global eclecticism – now more and more make of the world an actual 'oyster' in the way Shakespeare had Pistol, four hundred years ago, boast of it, metaphorically, to Falstaff. Hence, from an ideology of totalizing 'places', one moves to an actuality of individuals and groups entering and leaving spaces. Or, in the terminology of Marc Auge, it is 'non-places' that have become the real measure of our time (1995:79). Here are transit points and temporary abodes: wastelands, building sites, waiting-rooms, refugee camps, stations, malls, hotels, where travellers break step and thousands of individual itineraries momentarily converge. It is not, Auge admits, that socio-cultural places (groups, goods and economies) cannot reconstitute themselves in practice, but that place and non-place now represent ongoingly contrastive modalities. Certainly in terms of individual awareness, even if not of universal practice, movement has become fundamental to modern identity, and an experience of non-place (beyond 'territory' and 'society') an essential component of everyday existence.

Home

If population movement, travel, economy and communication make the globe a unified space, then, for Auge, no place is completely itself and separate, and no place is completely other (cf. Massey 1991, 1992). And in this situation, people are always and yet never 'at home': always and never 'at ease with the rhetoric of those with whom they share their lives' (Auge 1995:108). In John Berger's commentary, in a quintessentially migrant age, the idea of 'home' undergoes dramatic change at the least.

Salient among traditional conceptualizations of home was the stable physical centre of one's universe – a safe and still place to leave and return to (whether house, village, region or nation), and a principal focus of one's concern and control. Even if the potential mobility of home was attested to – the tent of the nomad – still the focus was on the necessary controlling of space. 'Home' easily became a synonym for 'house', within which space and time were structured functionally, economically, aesthetically and morally, so that the coordinated workings of home were seen to give on to an 'embryonic' or 'virtual community' (Douglas 1991).

As Douglas elaborated, home could be defined as a pattern of regular doings, furnishings and appurtenances, and a physical space in which certain communitarian practices were realized. Homes began by bringing space under control and thus giving domestic life certain physical orientations: 'directions of existence' (Douglas 1991:290). Homes also gave structure to time and embodied a capacity for memory and anticipation. In short, homes could be understood as the organization of space over time, and the allocation of resources in space and over time. Then again, the routinization of space–time was also aesthetic and moral; it provided a model for redistributive justice, sacrifice, and the common, collective good. Homes were communities in microcosm, which coordinated their members by way of open and constant communication, a division of labour, rights and duties, a commensal meal, and a rotation of access to resources. They encompassed total prestatory systems that exerted possibly tyrannous control over their members' minds, bodies and tongues in their search for solidarity.

However, to understand homes in this way – as being synonymous with Durkheimian notions of solidary communities and coercive institutions in microcosm – is anachronistic, and provides little conceptual purchase on a world of contemporary movement. A broader understanding is possible and necessary, one concerned less with the routinization of space and time than with their fluidity and with individuals' continuous movement through them (cf. Minh-ha 1994:14). In essence, a far more mobile conception of home should come to the fore, as something 'plurilocal' (Rouse 1991), something to be taken along whenever one decamps. As Berger describes, for a world of travellers, of labour migrants, exiles and commuters, home comes to be found in a routine set of practices, a repetition of habitual interactions, in styles of dress and address, in memories and myths, in stories carried around in one's head. People are more at home nowadays, in short, in 'words, jokes, opinions, gestures, actions, even the way one wears a hat' (Berger 1984:64). 'Home', in Bammer's words, 'is neither here nor there (. . .) rather, itself a hybrid, it is *both* here *and* there – an amalgam, a pastiche, a performance' (1992:ix). Or else, in a reactionary refusing of the world of movement, one is at home in a paradoxical clamouring for 'particularisms': in a multiplicity of invented, 'primordial', places for which one is perhaps willing to kill and die (Auge 1995:35; cf. also Harvey 1989). Here, in Robins' depiction (1991:41), is 'the driving imperative to salvage centred, bounded and coherent identities – placed identities for placeless times'.

Through different case-studies of contemporary identity, its local conceptualization and management, we shall explore ideas such as Auge's and Berger's on the relations between notions of home and movement across the globe, and on the changing nature of these notions. We examine home as part of local discourse. We study the 'narratives' of home of various kinds (orderly spoken scenarios, official communiqués, habitual social exchanges, routine behavioural practices) that individuals today 'write' (transcribe, enact, embody) for themselves. One writes, as Strauss puts it (1984:103), 'in order gradually to create for oneself an intellectual home (*eine geistige Heimat*)'. To traverse the globe with their informants, then, is for anthropologists to record the 'moving' homes of various kinds, behavioural and ideational, that individuals construct and enact. Here are routine practices and narrations that do not merely tell of home, but represent it: serve, perhaps, as cognitive homes in themselves.

We also discuss the viability of 'home' as an analytical construct. Our reasons for this are rooted in the expressive deficiencies of traditional classifications of identity, such as locality, ethnicity, religiosity and nationality. First, none of these terms conveys the universally affective power of home. While it may sometimes come laden with reactionary resonances, 'home' should not be ceded to the political Right; 'home', as Torgovinick argues (1992:133), is one of the few remaining utopian ideals, and does not need to be replaced by more abstract analytical terms. Secondly, and as importantly, in a situation where traditional classifications of identity often fail to provide adequate understandings of proximate behaviours – adequate appreciations of individual actors' world-views and their drives to new (often multiple and paradoxical) sites and levels of association, of incorporation and exclusion – 'home' may be of use.

'Home' can serve to encapsulate, but also to link and transcend, traditional classifications. Similarly, as a concept, 'home' can and must compass cultural norms and individual fantasies, representations of and by individuals and groups (cf. Wright 1991:214); it can and must be sensitive to numerous modalities, conventional and creative, and to allocatings of identity that may be multiple, situational and paradoxical. 'Home' brings together memory and longing, the ideational, the affective and the physical, the spatial and the temporal, the local and the global, the positively evaluated and the negatively. As Simmel sums it up, 'home' involves a 'unique synthesis': 'an aspect of life and at the same time a special way of forming, reflecting and interrelating the totality of life' (1984:93–4).

The paradoxes surrounding the concept of home may be of a number of kinds. Firstly, there is the paradox, already alluded to, that an increase in movement around the world, and the freeing up of restrictive boundaries to travel, is accompanied by an increase in renascent particularisms. In Hobsbawm's terms (1991:63), home as an essentially private and individual routine, fantasy, memory, longing or presence – *Heim* – is impacted upon by *Heimat*: an attempt publicly and collectively to impose home as a social fact and a cultural norm to which some must belong and from which others must be excluded. Hence, 'exiles' and 'refugees'; and hence, too, tramps and 'bag-people' expelled from the ranks of those felt deserving of combining house and home.

There is also the paradox that it is perhaps only by way of transience and displacement that one achieves an ultimate sense of belonging. To be at home 'in one's own place', as Kateb (1991:135) puts it, it is necessary to become alienated and estranged to some degree, mentally or spiritually. Exile is a resource inasmuch as it gives on to that vantage-point from which one is best able to come to know oneself, to know oneself best (cf. Sarup 1994:96). It is for this reason too that home 'moves' us most powerfully as absence or negation (cf. Hobsbawm 1991:63; Rapport 1994a).

Finally, there is the paradox concerning whether the movement to which home is party is linear or circular. Chambers (1994a) is definite that the migratory processes of the world are linear, since no returns are possible or implied. The journey of our lives is not between fixed positions, and there is no itinerary affording routes back again. And yet, while it may be true that 'the destiny of our journeys' is not circular, still home represents both 'the place from which we set out and to which we return, at least in spirit' (Hobsbawm 1991:65). We engage in ongoing transgression partly out of a desire to overcome it, and find our end in our beginning.

Perhaps it is part-and-parcel of an appreciation of the way that individuals live in movement, transition and transgression, that its conceptualization, as 'home', is to be similarly paradoxical and trans-gressive. 'Home', we suggest as a working definition, 'is where one best knows oneself' —where 'best' means 'most', even if not always 'happiest'. Here, in sum, is an ambiguous and fluid but yet ubiquitous notion, apposite for a charting of the ambiguities and fluidities, the migrancies and paradoxes, of identity in the world today.

The structure of this book is as follows:

In an introductory chapter, 'Home and Movement: A Polemic', the volume editors speculate in greater detail upon some of the possible relations between movement (physical and cognitive) and identity (individual and social), and how these relations may be seen to be changing in a contemporary cultural milieu of globalization. Beginning with Batesonian notions of the connections between movement and perception, and perception and the ordering of identity, the piece proceeds with a consideration of anthropological appreciation of movement, traditional and current. This is followed by the introduction of 'home' as a phenomenon, that 'mysterious atmosphere of a personal kind', in Stanley Spencer's word-painting, by which procedures and surroundings are made known as one's own.

The chapter concludes with a discussion of the classic sociological text, *The Homeless Mind*, where, some twenty years ago, P. and B. Berger and H. Kellner sought a link between modernity and a particular kind of consciousness. In transit between a plurality of life-worlds, they contended, modern individuals come to be at home in none. Hence, the loss of an absolute reality in a unified traditional life-world gives rise to 'homeless minds'. Rapport and Dawson argue, however, that while this remains a challenging thesis, it is ethnographically ungrounded. Being 'at home' and being 'homeless' are not matters of movement, of physical space, or of the fluidity of socio-cultural times and places, as such. One is at home when one inhabits a cognitive environment in which one can undertake the routines of daily life and through which one finds one's identity best mediated – and homeless when such a cognitive environment is eschewed. Most common, then, is to find individuals at home in the story of their lives: in the narrative of identity with which and through which they traverse their social environments (cf. Sarup 1994:95).

Following this introduction, Part II of the book comprises eight substantive chapters, each of which approaches the notion of 'home' from the vantage point of, and in relation to, a particular symbolic universe. The chapters stretch across a broad ethnographic range: the Cayman Islands (Amit-Talai); an Israeli development town (Rapport); the diasporic contexts of Yugoslav *émigrés* (Jansen); the Czech Republic (Holy); an English Midland town (James); households in Greater London (Hirsch); inner-city London (Wallman); and coal-mining towns of north-east England (Dawson). They focus upon a range of levels of sociation (from individual to community), and treat a range of discourse types (from formal (official) ideology to everyday conversation). Thus 'home' appears as a dominant symbol with polysemic content in a variety of contexts of use: Home and the Expatriate (Amit-Talai); Home and the Immigrant (Rapport); Home and the Dissident (Jansen); Home and the Nation (Holy); Home and the Child (James); Home and the House (Hirsch); Home and Urbanity (Wallman); Home and Community (Dawson).

Notwithstanding the above manifoldness, it may be objected that the chapters' ethnographic foci concentrate upon narrowly 'Euro-American' populations. However, we would challenge the analytical appropriateness of an essentializing, 'occidentalizing' demarcation of this kind (cf. Carrier 1994). What comes across strongly in the ethnographic accounting is not the homogeneity and coherency (historical, social or cultural) of behaviour that may be identified as 'Western' so much as its diversity and incoherency: 'homogeneity' and 'coherency' speak more to the prejudicial concerns of those epistemic communities that come together to study particular 'culture areas' than to anything more real (cf. Appadurai 1988; Fardon 1990). What also becomes clear is that deriving actors' identities and experiences from supposedly deterministic general sociological categories is a hangover from an analytical style that is no longer adequate: it is to confuse form with meaning. Part-and-parcel of an appreciation of contemporary migrancy ought to be an eschewing of vulgar, totalizing ways of theorizing identity, then, and an acceptance of its potentially radical individuality (cf. Rapport 1997). To adapt E. D. Hirsch (1988:258), 'the distance between one [socio-cultural milieu] and another is a very small step in comparison to the huge metaphysical gap we must leap to understand the perspective of another person in any time and place'.

At the core of the book is each chapter's consideration of the attainment of home as an individual search, involving either or both physical and cognitive movement. However, they also come together through exploration of a series of additional but related and interconnecting themes. One of these is 'home-making'. A range of the media and types of resource that people utilize in making their homes are considered: physical, from iconic imagery in architecture (Holy) to the clothes people wear (Jansen); textual, from autobiographical monographs (Jansen) to poetry (Dawson); verbal, from the orchestrated performance of song (Dawson) to routinized conversation (Rapport); and conceptual, from the state's imagings of the nation as home and family (Holy) to individual imaginings of new forms of collective identity (Jansen).

A second issue is that of the 'politics of home'. The chapters consider a range of sites in which people struggle to make and define home. There is the global labour market, in which individuals seek, often fruitlessly, to secure a home against the background of an absence of infrastructural protection (Amit-Talai). There are statal (Jansen, and Rapport) and local governmental (Wallman) visions of home that are resisted by communities and individuals. There is the material culture of heritage museums, in which class-based groups seek to freeze, in perpetuity, competing visions of the home community (Dawson). And there are the struggles involving children, parents and teachers over the imaging of the household home from which the child's identity is read (James), and the intrafamilial struggles surrounding new computerized technologies that shape and pattern family home life (Hirsch).

Finally, since the search, the making and the struggle for home do not necessarily result in resolution, a further issue is that of homelessness. Both Jansen and Rapport explore how the centralizing and essentializing practices of nation-states attempt to deny individualized senses of home. And, most poignantly, Amit-Talai problematizes the often rosy picture of the cosmopolitan; she depicts the modern-day labour migrant as facing a situation where neither place of origin nor work role constitute an adequate basis of identification through which to cultivate a sense of home.

More precisely:

1. In *Risky Hiatuses and the Limits of Social Imagination: Ex-Patriacy in the Cayman Islands*, Vered Amit-Talai provides an examination of the interaction between globalization and protectionism in the Cayman Islands: the way in which Cayman is home to both 'true' Caymanians and long-standing 'temporary residents', in a situation of highly mobile financial interests. The Cayman Islands are today home to one of the world's largest offshore financial centres and a thriving tourism industry. To meet the labour needs of these sectors, Cayman has recently shifted from being a population exporter – traditionally, most Cayman men would go to sea, in other countries' merchant marines – to importing a substantial part of its labour force. Nearly 40 per cent of Cayman's long-term residents are now 'temporary': foreign contract workers and their families. As a result of this, coupled with the return to Cayman of former expatriates who had meanwhile settled in other parts of the Caribbean, the United States and Canada, the Cayman population has increased threefold over the last three decades.

This chapter traces the interaction of two principal consequences of this transformation of economic and social organization. On the one hand, Cayman appears to be an archetype of globalization. Its economy is dependent on foreign labour and capital; its inhabitants maintain extensive personal and professional networks outside Cayman. On the other hand, access to full enfranchisement and rights of residency on Cayman are rigorously husbanded, and seen as the prerogative only of 'true' Caymanians. Thus the prosperity and claimed political stability ushered in by economic globalization has been accompanied by a sub-text of uncertainty and insecurity: the insecurity of a sizeable proportion of 'temporary residents', the uncertainty of 'full Caymanians' in danger of being overwhelmed.

At the core of the chapter is an exploration of the conditions faced by the temporary residents and an engagement with recent literature on migrancy and cosmopolitanism. Amit-Talai questions whether spatial displacement engenders new forms of imagined community or home. She argues that in the case of the temporary residents of the Cayman Islands, at least, few people possess adequate mobile bases for identification, while the category of homelessness itself is by no means an automatic condition for new forms of affiliation.

2. In *Coming Home to a Dream: A Study of the Immigrant Discourse of 'Anglo-Saxons' in Israel*, Nigel Rapport examines attempts to reconstruct cognitive and physical homes by a set of recent American immigrants in the small Israeli development town of Mitzpe Ramon. He explores the way in which these newcomers deal with their immigrant status – how they maintain ties to the United States, reformulate their decision to emigrate, organize and build local community boundaries around themselves.

In particular, the chapter analyses 'mother-country imagery': the way old homes in America are brought into metaphorical contact with new so as to afford bases of commonsensical expectation in the present, concepts of propriety and possibility, and sources of self-image; it is through a distilling of the essence of their past American selves that new migrants begin to be at home and imagine futures for themselves in Israel. To live in Israel is, in short, to come to terms with paradox: the dream of 'Next Year in Israel' is now; they are 'Anglo-Saxons' in the Middle East.

Hence, paradox comes to be enunciated as something of a national and ethnic trait: a wily Jewish way of getting around rules, furthering self-interest and feeling at home in marginal social settings. It is in recognizing their self-contradictions that these American immigrants come to realize their identities as new Israelis.

3. In *Homeless at Home: Narrations of Post-Yugoslav Identities*, Stefaan Jansen explores the interplay between the narratives of the new Croatian and Serbian states and the personal narratives of a group of privileged, non-nationalistic refugees from the former Yugoslavia.

He demonstrates how, through the states' narrations of a discursive break between before and after the national project, the refugees face a threefold crisis. First, they are delegitimized as 'Yugo-Zombies', nostalgic for a Yugoslavia now gone, and unwilling to participate in collective processes of amnesia that seek to obfuscate pan-nationalist Yugoslav history. Secondly, cultural homogenization and collectivization serve to rob them of their chosen forms of identification and their senses of individuality. Finally, the combination of these processes, aligned to the erection of national borders where once none existed, leaves the refugees feeling an ambiguous sense of being 'homeless at home'.

Jansen then goes on to explore the myriad ways in which the refugees confront their crises: through minute acts of resistance, such as the wearing of non-nationalist styles of dress; through clamourings for new forms of collective identity, such as refugee, East European and writer; and, most importantly, through the act of writing personal narratives. These last provide a means of continuity to a pan-nationalist past and, in effect, serve as new cognitive homes.

4. In *The Metaphor of 'Home' in Czech Nationalist Discourse*, Ladislav Holy examines the way in which Czechs rhetorically equate 'home' and 'homeland'. Amidst the ambiguity surrounding place brought about by the end of the Czechoslovak Republic, Czechs have seized upon an understanding of home as referring to a specifically sentimentalized place. This chapter explores the political implications of employing 'home' in this strategic and spatial sense in the context of the new Czech Republic.

Space enters into the conceptualization of 'homeland' in ways in which it does not enter into conceptualization of 'nation'. This enables Czechs to construct the concept of a homeland that mediates between a naturally constituted 'nation' and an artificially created 'state'. The mediating role of 'homeland' further enables Czechs to draw a sharp conceptual distinction between patriotism (love of one's homeland) and nationalism (identification with one's nation and feelings of superiority towards other nations). It is this positively valued concept of patriotism that then makes it possible for Czechs to engage in a vigorous nationalist discourse while denying their own nationalism, and only ascribing it to 'others' with whom they share Central European space (Slovaks, Germans). By invoking familial and spatial images particular to themselves – ranging from places associated with the earliest Czech history to places associated with the most recent political events – Czechs are today able to construct a nationalist discourse, a discourse of homeland, that is culturally specific.

5. In *Imaging Children 'At Home', 'In The Family' and 'At School': Movement Between the Spatial and Temporal Markers of Childhood Identity in Britain*, Allison James explores how it is, metaphorically, to be a child: what it is to 'be a child' in Britain today. If metaphors provide us with ways of structuring not only how we speak but also how we think and act, then this chapter is an attempt to tease out the current metaphorization of the dependency of 'the child'. Answers are sought with reference to the concepts of 'family' and 'home', particularly as they are articulated by parents, children and their teachers. If 'home' is that conceptual and physical space where identities are worked on, then the child is ideologically at home in 'the family'. Thus, conceptual links between 'home' and 'family' are mutually reinforcing. Moreover, such links protect the concepts from change. The ideal form of the family bears

little resemblance to contemporary family life, to the fluidity and dissolution of ties of kinship and marriage. And yet a traditional family ideology continues publicly to dominate our thinking. This is effected (metaphorically) by the notion of 'home' providing a setting for a normalizing of our understanding of family life and a reconciliation between the actual and the ideal. Similarly, home provides, ideally, a physical and emotional setting for private life; and yet new technologies and conditions of employment blur the boundaries between public and domestic almost beyond recognition. Notwithstanding, 'family life' continues (metaphorically) to reconstitute home even as physical locations and members change.

Finally, 'home' and 'the family' rest metaphorically on the dependency and immobility of the child. To be a child in Britain is to be dependent and non-mobile, and it is through a continued construction of this stasis that the British 'family home' survives.

6. In *Domestic Appropriations: Multiple Contexts and Relational Limits in the Home-Making of Greater Londoners*, Eric Hirsch begins with the observation that a sense of ever-present change and movement, of persons and objects moving speedily both in time and space, is one that continually throws into relief the home as a resting place – 'a haven in a heartless world'. Furthermore, inasmuch as 'we increasingly live with institutions and objects that we do not see ourselves as having created' (*apres* D. Miller), there is a further sense in which the home is a place in which we work to invest such entities with our own agency and direct them towards our own purposes. Through a series of case-studies of seven London families, and in particular their relations with Information and Communication Technologies (telephones, televisions, videos, above all, computers), the chapter examines the veracity of these senses of the home; it points up an important distinction between 'the home' (as house) and 'home' as such, and emphasizes the contextual slipperiness and multiplicity of the latter concept, and also its non-physicality.

The chapter argues, in particular, for a re-thinking of the notions of appropriation and alienation. Using an object (a computer, in a London house) may involve no alienation intrinsic to the operation, but may involve attempting to 'appropriate' other forms of alienation. Inasmuch as the social world is made up of a plurality of overlapping contexts and domains, individuals may find themselves potentially 'alienated', at any given time, in several, partially connected, ways. To the extent that a multitude of different social relations may overlap with and impinge upon the domestic environment of the home, so particular modes of domestic appropriation (using a computer in a London house) may be understood in terms of treating senses of alienation at work, in the past, with one's children, and so on.

The phenomenology of contemporary object-use calls for a subtle appreciation of individuals, attending to their being 'at home' in a number of seemingly discrete social spaces. Appropriating objects, they come to be at home in-between.

7. In *New Identities and the Local Factor* − OR *When is Home in Town a Good Move?*, Sandra Wallman pursues the notion that 'home' is a proxy for identity and that it is compounded of place and belonging. The notion is explored in terms of the variations, and the conditions of variation, surrounding peoples' constructions of urban homes.

The first level of variation that the chapter considers is cultural. It is approached through the question, 'Is city-ness as such a good or a bad thing?'; and, therefore, is living in the city taken as a sign of success and a source of self-esteem − a positive identity − or a lower-status, negative identity? (Contrasts may be drawn, for example, between English anti-urbanism and Italian suspicion of and contempt for the (literally) uncivilized rural person.) The second level of variation considered is structural, or better, systematic. It is approached through the question, 'Which kind of city-ness do people identify with, feel good about and make a home in?'

Both questions are addressed with ethnographic examples drawn from different London neighbourhoods. Discussion combines cultural ideals with the specifics of each urban milieu, and their differences in terms of: their degrees of 'compression', the 'open–closedness' of their networks, and their distribution of 'resources of identity'. The relationship between people and place is specified according to three modalities: (1) new identities being forged − 'moving in to stay'; (2) old identities being defended − 'refusing to move'; and (3) identity continually redefined − 'keeping moving'.

8. In *The Dislocation of Identity: Contestations of 'Home Community' in Northern England*, Andrew Dawson considers the processes that surround the right to define the 'community' one calls one's home: who owns these rights and how they are seen to be ascribed. Ethnographically, the chapter is focused on a town in the heart of industrial north-east England, where coal-mining has come to represent that central referent of local community. Analytically, the chapter focuses on the competing definitions of community articulated by groups of 'working-class', former mining people on the one hand, and local, 'middle-class' intelligentsia on the other. This definitional competition has come to the fore in recent years as Government has sought the participation of local people in the

design of post-mining 'community development' projects, such as the construction of a heritage museum.

The chapter elucidates two key processes. First, the rights that working-class groups see themselves as possessing to define their home community – based on direct erstwhile involvement in mining – are increasingly under challenge from a middle-class mastery over those cultural forms and symbols still associated with mining. Second, the rights that middle-class groups see themselves as possessing to define their community – based on ideas of unbroken residency of long duration – are challenged by the insistence of working-class groups that a defining referent of local belonging is migrancy.

At the heart of the chapter is a discussion of how definitional competition involves a process of location and dislocation of personal and community identities from their objective referents. This in itself involves engagement in forms of social, spatial and temporal cognitive movement.

Following these substantive case-studies, Part III of the book contains a review of the preceding chapters, or Response, in which overlapping theoretical insights and themes are drawn out. In *Contested Homes: Home-Making and the Making of Anthropology*, Karen Fog Olwig – with experience of Creole identities in the Caribbean (on the American Virgin Islands, and Nevis in the Leeward Islands) and also of diasporic identities (in migrant Nevisian communities in Connecticut and England) – assesses the book's argument concerning the relationship between home and movement, migrancy and identity.

In particular, Olwig draws attention to the important differences between home as a conceptual or discursive space of identification, and home as a nodal point in concrete social relations. Whereas in the life of fairly well-to-do individuals around the world (and their anthropologists) the former understanding of home may bring to mind a somewhat abstract domain of self-knowledge and individual narration, for the less well-off and disenfranchised, home may amount to a contested space of social rights and obligations, of knowledge of self and community that excludes and includes according to the dictates of powerful, significant others. In their studies of home, she concludes, anthropologists must be careful to emphasize the diversity of the different 'identity spaces' that their informants may call home, and how, through movement, informants may make manifest their awareness of this diversity and also their variable abilities to assert and select a home of their choice. In short, in a world in movement, home becomes 'an arena where differing interests struggle to define their own spaces within which to localize and cultivate their identity'.

Home and Movement: A Polemic

Nigel Rapport and Andrew Dawson

[O]ne comes to recognize the existence of an actual immortality, that of movement . . .

Friedrich Nietzsche: *Human, All Too Human*

Consequently anthropology is only a collection of traveller's tales.

A. R. Louch: *Explanation and Human Action*

Introduction

Michel Butor once suggested that anthropology and narratology meet under the rubric of a new overriding discipline of 'iterology': a science of journeys (1972:7). In this chapter, by way of introducing a number of the intentions and contentions of the volume as a whole, we outline the logic, or a logic, for iterology. We take Butor's suggestion to imply that the study of social life and the study of story-telling might be seen to be bound together by a commensurate interest in the relationship between movement and identity.

Movement and Perception

Quite a long time ago now, Gregory Bateson put it like this: the human brain thinks in terms of relationships. Things and events are secondary, epiphenomena: 'all knowledge of external events is derived from the relationship between them': from the relationships that the brain conceives between them (Bateson and Ruesch 1951:173). To conceive relationships (and so create things) is to move or cause to move things relative to the point of perception (the brain) or relative to other things within the field

19

of perception. Movement is fundamental to the setting up and the changing of relations by which things gain and maintain and continue to accrue thingness. Indeed, since one of the 'things' that thus comes to exist as an identifiable thing is 'oneself' (the perceiving brain as objectified 'out there'), movement is also fundamental to the thingness, the identity, of the self. Subject and object, perceiver and perceived are intrinsically connected.

Another way of saying this is that the mind operates with and upon differences. Relationships are about differences. Indeed, the word 'idea' is synonymous with 'difference'. If the mind 'treats ideas' (is an aggregate of ideas), then the mind is an aggregation of differences: between ego and alter, between objects in the world. If the mind 'gathers information', then this is data about differences that are seen as making a difference at a particular time.

There are a number of corollaries of this thesis. The first is, that the things that thus derive from movement, relations and differences are material and immaterial alike. Ponds, pots and poems, to the extent that each figures in the life of a social milieu, are all the outcome of engineering movement relative to a point of perception. As Bateson phrases it, all phenomena are 'appearances', for in the world of human behaviour 'to be is to be perceived' (1958:96). Constant movement is the essential characteristic of the way an individual mind perceives and so constructs an environment, whether 'natural' or 'cultural' (cf. Bourdieu 1966:233).

A second corollary is precisely that the mind is 'individual' in this regard. The movement that is engineered is relative to the individual perceiver. Bateson recognizes this by describing the individual mind as 'an energy source' (1972:126), responsible for energizing the events in the world, the movements, that underlie the perception of difference; it is not that the mind is merely being impacted upon by environmental triggers (cf. Minh-ha 1994:23). More generally, each human individual is an 'energy source', inasmuch as the energy of his acts and responses derives from his own metabolic processes, not from external stimuli. It is with this energy, through this movement, and by this construction of relations and objects, that individuals create order and impose it on the universe: human individuals are active participants in their own universe.

A third corollary, then, is that what can be understood by 'order' is a certain relationship, a certain difference, between objects that an individual mind comes to see as normal and normative; it is one of an infinite number of possible permutations, and it is dependent on the eye of the individual perceiver; this may not be what others perceive as orderly. What is random or 'entropic' for one perceiver is orderly, informational, negatively entropic for another. 'Disorder' and 'order' are statements of relations between a purposive perceiving entity and some set of objects and events; they are determined by individuals' states of mind.

What Bateson established (at least: translated into an anthropological environment from an Existential one) was the fundamental relationship between movement and perception, between movement and energy, between movement and order, and between movement and individuality.

Stationariness and Identity

If these ideas have long been known or at least in circulation within anthropology, then the implication usually drawn from them has been, paradoxically, the relationship between identity and fixity: necessarily and universally finding a stationary point in the environment from which to engineer one's moving, perceiving, ordering and constructing. If we may use the concept of 'home' to refer to that environment (cognitive, affective, physical, somatic, or whatever) in which one best knows oneself, where one's self-identity is best grounded – or worst, or most, or most freely, or most presently, as one deems fit – (cf. Douglas 1984:82; Silverstone, *et al.* 1994:19), then the conventional anthropological understanding has been that to be at home was tantamount to being environmentally fixed. In the construction and promulgation of essential cultures, societies, nations and ethnic groups, being at home in an environment meant being, if not stationary, then at least centred.

Hence the environment comes to be anthropologically depicted as fanning out around the perceiver in concentric circles of greater and lesser degrees of consociality and morality. From Sahlins, then, we get a demarcation of the social groupings of an environment mapped out from a perspectival centre as follows: from 'house' to 'lineage' to 'village' to 'tribe' to 'other tribes' (1968:65). Or again, in terms of the language with which the perceiver classified his environment, Leach offers us a continuum of related terms that place ego 'reassuringly' at the centre of a social space and fan out from there: from 'self' to 'sibling' to 'cousin' to 'neighbour' to 'stranger'; also from 'self' to 'pet' to 'livestock' to 'game' to 'wild animal' (1968:36–7). To be at home in an environment, in short, was to situate the world around oneself at the unmoving centre, with 'contour lines of relevance' in the form of symbolic categories emanating from a magisterial point of perception (cf. Schuetz 1944:500–4). To know (oneself, one's society) it was necessary to gain a perspective on an environment from a single, fixed and homogeneous point of view: to know was to see the world as singular, made proportionate and subjected to the individual eye, sight and site of the beholder. In short, knowledge was validated by making the eye (and hence the 'I') the still centre of a visually observed world (cf. Ong 1969; Strathern 1992: 9–10).

Even if the actors were nomads, their myths were regarded anthropologically as making of the environment through which they passed a known place, an old place, a proper place, not only fixed in memory but to which their belonging was stationary because permanent, cyclical, normative and traditional; cognitively, they never moved. And even if the actors engaged in ritual journeys outside everyday space and time – rites of passage; pilgrimage; vision quests – in search of sacred centres to their lives (Eliade 1954:12–20), these anti-structural events served in fact to fix them even more; as special, extraordinary, aberrant experiences, the rituals merely emphasized and legitimated an everyday identity that derived from fixity in a social environment. Ritual pilgrims used their moments of (imagined) movement to establish routinely fixed orientations to a world around them (cf. Myerhoff 1974; Yamba 1992). Similarly anti-structural and marginal, finally, were the journeys undertaken between status-groups by actors in hierarchically organized societies (between classes, between professions, between age-grades), for here was movement whose experiential purpose, whose successful conclusion, was eventual stasis. In short, as Lévi-Strauss concluded, myths should be understood as machines for the suppression of the sense of passing time and space, giving on to a fixed point from which the world took and takes shape (1975:14–30); a conclusion Leach would then extend to ritual acts in general (1976:44).

Movement was thus mythologized in anthropology as enabling fixity (cf. Strathern 1981). As cultures were things rooted in time and space (embodying genealogies of 'blood, property and frontiers' (Carter 1992:7–8)), so cultures rooted societies and their members: organisms which developed, lived and died in particular places. Travel, as Auge quipped (with Lévi-Strauss in mind), was something 'mistrusted to the point of hatred' (1995:86).

However, of late there has been a conceptual shift in the norms of anthropological commentary – brought about, perhaps, by the communications revolution of the past forty years and the perspective this gives on to (and itself evinces) of the globalization of culture, of multi-culture replacing national culture: world markets, goods and labour, world polities, world music, taste and fashion, and, not least, world movement; or else brought about by the recent communicative revolution within anthropology *per se*, 'the reflexive turn' which, paradoxically, has seen the discipline look beyond itself, 'globally', to a world of other disciplines (Literature, Psychoanalysis, Biology) in terms of which it can hope to know itself better.

For a complex movement of people, goods, money and information – 'modernization', the growing global economy, the induced, often brutally enforced, migrations of individuals and whole populations from 'peripheries' towards Euro-American metropolises and Third World cities (cf. Chambers 1994a:16); the migration of information, myths, languages, music, imagery, cuisine, décor, costume, furnishing, above all, persons (cf. Geertz 1986:120–1) – brings even the most isolated areas into a cosmopolitan global framework of socio-cultural interaction. Here, with ways of life 'increasingly influencing, dominating, parodying, translating and subverting one another', there are no traditionally fixed, spatially and temporally bounded cultural worlds from which to depart and to which to return: all is situated and all is moving (Clifford 1986:22).

As Keith Hart argues (1990), the world can no longer be divided up into framed units, territorial segments and the like, each of which shares a distinctive, exclusive culture, a definite approach to life; rather, everyone is now caught between local origins and a cosmopolitan society in which 'all humanity participates'. Emberley concludes (1989:741–85) that notions of space as enclosure and time as duration are 'unsettled', and redesigned as a field of infinitely experimental configurations of 'space–time'; here the old order of 'prescriptive and exclusive places' and 'meaning-endowed duration' dissolves (cf. Kearney 1995).

John Berger (1984) therefore suggests that movement around the globe represents our quintessential experience, while for Minh-ha: 'our present age is one of exile' (1994:13–14). Exile, emigration, banishment, labour migrancy, tourism, urbanization and counter-urbanization are the central motifs of modern culture, while being rootless, displaced between worlds, living between a lost past and a fluid present, are perhaps the most fitting metaphors for the journeying, modern consciousness: 'typical symptoms of a modern condition at once local and universal' (Nkosi 1994:5).

Moreover, to bring together current forms of movement in this fashion, as Berger does, is not inevitably to essentialize movement: to claim 'it' is somehow always the same, an effect *sui generis*. Movement remains a polythetic category of experience: diverse, and without common denomination in its particular manifestations. Nor is it to underrate either the forces eventuating in large-scale population movement in the past (famine, plague, crusade, imperial conquest, urbanization, industrialization), or the forces arrayed against movement in the present (restrictive or repressive state or community institutions, state or community borders *per se*). To talk about the ubiquitous experience of movement is not to deny power and authority, and the differential motivations and gratifications in that experience that hierarchy might give on to. Rather, what Berger draws our attention to is the part movement plays in our modern imagination, and in our imaging of the modern. Movement is the quintessence of how we – migrants and autochthones, tourists and locals, refugees and citizens, urbanites and ruralites – construct contemporary social experience and have it constructed for us. As Iain Chambers concludes, wandering the globe is not now the expression of a unique tradition or history, for the erstwhile particular chronicles of diasporas – those of the black Atlantic, of metropolitan Jewry, of mass rural displacement – have come to constitute the broad ground swell of modernity; modern culture is practised through, and the work of, wandering (1994a:16). And hence anthropology has had increasing recourse to such concepts as 'creolization' and 'compression', 'hybridization' and 'synchronicity', to comprehend the changes that such movement causes to social and cultural environments – and to apprehend relations between movement and identity.

Creolization and Compression

Let us allude explicitly, if briefly, to three of these recent anthropological expositions, those of Lee Drummond, Ulf Hannerz and Robert Paine.

The culmination of four hundred years of massive global migration, voluntary and involuntary, in the recent cultural impetus to modernize, urbanize and capitalize, and in movements of people and traffic in cultural items and information that have become continuous, have transformed most societies. However, the result of these transformations, Lee Drummond suggests (1980:352), is neither new integrations of what were once separate societies and features of societies, now fitting neatly together as one, nor pluralities whereby old separate societies simply retain their cultural distinctivenesses side by side. Rather, what results are socio-cultural continua or combinations: 'creolizations'. Societies are no longer discrete social spaces with their own discrete sets of people and cultural norms – if they ever were. They are now basically creole in nature: combinations of ways of life, with no invariant properties or uniform rules. A series of bridges or transformations now lead across social fences and cultural divisions between people from one end of the continuum to the other: bridges which are in constant use as people swop artefacts and norms, following multiple and incompatible ways of life. Here is a 'concatenation of images and ideas' (1980:363). And here, ultimately, is a world in which there 'are now no distinct cultures, only intersystemically connected, creolizing Culture'.

Hence, Hannerz continues, the traditional picture of human cultures as forming a global mosaic – of cultures as plural, bounded, pure, integrated, cohesive, distinctive, place-rooted and mapped in space – must now be complemented by a picture of 'cultural flows in space' (1993:68), and by 'a global ecumene' (1992:34): a world system, a single field of persistent interaction and exchange, a continuous spectrum of interacting forms, which combines and synthesizes various local cultures and so breaks down cultural plurality. That is, through mass media, objects of mass consumption, and the mass movements of people, culture now flows over vast distances. Indeed, it may be better to conceive of culture *tout court* as a flow. Thus, for Hannerz, the new world system does not result in socio-cultural homogeneity so much as a new diversity of interrelations: many different kaleidoscopes of cultural combinations, amounting to no discrete wholes, only heterogeneous and interpenetrating conglomerations. For people now draw on a wide range of cultural resources in the securing of their social identities, continually turning the erstwhile alien into their own; they select from the rich treasury of behaviours and beliefs that different cultural traditions now hold out to them, ranging between them, electing to have this and not that, to combine this with that, to move from this to this to that: to 'listen to reggae, watch a western, eat MacDonald's food for lunch and local cuisine for dinner, wear Paris perfume in Tokyo and "retro" clothes in Hong Kong' (Lyotard 1986:76); to make of each 'local' point a 'global' collage, a 'Kuwaiti bazaar' (Geertz 1986:121). In short, people make sense to themselves and others by continually moving amongst a global inventory of ideas and modes of expression.

However, such movement is not smooth, Paine insists (1992), nor is it singular. With individuals making different cultural selections and combinations – different from other individuals and different from themselves in other times and places; different in terms of particular items and their relative weighting, and different in terms of the willingness, loyalty and intensity of the selection – and combinations of elements not just previously separate but still incommensurable, so this movement amongst cultures can be expected to be volatile, and advocates of different selections to be exclusionary if not hostile. At the same time as there is globalization, therefore, and movement across the globe, between societies and amongst cultures, as never before –people treating the whole globe as the cognitive space within which they can or must imagine moving and actually do move, the space that they expect to 'know' – there is also 'cultural compression': an insistence on socio-cultural difference within the 'same' time and space; a piling up of socio-cultural boundaries, political, ritual, residential, economic, which feel experientially vital, and which people seek to defend and maintain. Here is a dialectic (not to say a Batesonian schismogenesis) between global movement and local compression (cf. Featherstone 1990). So that even if travel is ubiquitous, and one is 'at home' on the entire globe, to travel within one's home is to encounter a world of socio-cultural difference; even to stay home is to experience global movement.

Movement and Home

Moving from Drummond to Hannerz to Paine is not to meet perfectly commensurable expositions of the contemporary world, and there is disagreement over the extent to which a globalization of culture results in the continuing boundedness of social groups, as well as disagreement concerning the extent to which this globalization is experienced as colonial or post-colonial – as the imposition of a particular cultural way of being-in-the-world or as the opportunity to constitute and reconstitute the set of cultural forms that go to make up one's life-way (cf. Appadurai 1990). More significantly, there appears to be divergence concerning whether the thesis linking contemporary movement and identity is a historical one or a representational one. In particular, Drummond is happy to talk in terms of four centuries of change, while Paine's central motif is a comparison of could-be representations between E. M. Forster and Salman Rushdie. The historical argument would seem to be the harder one to make, and would also seem prone to the kinds of grand-historical reductionism that characterized conventional anthropology in its old dispensation (from 'fixity to movement' as from 'mechanical solidarity to organic', from 'community to association', from 'concrete thought to abstract', from 'hierarchy to individualism'). Certainly, Bateson's propositions claim universal pertinence, while the history and archaeology of frequent and global movement make generalizations about the uniqueness of the present foolhardy.

Where Drummond, Paine and Hannerz do meet is in a recognition of the contemporary significance of movement around the globe – its universal apperception, its ubiquitous relationship to socio-cultural identities. Whether or not this pertains to a historical shift, whether it is imposed or opportunistic, there is in the contemporary world a sense in which metaphors and motifs of movement are of the quintessence in the conceptualization of identity. In folk commentary as in social-scientific, there is a recognition of the fundamental relationship between movement and cultural practice and expression (cf. Dawson 1997).

More particularly, there is an implicit recognition in the above anthropological expositions of the changing relations between movement and home. Increasingly, one is seen as moving between homes, erstwhile to current; or as moving between multiple homes (from one compressed socio-cultural environment to another); or as being at home in continuous movement (amongst creolized cultural forms); and so one's home as movement *per se*.

This is certainly the explicit thesis of John Berger. For Berger, in an age that conceptualizes itself in terms of global movement, the idea of 'home' undergoes dramatic change. In place of the conventional conception of home as the stable physical centre of the universe – a safe place to leave and return to – a far more mobile notion comes to be used: a home that can be taken along whenever one decamps. For a world of travellers and journeymen, home comes to be found far more usually in a routine set of practices, in a repetition of habitual social interactions, in the ritual of a regularly used personal name (cf. Rapport 1994b). It might seem, in Heidegger's words, as if 'homelessness is coming to be the destiny of the world'; but it is rather that there develops another sense of being-in-the-world. (It is not that in an age of global movement, there cannot be a sense of homelessness – far from it – but that a sense of home or of homelessness is not necessarily related in any simple or direct way with fixity or movement.) One dwells in a mobile habitat and not in a singular or fixed, physical structure. Moreover, as home becomes more mobile, so it comes to be seen as more individuated and privatized; everyone chooses their own, and one's choice might remain invisible (and irrelevant) to others (cf. Dawson 1994; Rapport 1995). Home, in short, is increasingly: 'no longer a dwelling but the untold story of a life being lived' (Berger 1984:64).

To recap: the emphasis on a relationship between identity and fixity has been at least challenged in anthropology of late by representations of the relationship between identity and movement. Now we have 'creolizing' and 'compressing' cultures and 'hybridizing' identities in a 'synchronizing' global society. Part of this reconceptualization pertains significantly to notions of home; part-and-parcel of this conceptual shift is a recognition that not only can one be at home in movement, but that movement can be one's very home. One's identity is 'formed on the move': a 'migrant's tale' of 'stuttering transitions and heterogeneities' (Chambers 1994a:24, 1994b:246–7). And the personal myths and rituals that one carries on one's journey through life (that carry one through a life-course) need not fix one's perspective on any still centre outside one's (moving) self. As Berger concludes, one is at home not in a thing or a place but 'in a life being lived in movement', and in an 'untold story' (1984:64).

Home and Story

The link Berger would make between home and story we find very provocative; and his claim that the story remains untold we find highly polemical. Because a story, a narrative, can itself be conceived of as a form of movement; and because stories, narratives, can be approached from two very different directions, the one describing the art of narration as the orderly telling of people, objects and events that did not previously exist, the ultimate creative act, and the other claiming, in contradistinction, that it is narratives that do the telling, that pre-exist their particular narrators, speak through the latter's lives unbeknown to them, and to that extent remain 'untold'. Let us elaborate.

Narrative has been defined as: 'the telling (in whatever medium, though especially language) of a series of temporal events so that a meaningful sequence is portrayed – the story or plot of the narrative' (Kerby 1991:39). Also, narrative is the cultural form that is 'capable of expressing coherence through time' (Crites 1971:294). The content of narratives, then, treats a movement between events so as to give on to meaning and coherence in time. Also, the medium of narratives entails a movement from a start to a finish (if not a 'beginning' to an 'ending'), and is 'everywhere character-ized by movement': the passage of words, the slippage of metaphor, the caravan of thought, the flux of the imaginary, the movement of calligraphy (Chambers 1994a:10); the 'consecution' of linguistic signs, the movement of meaning (Arshi et al. 1994:226). To recount a narrative, in short, is both to speak of movement and to engage in movement. One tells of people, objects and events as one moves them through time and one moves from the start of one's account to its end. Narrative mediates one's sense of movement through time, so that in the telling one becomes, in Rushdie's (telling) observation (1991:12), an *émigré* from a past home.

But precisely who or what does the telling, and who or what is told? Two answers are suggested. For Kerby, it is the narrative that tells the self of the narrator, that gives that self identity in the movement of the telling. The self arises out of signifying practices, coming to know itself and the world through enculturated narrational acts. In a particular socio-cultural environment, the self is given content, is delineated and embodied, primarily in narrative constructions or stories. It is these that give rise to the possibilities of subjectivity: 'it is in and through various forms of narrative emplotment that our lives −. . . our very selves − attain meaning' (Kerby 1991:3). And being merely an outcome of discursive practice, the subject or self has no ontological or epistemological priority. Rather, 'persons' are to be understood as the result of ascribing subject status or selfhood to those 'sites of narration and expression' that we call human bodies. And the stories they tell of themselves and others are determined by the grammar of their language, by the genres of their culture, by the fund of stories of their society, and by the stories others tell and have told of them. In Crites's words (1971:295–7), consciousness 'awakes' to a culture's 'sacred story'. It is this story that forms consciousness and in which consciousness lives, rather than being something of which consciousness is directly aware. And it is of culture that this story tells, in the bodies and lives of its members: it is the story that tells, it is not told. In short, we are back with Lévi-Strauss: '[M]yths think in men, unbeknownst to them'; not to mention Heidegger: 'It is language that speaks, not Man. Man begins speaking but Man only speaks to the extent that he responds to, that he corresponds with language, and only insofar as he hears language addressing, concurring with him'; and Lacan: 'Man speaks, then, but it is because the symbol has made him man'; 'man is inhabited by the signifier'.

But there is another answer to the question of narrative, which allows that through narrative, human beings, individual men and women with agency, tell the world, and tell it anew, continuously reorganizing their 'habitation in reality' (Steiner 1975:23). Thus, for George Steiner, language might be conceived of as having a public and collective face; but more significant than this is its individual and private base. At the base of every language-act resides 'a personal lexicon', 'a private thesaurus' constituted by the unique linguistic 'association-net' of personal consciousness: by the fact that each individual's understanding of language and the world is different. Embodied in language, therefore, are the 'minute particulars' of individuals' lives: the singular and specific ensembles of individuals' somatic and psychological identities. All but the most perfunctory of language-acts represent personal narratives in which individual speakers tell of themselves and their world-views. Furthermore, it is the intensity of this personal association that causes individual users continually to make their language anew. Language, and discursive practice in general, is subject to mutation by its speakers at every moment and at bewildering speed; so that the concept of a normal or standard idiom in a community of speakers is a statistical fiction; and so that what is represented in the narratives that speakers and writers produce is the generation of a personal 'language-world' and a new reality (Steiner 1978:155–6). In sum: 'the language of a community, however uniform its social contour, is an inexhaustibly multiple aggregate of speech-atoms, of finally irreducible personal meanings' (Steiner 1975:46).

In these two approaches to narrative, it seems to us, we also find encapsulated the two notions of home that this essay has considered: home versus movement, and home as movement; and the two conceptualizations of identity that the essay features: identity through fixity, and identity through movement. That is, although both approaches recognize narrative as a form of movement in itself, recognize that movement is a ubiquitous feature of social life, the relationship each would posit between that movement and members of a social environment (the way each would posit individual narrators relative to that movement) is very different. The first approach, above, had the selves of narrators and recipients of a narrative fixed and stationary within a narrative, as it were. The narrative might move through them, but their identity derived from their maintenance of a position within it; if they were to move beyond the ambit of their culture's narrative constructions or their society's narrational acts, leave home as it were, they would no longer be recognizable 'sites of expression' and they would lose their ability to know, to perceive themselves and the world. This is equivalent to the traditional anthropological approach to the relationship between identity and fixity. Meanwhile, the second approach, above, has members of a socio-cultural community continuously moving between different 'habitations of reality' as they tell different stories, remaking their language in the process. They are at home in personal narratives that move away from any notion of fixity within a common idiom, and their identities derive from telling moving stories of themselves and their world-views. And this is equivalent to a contemporary anthropological recognition of the relationship between identity and movement in the world today.

When Berger speaks of notions of home in an age of movement as increasingly to be found in 'untold stories', he seems to be sitting on the fence between two opposed positions. For untold stories leave their narrators stationary as the stories unfold, while the experience of the narrators he is describing is 'quintessentially' to be found in global transience.

Of course we are not being fair to Berger. What he means, it is clear (cf. Berger 1975), is not (the post-structuralist point) that people in transit across the globe today do not tell stories because their condition is overdetermined by the systems of signification that make stories out of their lives and hence 'tell' them, but rather (the social-democrat point) that people in movement across the globe today do not have the resources (temporal, financial) to sit down and formally record the stories of their lives; and even if they did their stories would remain 'untold' because they would clamour for attention alongside millions of others; while those in a position to make their stories heard are deliberately suppressing them, or at least ensuring that it is their own that are instead broadcast, disseminated and recorded.

The Homeless Mind?

In this conclusion, John Berger comes close to that drawn by Peter Berger and his collaborators in the premonitory text *The Homeless Mind* (P. Berger *et al.* 1973). Modernity, the latter argued, could be characterized by a pluralization of social life-worlds between which individuals are in inexorable migration. Everyday life now consists of constant transition between a variety of divergent, discrepant, even contradictory, social milieux; so that there is no consistency concerning what is experienced as 'right' or 'true' between different contexts and life-stages. Moreover, once uprooted in this way from a first and 'original' social milieu, no succeeding one becomes truly home; in transit between a plurality of life-worlds, individuals come to be at home in none. Hence does the loss, under modernization, of a traditional, absolute and unified reality give rise to a 'spreading condition of homelessness' (1973:138). This condition is at the same time normative, spiritual and cognitive; the anomy of social movement correlates with a metaphysical sense of homelessness in the cosmos, which correlates with personal alienation on the level of consciousness. However, the 'homeless mind' is hard to bear, and there is widespread nostalgia for a condition of being 'at home' in society, with oneself, and with the universe: for homes of the past that were socially homogeneous, communal, peaceful, safe and secure. De-modernization movements of various kinds (Socialism, localisms, religious cults) therefore promise new homes where individual members are reintegrated within all-embracing, meaningful structures of social, psychical and metaphysical solidarity. There are also growing attempts by those with the wherewithal to reconstruct homes in private, closed havens that shut out the present and serve as subjective refuges of the self. Nevertheless, Berger *et al.* conclude, before 'the cold winds of homelessness' nostalgia proves to be fragile defence; de-modernization schemes that are not institutionalized and society-wide are mostly precarious buffers, given the finitude and mortality of the human condi-tion. In short, in a modern world in which 'everything is in constant motion' and where 'the life of more and more individuals [is] migratory, ever-changing, mobile', homelessness represents the deepening global effect (1973:184).

While *The Homeless Mind* remains a challenging thesis, it is steeped in a communitarian ideology that can decry modern 'ills' (individualism and pluralization, alienation and anomy) only to the extent that it posits an idyllic past of unified tradition, certainty, stasis, and cognitive and behavioural commonality. We would query the existence of that 'original life-world' of traditional absoluteness and fixity, where the individual is said to be first and 'truly' at home (cf. Rapport 1993; Phillips 1993: 149–56).

Not only does the thesis of modern homelessness involve a mythic past, it also remains ethnographically ungrounded in the present. In testing homelessness against the ethnographic record (below), we contend that the evidence points to a successful resilience of 'home', however this may come to be defined, and an inexorability of home-making – even as individuals and groups lead their lives in and through movement (cognitive and physical) and refrain from finally and essentially affixing their identities to places.

Movement and Anthropology

There is one further twist in this tale. When the philosopher A. R. Louch proposed in 1966 that anthropology should be seen as a collection of travellers' tales – and that this was perfectly fine, the tales were 'sufficient unto themselves' (1966:160) – few anthropologists would have been satisfied with his description. This has now changed. Again in conjunction with a description of the ubiquity of movement in the world, with 'our heightened awareness of global interdependence, communication, diffusion, integration, sharing and penetration' and our allowance that anthropologists are no more aware of 'the world cosmopolitan conscious-ness' and its operation than their transient ethnographic subjects (Marcus and Fischer 1986:viii,38,86), with an appreciation that there is no fixed and stable Archimedean point at which to stand and observe because we are all historico-socio-culturally situated, because all knowledge is in flux (cf. Clifford 1986:22), anthropology now conceives of its enterprise very differently. There is an acceptance that anthropology, in essence, is 'a kind of writing', 'a telling of stories', legitimate to the extent that it convinces its readers of the claim that its author and narrator has 'returned here' after 'being there': journeyed into 'another way of life' so as to inscribe 'what it was like There and Then in the categories and genres of the Here and Now' (Geertz 1988:1–5,140–5). Also that cultures need to be rethought 'in terms of travel' (Clifford 1992:101), so that 'returning home' is not to find oneself in the same place as before (Weil 1978:196). In short, there is now an acceptance that anthropological knowledge derives from movement and represents itself through movement; the identity of the anthropologist is inextricably bound up with his having undertaken a cultural journey – a journey into reflexivity, a journey alongside other cosmopolitan journeymen; and the proper home of the anthropologist is the narrative account of his journeying.

To the travelling of 'the other', the informant (whether exile, migrant, tourist or counter-urbanite), then, must be added 'the increasing nomadism of modern thought', no longer bolstered by sites and sightings of absolutism (Chambers 1994a:18), no longer persuaded by fixed, totalizing ways of thinking relations (cf. Strathern 1990:38). So that Louch's statement is now doubly true: anthropology as a study of travellers as well as by travellers.

Conclusion

It seems that the world in motion to which anthropology has now awoken (and begun to address conceptually through 'creolization', 'compression' and so on) brings to our attention something basic to the human condition, universal in human life, whatever the socio-cultural milieu, and whatever the conventions of representation; something that, over and against its history of conceptualization, has always been (and will always be) true of human beings; something that Gregory Bateson was fully aware of some forty or fifty years ago, but that has somewhat slumbered in our anthropological consciousness since; something to which our disciplinal theorizing, our will to fixed systems, has continued to blinker us. And that is the basic relationship between identity (knowledge, perception) and movement: the universal way in which human beings conceive of their lives in terms of a moving-between – between identities, relations, people, things, groups, societies, cultures, environments, as a dialectic between movement and fixity. It is in and through the continuity of movement that human beings continue to make themselves at home; seeing themselves continually in stories, and continually telling the stories of their lives, people recount their lives to themselves and others as movement.

Needless to say, this is something of which commentators outside anthropology have claimed manifest (and manifold) awareness:

People are always in stories.

John Berger

We live in a narrative from breakfast to bedtime.

Robertson Davies

We all live out narratives in our lives and (. . .) we understand our own lives in terms of the narrative that we live out.

Alasdair MacIntyre

Our lives are ceaselessly intertwined with narrative, with the stories that we tell and hear told, those we dream or imagine or would like to tell, all of which are reworked in that story of our lives that we narrate to ourselves in an episodic, sometimes semi-unconscious, but virtually uninterrupted monologue.

Peter Brooks

We dream in narrative, day-dream in narrative, remember, anticipate, hope, despair, believe, doubt, plan, revise, criticize, construct, gossip, learn, hate and love by narrative.

Barbara Hardy

Man is a sort of novelist of himself who conceives the fanciful figure of a personage with its unreal occupations and then, for the sake of converting it into reality, does all the things he does.

José Ortega y Gasset

To be human is to be in a story.

Miles Richardson

Reading the narrative that these extra-anthropological commentaries (on narrative) amount to, cushioned and calmed by the repeating syllables, is surely to find oneself at home in the notion that it is in the motion of narrative that people are at home. In Butor's 'iterology', anthropology might find a suitable home in which best to know itself and its subjects in the contemporary world.

References

Appadurai, A. (1988), 'Putting Hierarchy in its Place', *Cultural Anthropology*, 3(1): 36–49.

—— (1990), 'Disjuncture and Difference in the Global Cultural Economy', *Public Culture*, 2(2): 1–24.

Arshi, S., Kirstein, C., Naqvi, R. and Pankow, F. (1994), 'Why Travel? Tropics, En-tropics and Apo-tropaics', in G. Robertson *et al.* (eds), *Travellers' Tales. Narratives of Home and Displacement*, London: Routledge.

Auge, M. (1995), *Non-places*, London: Verso.

Bammer, A. (1992), 'Editorial', *New Formations: Journal of Culture/Theory/ Practice (The Question of 'Home')* 2(2): 1–24.

Bateson, G. (1958), 'Language and Psychotherapy', *Psychiatry*, 21: 96–100.

—— (1972) *Steps to an Ecology of Mind*, London: Intertext.

—— and Ruesch, J. (1951), *Communication*, New York: Norton.

Berger, J. (1975), *A Seventh Man*, Harmondsworth: Penguin.

—— (1984), *And Our Faces, My Heart, Brief as Photos*, London: Writers & Readers.

Berger, P., Berger, B. and Kellner, H. (1973), *The Homeless Mind*, New York: Random House.

Bourdieu, P. (1966), 'The Sentiment of Honour in Kabyle Society', in J. Peristiany (ed.), *Honour and Shame*, Chicago: University of Chicago Press.

Butor, M. (1972), 'Le Voyage et l'Ecriture', *Romantisme*, 4.

Carrier, J. (ed.) (1994), *Occidentalism*, Oxford: Oxford University Press.

Carter, P. (1992), *Living in a New Country*, London: Faber & Faber.

Chambers, I. (1994a), *Migrancy Culture Identity*, London: Routledge.

—— (1994b), 'Leaky Habitats and Broken Grammar', in G. Robertson *et al.* (eds), *Travellers' Tales. Narratives of Home and Displacement*, London: Routledge.

Clifford, J. (1986), 'Introduction: Partial Truths', in G. Marcus and J. Clifford (eds), *Writing Culture*, Berkeley: University of California Press.

—— (1992), 'Travelling Cultures', in L. Grossberg, C. Nelson and P. Treichler (eds), *Cultural Studies*, London: Routledge.

Crites, S. (1971), 'The Narrative Quality of Experience', *Journal of the American Academy of Religion*, XXXIX: 291–311.

Dawson, A. (1994) 'Cultural Identity and Economic Decision Making in Three Peripheral Areas of Europe: A Comparative Account', in J. Phelan, M. Henchion and P. Bogue (eds), *Constraints on Competitiveness in EC Agriculture: A Comparative Analysis*, Brussels: European Commission.

—— (1997) 'Identity and Strategy in Post-Productionist Agriculture: A Case-Study in Northern Ireland', in H. Donnan and G. MacFarlane (eds), *Anthropology and Public Policy in Northern Ireland*, Belfast: Institute of Irish Studies Press.

Douglas, J. (1984), 'The Emergence, Security, and Growth of the Sense of Self', in J. A. Kotarba and A. Fontana (eds), *The Existential Self in Society*, Chicago: University of Chicago Press.

Douglas, M. (1991), 'The Idea of Home: A Kind of Space', *Social Research*, 58(1): 287–307.

Drummond, L. (1980), 'The Cultural Continuum: A Theory of Intersystems', *Man*, 15: 352–74.

Eliade, M. (1954), *The Myth of the Eternal Return, or Cosmos and History*, Princeton: Princeton University Press.

Ellen, R. F. (1986), 'What Black Elk Left Unsaid: On the Illusory Images of Gree Primitivism', *Anthropology Today*, 2(6): 8–12.

Emberley, P. (1989), 'Places and Stories: The Challenge of Technology', *Social Research*, 5(3): 741–85.

Fardon, R. (ed.) (1990), *Localizing Strategies*, Edinburgh: Scottish Academic Press.

Featherstone, M. (1990), 'Global Culture: An Introduction', in M. Featherstone (ed.), *Global Culture: Nationalism, Globalization and Modernity*, London: Sage.

Foster, R. (1991), 'Making National Cultures in the Global Ecumene', *Annual Review of Anthropology*, 20: 235–60.

Geertz, C. (1986), 'The Uses of Diversity', *Michigan Quarterly Review*, 25 (summer).

—— (1988), *Works and Lives*, Cambridge: Polity.

Gupta, A. and Ferguson, J. (1997), *Anthropological Locations*, Berkeley: University of California Press.

Hannerz, U. (1992), 'The Global Ecumene as a Network of Networks', in A. Kuper (ed.), *Conceptualizing Society*, London: Routledge.

—— (1993), 'The Cultural Role of World Cities', in A. P. Cohen and K. Fukui (eds), *Humanizing the City?*, Edinburgh: Edinburgh University Press.

Hart, K. (1990), 'Swimming into the Human Current', *Cambridge Anthropology*, 14(3): 3–10.

Harvey, D. (1989), *The Condition of Postmodernity*, Oxford: Blackwell.

Hirsch, E. D. (1988), 'Faulty Perspectives', in D. Lodge (ed.), *Modern Criticism and Theory*, Longman: London.

Hobsbawm, E. (1991), 'Introduction', in A. Mack (ed.), *Home: A Place in the World, Social Research* (special edition), 58(1): 63–8.

James, A., Hockey, J. and Dawson, A. (eds) (1996), *After Writing Culture: Epistemology and Praxis in Contemporary Anthropology*, London: Routledge.

Kapferer, B. (1988), *Legends of People, Myths of State*, Washington DC: Smithsonian Institution Press.

Kateb, G. (1991), 'Exile, Alienation and Estrangement', in A. Mack (ed.), *Home: A Place in the World, Social Research* (special edition), 58(1): 135–8.

Kearney, M. (1995), 'The Local and the Global: The Anthropology of Globalization and Transnationalism', *Annual Review of Anthropology* 24: 547–65.

Kerby, A. P. (1991), *Narrative and the Self*, Bloomington: Indiana University Press.

Leach, E. R. (1968), 'Anthropological Aspects of Language: Animal Categories and Verbal Abuse', in E. Lenneberg (ed.), *New Directions in the Study of Language*, Cambridge MA: MIT Press.

——— (1976), *Culture and Communication*, Cambridge: Cambridge University Press.

Lévi-Strauss, C. (1975), *The Raw and the Cooked*, New York: Harper Colophon.

Louch, A. (1966), *Explanation and Human Action*, Oxford: Blackwell.

Lyotard, J.-F. (1986), *The Post-Modern Condition*, Manchester: Manchester University Press.

Marcus, G. (1995), 'Ethnography in/of the World System: The Emergence of Multi-sited Ethnography', *Annual Reviews of Anthropology*, 24: 95–117.

Marcus, G. and Fischer, M. (1986), *Anthropology as Cultural Critique*, Chicago: University of Chicago Press.

Massey, D. (1991), 'A Global Sense of Place', *Marxism Today*, June: 24–9.

——— (1992), 'A Place Called Home?', *New Formations: Journal of Culture/ Theory/Practice (The Question of 'Home')*, 17: 133–45.

Minh-ha, T. (1994), 'Other than Myself/My Other Self', in G. Robertson *et al.* (eds), *Travellers' Tales. Narratives of Home and Displacement*, London: Routledge.

Myerhoff, B. (1974), *Peyote Hunt*, Ithaca: Cornell University Press.

Nietzsche, F. (1994[1878]), *Human, All Too Human*, Harmondsworth: Penguin.

Nkosi, L. (1994), 'Ironies of Exile: Post-colonial Homelessness and the Anticlimax of Return', *Times Literary Supplement*, 4748: 5.

Ong, W. (1969), 'World as View and World as Event', *American Anthropologist*, 71: 634–47.

Paine, R. (1992), 'The Marabar Caves, 1920–2020', in S. Wallman (ed.), *Contemporary Futures*, London: Routledge.

Phillips, D. (1993), *Looking Backward. A Critical Appraisal of Communitarian Thought*, Princeton: Princeton University Press.

Pratt, M. (1986), 'Field Work in Common Places', in G. Marcus and J. Clifford (eds), *Writing Culture*, Berkeley: University of California Press.

Rapport, N. J. (1993), *Diverse World-Views in an English Village*, Edinburgh: Edinburgh University Press.

——— (1994a), 'Trauma and Ego-Syntonic Response. The Holocaust and the "Newfoundland Young Yids" 1985', in S. Heald and A. Duluz (eds), *Anthropology and Psychoanalysis*, London: Routledge.

——— (1994b), '"Busted for Hash": Common Catchwords and Individual Identities in a Canadian City', in V. Amit-Talai and H. Lustiger-Thaler (eds), *Urban Lives. Fragmentation and Resistance*, Toronto: McClelland & Stewart.

——— (1995), 'Migrant Selves and Stereotypes: Personal Context in a Postmodern World', in S. Pile and N. Thrift (eds), *Mapping the Subject: Geographies of Cultural Transformation*, London: Routledge.

——— (1997), *Transcendent Individual: Towards a Literary and Liberal Anthropology*, London: Routledge.

Robins, K. (1991), 'Tradition and Translation: National Culture in its Global Context', in J. Corner and S. Honey (eds), *Enterprise and Heritage*, London: Routledge.

Rouse, R. (1991), 'Mexican Migration and the Social Space of Postmodernism', *Diaspora*, 1(1), p. 8.

Rushdie, S. (1991), 'Imaginary Homelands', *Granta*, 9–21.

Sahlins, M. (1968), *Tribesmen*, Englewood Cliffs: Prentice-Hall.

Sarup, M. (1994), 'Home and Identity', in G. Robertson *et al.* (eds), *Travellers' Tales*, London: Routledge.

Schuetz, A. (1944), 'The Stranger: An Essay in Social Psychology', *American Journal of Sociology*, 49(6).

Schwartz, T. (1975), 'Cultural Totemism', in G. de Vos and L. Romanucci-Ross (eds), *Ethnic Identity*, Palo Alto: Mayfield.

—— (1976), 'Relations among Generations in Time-Limited Cultures', in T. Schwartz (ed.), *Socialization as Cultural Communication*, Berkeley: University of California Press.

Silverstone, R., Hirsch, E. and Morley, D. (1994), 'Information and Communication Technologies and the Moral Economy of the Household', in R. Silverstone and E. Hirsch (eds), *Consuming Technologies. Media and Information in Domestic Spaces*, London: Routledge.

Simmel, G. (1984[1911]), 'Female Culture', in *Georg Simmel: On Women, Sexuality and Love*, ed. G. Oakes, New Haven: Yale University Press.

Steiner, G. (1975), *After Babel*, London: Oxford University Press.

—— (1978), *On Difficulty, and Other Essays*, Oxford: Oxford University Press.

Strathern, M. (1981), *Kinship at the Core*, Cambridge: Cambridge University Press.

—— (1990), 'Proposing the Motion that "The Concept of Society is Theoretically Obsolete"', *Group for Debates in Anthropological Theory*, Dept of Social Anthropology, University of Manchester.

—— (1992), 'Writing Societies, Writing Persons', *The History of the Human Sciences*, 5(1): 5–16.

Strauss, B. (1984), *Paare Passantem*, Munich/Vienna: Hanser.

Torgovinick, M. (1992), 'Slasher Stories', in *New Formations: Journal of Culture/ Theory/Practice (The Question of 'Home)*, 17: 133–45.

Weil, S. (1978), 'Anthropology Becomes Home; Home Becomes Anthropology', in A. Jackson (ed.), *Anthropology at Home*, London: Routledge.

Wright, G. (1991), 'Prescribing the Model Home', in A. Mack (ed.), *Home: A Place in the World, Social Research* (special edition), 58(1): 213–25.

Yamba, C. B. (1992), 'Going There and Getting There: The Future as a Legitimating Charter for Life in the Present', in S. Wallman (ed.), *Contemporary Futures*, London: Routledge.

Part II
Perceptions of
Identity in a World
of Movement

1

Risky Hiatuses and the Limits of Social Imagination: Expatriacy in the Cayman Islands

Vered Amit-Talai

Monique originated from Montreal, but in 1995, she had been resident in Grand Cayman for eight years, following a two-year sojourn in Bermuda.[1] Monique had met and married her British husband in the Caribbean. They both held full-time jobs, owned a house and were raising their children in Cayman. Although she had been trained and educated in Montreal, Monique's entire adult working life had been spent outside Canada. Monique doubted that she would have been able to command a comparably high salary in Quebec; but in spite of this, she complained that 'We never manage to save anything, we just spend it.' She was expecting to return to Montreal, but wasn't sure when. She and her husband wanted to save some money before 'returning', because both wanted to continue their education in Canada. They had no desire to 'leave any strings behind' in Cayman, so they were planning to sell their house when they did finally leave. Monique was looking forward to the move to Montreal; but she also feared it. It was difficult to go back in some ways. She knew other people who had gone back to Canada, but had returned to Cayman after only a year away. 'It's [the return to Montreal] going back to *reality*.'

So a significant portion of Monique's life, the period during which she had held her first full-time job, married, given birth to and started to raise children had not been quite *real*, or at least not as fully real as life

1. Aliases have been used throughout in place of real names so as to preserve the confidentiality of interviewees on Grand Cayman.

in Montreal. Not all expatriates in Cayman expect or wish to return to
their country of origin; but Monique's interpretation of transnational
movement as a state of liminality and Cayman as a place outside normal/
'real' life frequently recurs in the migration narratives of other foreign
workers residing in the Islands. It is a rendition that is encouraged by
enactments of Caymanian government policies that largely proscribe long-
term immigration. It is also an image used by both clients and hosts to
define and transact the stays of the million or so tourists who visit Cayman
every year.

    In what follows, I offer an ethnographic portrait of institutionalized
transience in Cayman as a cautionary tale against assumptions that spatial
displacement and increased border crossings necessarily or easily
engender new forms of imagined community, even when old notions of
'home' lose their salience. Further, I want to consider the political and
personal implications of migration approached as liminality: the unintended and often unwelcome ways in which expectations of temporary
interstitiality position people and places within a global economy and
political geography that they cannot, after all, step out of.

Ethnography of Transnationalism

Flows of images, voices and data 'more real than the real' (Featherstone
and Lash 1995:9), hyperspaces with 'no sense of place' (Luke 1995:97),
habitations in 'the beyond' (Bhabha 1994:7), an explosion of hybridity
in a world in which 'nothing is fixed, given, [or] certain' (Lash and Urry
1994:10): these are metaphors regularly invoked in a range of scholarly
commentary on the late twentieth-century human condition. While
anthropologists have hardly been immune to the millennialist hyperbole
of global fluidity (Rosaldo 1989; Appadurai 1990; Gupta and Ferguson
1992), it is also not difficult to understand why the practitioners of a
discipline that has more often focused on the finely observed details
of face-to-face social relations might find this ungrounded vision
unsatisfying.

    Yet anthropologists have also spent the better part of the last two
decades trying to escape from or redeem a legacy of overly fixed and
bounded ethnographic subjects. How then to reconcile the usual siting
of ethnographic work in particular places and the prosaics of everyday
life with engagement in a wider scholarly quest for global contextualiza-
tion, especially when the price of failure sometimes seems to be
intellectual marginalization in the 'neoworld order' (Featherstone and
Lash, 1995) of informational 'flows' (Castells 1989, 1996)?

The effort to find a *rapprochement* is earnestly apparent in a particular version of transnationalism that appears to be gaining currency, particularly in American migration literature. Here, the focus is on migration from the postcolonial states of the Caribbean, Pacific Rim or Latin America to world cities like New York or Los Angeles. Neither 'temporary' labour migrants, nor 'permanent' immigrants, these 'trans-migrants' maintain ongoing personal networks and investments that cross state boundaries. In spite of the occasional reference to, or example of, networks spanning more then two countries, for the most part this literature is concerned with bi-statal affiliations that extend only between the migrant's country of origin and one country of settlement, i.e. the United States (Kearney 1995:559).

There are some important continuities between this dual focus and previous anthropological, and in particular earlier British, research on migration. In 1977, a volume edited by James Watson and entitled *Between Two Cultures* refigured contemporary invocations of inter-stitiality and featured accounts of ethnographic research conducted by the same researcher at both the sending and the receiving ends of migration streams. Fields of social relations crossing geographic, cultural and economic borders were maintained by rural migrants encountered by British anthropologists in a variety of African urban settings (cf. Mitchell 1969; Mayer 1961). And as Basch *et al.* themselves have noted, scholarly recognition of the rotating circulation and continuing remittances home of Caribbean migrants has been long-standing (1994:31).

But contemporary ethnographers of transnationalism are more likely to insist on the discontinuities between their and previous approaches, to emphasize that they have moved beyond the mystifications of previous bounded visions of culture and society and the limitations attendant upon conflations of place, culture and identity (Basch *et al* 1994; Olwig 1997). They are analysing emergent fields of political and social relations from new global perspectives that problematize the siting of culture, rather than treating it as a local given (ibid.).

Significantly, the ethnography of transnationalism resists the indulgences of free-flowing discussion more grounded in metaphor than empirical description. Far from simply invoking disjunction and interstitiality, much of this literature is informed by a cross- disciplinary political economy, and embeds particular places and people within global labour and financial markets (Basch *et al.* 1994; Szanton Blanc *et al.* 1995; Gardiner Barber 1995; Rouse 1995). Thus contemporary migration is situated within a fragmented and dispersed international system of production that disrupts local labour markets and displaces workers in postcolonial countries at the same time as it establishes political and economic links with 'core' economies (cf. Sassen 1988, 1991, 1994; Waters 1995). Workers from these countries who have migrated to global cities like New York are positioned within an urban workforce increasingly polarized between a corporate business service élite on the one hand and a growing presence of marginalized, disadvantaged economic actors on the other (Sassen 1996). As Saskia Sassen has noted, '[M]ajor cities in the highly developed world are the terrain where a multiplicity of globalization processes assume concrete, localized forms' (1996:210). The ethnographers of the 'new' migration and the ensuing transnational networks are certainly helping to document at least some of these localized forms.

And yet there is still an inescapable sense here of missed opportunities; of traditional research ambits recycled in new euphemisms. Migrants from the Caribbean, with its long-standing tradition of circular migration, continue to predominate, particularly in the American incarnations of this literature. In their determination to document emergent structures of interstitial affiliations, the ethnographers of transnationalism appear instead to have sought out familiar networks of relations that can be readily 'reinterpreted' within the new canons. The ironic result is that relatively stable and often venerable systems of bi-statal circular migration are being used as a paradigm for the analysis and representation of recent forms of destabilization. And very little attention is being paid to newer forms and directions of migration that have emerged in response to new informa-tion technologies and global restructuring of production and financial markets: American firms 'bodyshopping' for bargain basement Indian software writers (Rapaport 1996); an increase in high-level professional movements between EC countries or between global cities (Salt 1992a; Beaverstock 1994); the growing convergence between business travel and migration (Salt 1992b), which has been a factor of the explosion of international consultancy work; and the migration of skilled workers, managers and professionals from older developed economies to new zones of economic activity in newly industrialized countries, export processing centres, and offshore financial centres such as Grand Cayman.

Even more disappointing, the ethnography of transnationalism does not fully engage with recent processes of displacement that the literary theorists, for all their nebulous, expansive rhetoric, have aptly identified. One can but heartily agree with Hastrup and Olwig when they assert that it is about 'time that anthropology recognized its duty to deal with de-stabilization . . .'(1997:6). Karen Fog Olwig may also be right that 'sociocultural contexts of greater permanence and sustenance' are emerging in the interstices between local and global conditions of life

(Olwig 1997: 35), at least in respect to migrants from the West Indian island of Nevis where she conducted fieldwork. And she is probably right that such cultural sites are not unique to Nevis or the West Indies.

But I am not sure that such a focus, in and of itself, takes us very far in understanding either the nature or the sources of the very real insecurities produced both within and across state borders by recent global economic restructuring. It is not only that an increasing number of migrants experience successive movements to second, third and fourth countries of 'settlement' (Bhachu 1996), that the distinction between migration and other forms of movement has become less evident or that the relationship between workplace and home has also become unsettled for many people who will never venture much beyond one state's boundaries. It is also that these increasing economic pressures for a 'flexible' global workforce have not by and large been accompanied by the development of new institutional infrastructures that recognize or respond to the conditions imposed by such labour mobility. An increasing number and variety of workers have thus become caught in the crossfire between structural pressures towards career and geographic mobility, on the one hand, and worker and citizenship entitlements still predicated on the assumption/principle of stable employment and residence, on the other. The result has been a ramification, up the socio-economic hierarchy, of the precariousness long experienced by the most marginalized workers of capitalist economies. This chapter explores the circumstances, expressions and responses that these insecurities have generated among some expatriate contractual workers in the north-west Caribbean island of Grand Cayman.

The Cayman Islands

The Cayman Islands are one of six Caribbean territories that still retain their British colonial status. Until the 1970s, the islanders largely relied on a maritime economy, first exploiting giant turtles in local waters and then, when these were depleted, gradually venturing further and further afield in turtling expeditions to the south coast of Cuba or the cays off Nicaragua. During the twentieth century, a growing number of Caymanian men sought work in foreign merchant marines, and the economy of the Islands became increasingly dependent on their remittances home. Some of these seamen, however, eventually settled abroad, forming part of a constant stream of emigration from Cayman. Until the 1970s, then, the Cayman Islands were net exporters of population to other islands in the region, as well as to North America.

During the 1970s, this situation began to change rapidly with the adoption of new banking legislation and the alleviation of the mosquito problem. The former facilitated the development of the Cayman Islands as an offshore banking centre, while the latter enabled the development of the tourism industry. Today, luxury condominium and hotel complexes thickly line the Seven Mile Beach tourist strip; traffic jams are a ubiquitous presence; and the Cayman Islands are ranked as the world's fifth largest financial centre. These developments have entailed dramatic shifts in lifestyles and consumption patterns for most Caymanians, including one of the highest per capita incomes in the western hemisphere. But the economic monopoly of tourism and finance has sustained and increased the Islands' reliance on foreign capital, while also creating a new dependence on the import of labour.

Over the last two decades, Cayman's residential population has more than doubled, and much of that increase has come through inmigration. As the influx of migrants has increased, Cayman's immigration regulations have been applied with increasing exclusivity and severity. The vast majority of recent newcomers to Cayman will not be able to settle permanently in this territory. They and their dependants are limited to the duration of short-term, albeit frequently renewable, work contracts with initial terms of between a few months and a few years. In 1994, according to estimates provided by the Government Economics and Statistics Office, non-Caymanians, i.e. residents without permanent Caymanian status, made up 40.4 per cent of the total labour force.

Expatriates work in every sector of the economy, from construction to offshore finance. They fill many of the positions in the civil service, and their labour is essential to the tourism industry. The majority of these workers come from Jamaica, Honduras, North America, Britain and Ireland. The foreign labour force is, in large part, skilled, with skilled workers and professionals accounting for 42 per cent and 17.4 per cent respectively of all work-permit holders (Shah 1995:510–11). The largest group of unskilled expatriate workers in Cayman are domestics, who make up approximately 60 per cent of this category. Many domestic workers come to Cayman from other parts of the same region, and as such are part of the long-standing stream of Caribbean emigration that anthropologists have encountered in the United States and Britain. This chapter is however concerned with the factors involved in prompting the smaller but growing migration of workers in the opposite direction, moving from North America and Europe to take advantage of the opportunities arising from the development of tourism and offshore banking in a number of Caribbean islands.

Inescapable Marginalization

In Grand Cayman, there are hundreds of young twenty-something migrants from North America and Europe working on temporary labour contracts in the shops, dive boats, restaurants and hotels that cater to their older tourist countrymen and women. For many this is a temporary interlude between one year and the next of their studies; for others this is but one stop-over on a long, multi-sited world tour combining work and travel; and for still others, a visit to Cayman, intended as a pause to consider longer-term work and migration possibilities, becomes progressively extended as the uncertainties that brought them to the Islands fail to clarify.

These young travellers in Cayman are a small segment of a generation of youth in many postindustrial economies, often highly educated, for whom long-term salaried jobs appear increasingly out of reach. Downsizing and contracting out, by private corporations as well as by governments bent on deficit reduction, have succeeded in virtually eliminating a whole rung of middle-level positions, while increasing dependence on short-term consultancy work for white-collar and skilled jobs that would once have been provided in-house. In the name of organizational flexibility, the economic marginalization and precariousness that Saskia Sassen has noted for the blue-collar force manning the informal economy of global cities has been progressively extended to include an ever-wider range of workers in many more locales.

Not all the peers of the young expatriates in Cayman respond, however, by venturing abroad. Most take on, instead, a series of similarly short-term contracts and/or temporary jobs, but for firms in their locality. By definition, however, this structural disposability is associated with an uneven and insecure supply of work. As Kimiko Hawkes, a Montreal graduate student, explained, 'Even when you're making a living, it's like being unemployed all the time, because you're always looking for jobs.' A perennial hunt for temporary contracts and jobs locally can therefore quickly expand spatially in ever-widening parameters, increasing the likelihood that a multiplicity of employers will also be associated with a multiplicity of places. 'Flexible' labour increasingly means geographically mobile contract workers. But this transience of both place and work and the continuous physical and social displacement it involves can operate *within* state boundaries as well as across them.

It is not hard to find echoes among youthful workers who have *not* left Montreal of that same sense of limbo, of not having yet arrived at a 'real' destination of permanence and stability, that appeared in Monique's account of her time in the Cayman Islands and her expectations of a return to Canada.

Escaping Marginalization

There is another kind of foreign worker in Cayman. Also from North America and Europe and to a lesser extent from other islands in the Caribbean region, these are skilled workers and professionals in their thirties and forties. Many in this category of migrants held full-time, long-term jobs in their countries of origin before applying for and then taking up a short-term contract position in the Cayman Islands. Why move, then? High, tax-free salaries and pleasant living conditions are certainly attractive enticements; but expatriates like Ann, John and Mary, or Christine were among a number who also reported a longing to get away, for new opportunities, for 'adventure', to escape jobs that had reached a dead end; these were aspirations and needs that predated any notice of the Cayman Islands.

Ann and her husband, both British-born, had met in Germany, where he was working at the time. They had lived in Germany for a while, but Ann didn't want to stay because she couldn't find work there. They returned to England but even though they both found jobs, they continued to dream of being able to live abroad . They came to Cayman, not because they thought it was 'a jewel in the Caribbean', but because it offered job opportunities and the chance of a foreign 'adventure'. Their original intention had been to come for only two years; and this, indeed, was what they had promised their young son. By 1996, however, they had been living in Cayman for nearly five years, and now they had the 'wanderlust'. They were thinking of New Zealand as a possible destination, and had just recently sold their house in Britain. Ann said that an American friend, an artist who lived in Cayman Brac, had once told her that when you live in the Cayman Islands for a few years, 'you become homeless', and Ann could now see what she meant. 'Because you no longer feel at home in your own country, and I certainly don't feel comfortable here.'

John and Mary were also both British-born. John had first arrived in the Cayman Islands in 1982 as a 23-year-old. He had seen his job advertised in Britain, but had never heard of the Cayman Islands before that. In fact, he had to go the library to look it up, and there wasn't much information available. He had come, not knowing what to expect, for 'the adventure aspect of it, the sun, sea, sand, to see the world'. It had been his first extended period outside England. Like many of the younger migrants currently in Cayman, he originally expected to come for a temporary visit before 'dotting' around the world; but 'Cayman had been so good', he stayed on. Mary had met John while visiting a relative in Grand Cayman and eventually she returned to take up a temporary job. According to Mary, 'I had a very good job in England, but I had gone as far as I could go in this job and I couldn't go any further. Life was pretty stale. I was looking for a change, for adventure, something different. I was sick of not earning much money, of not being able to travel. Having a relative here gave me access to living here for a while without a work-permit.' In 1995, when I met them, Mary had left her job to have a baby; but this also coincided with her replacement by a Caymanian (Caymanians having first preference), so her post was no longer available. John had recently been informed that his contract would not be renewed, because there were now qualified Caymanians available to fill this position. He was actively looking for another job. Britain was, according to John, 'a default place to be'. If all else failed, they could always go back; but whether they stayed in Cayman, returned to Britain, or moved to a third country depended on employment prospects. 'We would go wherever work is. We don't feel very tethered.' John and Mary had bought a small house in Georgetown, the Cayman capital. 'We gambled', said John, 'but we didn't bet the whole farm. We could have afforded to lose the $10,000 land transfer tax if we had to. If we knew we were staying here for another 10 years, we would probably have bought some place nicer, a larger place, maybe with a pool. We would go on more holidays. Now, we only go to England every 18 months . . . we're very conscious of money.' When he goes back to Britain, John said, 'it feels like home', because it's so familiar; but he also feels distanced. 'It's a very strange feeling going back to England.'

Christine had worked in Ottawa within the Canadian federal civil service for nearly two decades before moving to the Cayman Islands to take up a similar position. Her application for a job in Cayman had been part of a larger search that she had undertaken for employment in the Caribbean region. 'It was a concentrated effort on my part to get out of Canada and do something interesting.' Christine had been coming to the West Indies since the 1970s, when she had first holidayed in Jamaica, and had then subsequently worked and lived there for several months at a time in repeated visits. By 1991, Christine felt that Jamaica had become too violent a place to raise her child; and, while she was willing to consider a move to another region, she preferred to continue living in the Caribbean if possible. In 1995, she had been living in Grand Cayman for three years, and while she expected to stay on for a little longer, she was looking at some other possibilities of employment that would allow her to visit Canada more often, because her son was going back to attend school there. 'Ideally I'd like to maintain a base in Canada and a base in the Caribbean.' She had sold her house in Canada before moving, and had bought a small house in Cayman that she expected to keep, probably over the long term. At one point Christine considered a business venture on another Caribbean island; but this, as well as a position with a private consulting firm, did not prove to be financially viable. She has therefore stayed on in her Caymanian civil service job. Meanwhile, in the face of a contracting Canadian civil service, many of her friends and former colleagues in Canada have moved into freelance consulting work. 'Home' according to Christine, is the Ottawa Valley, where she can trace six generations of ancestors; but she feels most 'sentimental' and 'patriotic' about Montego Bay, even though she sees no reasonable prospect of living there.

In seeking an escape from contracting economies, professional migrants like Christine, Mary, John and Ann exchanged stale routines and capped salaries for more lucrative but insecure positions in the expanding economy of the Cayman Islands. Years later, they find that they cannot go backwards and they cannot go forwards. The jobs they left are no longer there to return to; they no longer feel comfortable or at ease in their country of origin, but finding a job in another country has proved difficult. That stalemate, however, reflects the very structural conditions that facilitated their migration to Cayman. The presence of foreign teachers, nurses, engineers, social workers, conservators, office managers and other such professionals in the Cayman Islands reflects the interplay between a shrinking social service system in many Western industrial countries and the infrastructural gaps engendered by an enlarging foreign service economy and limited indigenous manpower resources in Cayman. These conditions have persisted, and therefore continue to undermine the economic viability of either a return by these professionals to their country of origin or migration to a country with a similarly developed economy. In Cayman, moreover, they have become used to large, tax-free salaries and a high standard of living, perks not necessarily available in other developing economies with shortages of professionals, or even, for that matter in many affluent postindustrial economies. They are thus caught in the squeeze between the distribution of professional positions within the global economy and their own raised lifestyle expectations. So, here again, Monique's original characterization of leaving Cayman as a 'return to reality' is echoed.

However, expatriate professionals working in Cayman's offshore banking and business service sectors are involved in a somewhat different dynamic. The growth of offshore finance in Cayman has been emblematic of the dramatic expansion of the financial industries globally. Propelling this growth has been an increased mobility of capital that has been facilitated by a deregulation of capital markets (Campbell 1993:274), the internationalization of banking (Langdale 1985), and new information technology. These regulatory and technological shifts have made the financial industries so profitable that they have assumed an increasing centrality in the world economy at the expense of manufacturing and trade (Sassen 1994). Cayman's financial industries are, however, satellites of major financial and business centres such as New York, London and Tokyo. Expatriates working in this sector of the Caymanian economy are therefore operating outside the loop, or at the very least on the relative margins, of personal and occupational networks available to specialists moving between global cities. But, given the high salaries commanded by foreign professionals in Cayman, neither are they likely to be attractive prospects for 'bodyshopping' firms on a transnational search for bargain basement expertise.

Rather than offering a ready pathway to new employment and residential possibilities, the 'opportunities' offered by the thriving Caymanian economy can become a tenuous stalemate for expatriate professionals and skilled workers. Old homes seem distant and increasingly unfamiliar; the conditions that prompted their initial migration persist; and job prospects both in their countries of origin and in third countries are not always easy to access from the remove of the Cayman Islands. But neither can they remain where they are. Sooner or later, their contracts will not be renewed and they will have to leave.

Displacement and Partial Deterritorialization

The displaced do not experience temporary absences only to be confirmed in the well-ordered structure of normal life. Theirs is a more or less permanent experience of not being *in situ* as they negotiate a diversity of experiences in a deterritorialized world (Olwig 1997:34).

Much of Olwig's description of displacement is as pertinent to expatriates in Cayman as it is for Nevisians in Connecticut, Leeds, or the US Virgin

Islands. However, the displacement which she describes, the sense of not being *in situ*, is less a reflection of a deterritorialized world than of its very *partial* deterritorialization. Citizenship entitlements, social security provisions, pension benefits, rights of residence and, most particularly, migration are still more often predicated on national models of stable employment and populations than of deterritorialization. Meanwhile, many of the travellers following the trail laid by the fragmentation and dispersal of corporate production as well as increasingly mobile capital are doing so on a contractual basis rather than within the protective confines of corporate internal labour markets. Economic restructuring is undoubtedly producing transnational links and new fields of relations; but it is also ensuring that much of the labour mobility incited by this reorganization is being conducted without an institutional safety net and across state borders firmly retrenched against a free flow of migration. Nor is this institutional disjunction entirely accidental, for the whole point of contracting out is to reduce and limit corporate and state responsibilities towards labour, not to create new ones.

Expatriates in the Cayman Islands, like their mobile counterparts in emerging economic zones elsewhere, are therefore trying to navigate the incongruities of a world in which economic activity and property rights are increasingly denationalized while civil entitlements still remain quite firmly positioned within state and regional boundaries. Their allusions to a state of limbo, of homelessness, of neither leaving nor staying, appear to be quite reasonable descriptions of the interstitiality that can be occasioned by this partial deterritorialization. Without the benefit of statutory protections, as the stories above indicate, individuals like Ann, John, Mary and Christine employed a variety of quite divergent strategies to cushion the effects of the attendant insecurities: investing in Caymanian real estate or alternatively ensuring only a limited property investment; maintaining property in the country of origin or selling that property to facilitate mobility to a third country; investing the funds in Cayman's offshore financial sector, and so on. But even when foreign professionals maintained ownership of a house in their country of origin, as did many of the British migrants in Cayman, this property rarely constituted the linchpin of a set of kinship relations, as often occurs with Caribbean transmigrant networks (Basch *et al.* 1994; Olwig 1997). Nor was it a house they necessarily expected to live in again. Rented out to strangers, it certainly provided a foothold in the country of origin – but one of equity and financial security rather than an affective home or a stable anchor of cultural attachment in its own right.

Yet neither was Cayman home. It is important to recognize that the attenuation of many expatriates' attachment to Cayman reflected not only their tenuous legal status, but the degree to which their notion of home continued to be identified with a place of permanence and stability for both work and residence. In spite of a growing affective and social distanciation from old homes, many foreign workers in Cayman were unwilling to make an unequivocal emotional and/or financial investment in a place where they had no long-term security. Notwithstanding, most of the expatriates I spoke to still hoped eventually to 'land' in a secure situation, even as, for some of them, the years sped on without the materialization of these possibilities. Concomitantly, the experience in Cayman continued to be defined as liminal, a fare stage towards 'real' settlement somewhere else: a definition underlined by the dogged determination of the Caymanian government to deny permanent settlement to the vast majority of resident foreign workers.

All this, however, prompts the question why new, non-territorial forms of affiliation, identification and belonging have not developed. Given such ongoing uncertainties, their attenuated attachments to both their old and their current places and the openness that a number of expatriates expressed towards potential opportunities in entirely new locations, why is itineracy itself not presenting an alternative basis of identification and association for transmigrants? That the latter does not appear to be occurring among foreign workers in Cayman is not, I would argue, an indicator of their insensibility to the local situation or its wider context so much as of the limitations of displacement and transience alone as bases for collectivity.

New Collectivities?

In considering the barriers as well as the incentives to the emergence of new forms of collectivity that can act as mobile social anchors for people in precarious motion, it is useful, for a moment, to consider the location of our analytical perspective. Here I am as much, if not more, concerned with the anthropological gaze as with those of expatriate professionals in Cayman. I began this chapter by noting the challenges of reconciling the usual anthropological research orientation towards particular places and everyday life with an analysis of global systems. One response to this challenge, I suggested, has been a somewhat distorting recourse to the familiar ground of long-standing systems of circular migration between two places. But anthropologists in search of templates for transnational networks are as likely to be misled by their own occupational practices as their research sites. Like most academics, anthropologists operate within a highly structured and managed transnational field of professional organizations and interpersonal contacts. In the course of their training, professional appointments, scholarly production, intellectual communication and teaching, most anthropologists will regularly cross state boundaries. Their transnational presences are not, however, only or even primarily a product of personal journeys and communication. They are managed and supported by numerous professional associations, formal institutional affiliations, informational and communication systems, government programmes and funding explicitly oriented towards the creation and sustenance of transnational connections. While the proliferation and failure of institutions virtually guarantees that no one practitioner can have a comprehensive knowledge of the entire global anthropological organizational inventory, this is, nevertheless, a clearly bounded field demarcated by a predictable calendar of regular events and internationally recognized institutions and personages. There are certainly also many analogues to this kind of transnational organizational field outside academia: other professional associations, business and corporate alliances, the occupational, political and financial networks generated by bureaucracies like the World Bank or the IMF, and so on.

However, many of the people moving through the global labour market are doing so without the backing or signposts afforded by a clearly demarcated and synchronized associational field. They are moving through a market-place dominated by competing corporate and state actors and structured by contradictory epistemes governing the movement of labour and capital. And they are moving more often as individuals or small family units than as members of transnational organizations. Indeed, as I have noted earlier, an effect of global economic restructuring has been to increase the numbers of 'freelancers' providing services to corporate clients and their smaller affiliates. Far from having access to a transnational *habitus* of synchronized activities, the attention of many transmigrants is devoted simply to trying to map out what is happening, and when and where it is possible to go. As Lash and Urry (1994) have noted, the complexity and structurally contingent and fragmented nature of late twentieth-century global economic processes demand an increasing reflexivity from the subjects navigating them. But the very circumstances propelling that increased reflexivity can as easily dislocate a sense of belonging and rootedness as redirect it .

Ironically, one of the greatest barriers to the formation of new social identities and political associations may be the very ramification of displacement into an increasing range of sectors and classes. Professional expatriates in Cayman, newly minted university graduates in Canada, recruits to the growing army of international 'consultants' or pieceworkers in the garment industries of New York and Miami, are now often experiencing chronically uneven, dispersed and insecure supplies of work. But these are very different experiences of insecurity, and they imply divergent resources and responses. Foreign workers in Cayman may well recognize that Caymanian immigration and labour policies impose structural insecurities of place and work on *all* expatriates; but this has not translated into a common cause between American bankers working in offshore finance and the Jamaican maids who clean their homes.

Imagination, Boundaries and Resistance

For many labour migrants, place of origin or work roles and occupational relationships provide limited and not necessarily portable bases of cultural identification. The invention of alternative forms of non-localized community, however, can require a Herculean task of selective aggregation in the context of an accelerating circulation of people, objects and signs along increasingly extended routes (Lash and Urry 1994:2). There are limits to the social imaginary, and limits even further to actualizing what *can* be imagined. Madan Sarup was correct when he noted that the notion of home (and hence by extension of homelessness) is tied to the notion of identity, but equally correct in asserting that 'identities are not free-floating, they are limited by borders and boundaries' (1994:95). Such boundaries need not necessarily be linked to specific places, nationalities or ethnicities; as most anthropologists know from personal experience, they can also demarcate transnational, multi-ethnic fields of exchange, movement and interaction. However, enthusiastic exhorters of identity 'across the hyphen' or 'counter-communities' positioned in the 'risky experience of travel and transit' (Chambers 1996:53) often appear to confuse the relationship between uncertainty, deterritorialization, and boundary. In celebrating, as a basis for collective identity, the interstitiality that is frequently a product of competing pressures for de- and re-territorialization, they can end up being quite cavalier about the necessary and often immensely difficult conceptual and organizational work that is required to construct the boundaries of new forms of identity. They are also naive about the political and personal costs of failed or stillborn efforts at creating these new boundaries.

Precarious traversals of borders, tenuous legal statuses and rights, complicated evaluations of the opportunities and risks entailed in movement, can make old forms of belonging, of being 'at home', increasingly irrelevant or ineffective. In turn, this redundancy may generate a search for alternative bases of collective identification. But 'homelessness' is neither a sufficient nor, as the case of expatriates in Cayman indicates, by any means an automatic condition for new forms of affiliation. The latter require further, often unrealized, leaps of purposeful imagination as well as the delineation of new socially recognized boundaries.

What then of political resistance to economic processes that treat human beings as disposable: that demand mobility but leave mobile workers impaled on the national borders so easily traversed by capital? Evident throughout much of the literature on globalization is a hunger for a glimpse of new sites and prospects of resistance. For Rob Wilson and Wimal Dissanayake, it is local spaces, however reconfigured by global processes, that offer 'resources of hopes' (1996:4). For Basch *et al.*, transnational practices provide the basis for potential, if as yet largely unrealized, critiques of the domination by an emerging global capitalist class (1994: 291). For Stanley Aronowitz, postmodern social movements incorporate radical new conceptions of historical agency, speaking against the power of the multinationals as well as the national state (1992). Maybe . . .

Yet these claims appear to speak more often to the disorientation of many intellectuals in the face of *fin-de-siècle* economic and political shifts than to persuasive empirical accounts of popular resistance. It is, however, precisely in respect to this field, the investigation of the dynamics of collective consciousness and mobilization, that I think the traditional strength of anthropology, its attention to the prosaics and poetics of everyday life in an extraordinarily diverse range of situations, is most vital. The breadth of our ethnographic experience offers a scope for imagining political possibilities and social formations that others have not yet considered. But the depth of our ethnographic experience provides a sobering index of the gap between imagining and actualizing these possibilities. This concern with social practice, with the 'intersection between everyday life and the structures of power that impinge upon it' (Herzfeld 1997:158), can therefore furnish a powerfully grounded critique of globalizing processes that moves beyond sweeping invocations of fluidity or proclamations of faith in the imminence of radical resistance. As such, it is as likely to reveal the complex processes involved in *impeding* the formation of new transnational identities and affiliations as of *inciting* them.[2]

2. The research on which this chapter is based was funded by a grant from the Social Sciences and Humanities Research Council of Canada.

References

Appadurai, Arjun (1990), 'Disjuncture and Difference in the Global Cultural Economy', in Mike Featherstone (ed.), *Global Culture: Nationalism, Globalization and Modernity*, pp. 295–310. London, Newbury Park; New Delhi: Sage Publications.

Aronowitz, Stanley (1992), *The Politics of Identity: Class, Culture, Social Movements*. London and New York: Routledge.

Basch, Linda, Glick Schiller, Nina and Szanton Blanc, Cristina (1994), *Nations Unbound: Transnational Projects, Postcolonial Predicaments and Deterritorialized Nation-States*. Basle, Switzerland: Gordon and Breach Science Publishers.

Beaverstock, Jonathan V. (1994), 'Re-thinking Skilled International Labour Migration: World Cities and Banking Organisations', *Geoforum*, 25(3): 323–38.

Bhabha, Homi K. (1994), *The Location of Culture*. London and New York: Routledge.

Bhachu, Parminder (1996), 'The Multiple Landscapes of Transnational Asian Women in the Diaspora', in Vered Amit-Talai and Caroline Knowles (eds), *Resituating Identities: The Politics of Race, Ethnicity and Culture*, pp. 283–303. Peterborough, Ont.: Broadview Press.

Campbell, Duncan (1993), 'The Globalizing Firm and Labour Institutions', in Paul Bailey, Aurelio Parisotto and Geoffrey Renshaw (eds), *Multinationals and Employment: The Global Economy of the 1990s*, pp. 267–91. Geneva: International Labour Office.

Castells, Manuel (1989), *The Informational City*. Oxford: Blackwell.

—— (1996), 'The Net and the Self: Working Notes for a Critical Theory of the Informational Society', *Critique of Anthropology*, 16(1):9–38.

Chambers, Iain (1996), 'Signs of Silence, Lines of Listening', in Iain Chambers and Lidia Curti (eds), *The Post-Colonial Question: Common Skies, Divided Horizons*, pp. 47–62. London and New York: Routledge.

Featherstone, Mike and Lash, Scott (1995), 'Globalization, Modernity and the Spatialization of Social Theory: An Introduction', in Mike Featherstone, Scott Lash and Roland Robertson (eds), *Global Modernities*, pp. 1–24. London, Thousand Oaks; New Delhi: Sage Publications.

Gardiner Barber, Pauline (1995), 'Invisible Labour, Transnational Lives: Gendered Work and New Social Fields in Coastal Philippines', *Culture*, XV(2)5–26.

Gupta, Akhil and Ferguson, James (1992), 'Beyond "Culture": Space, Identity and the Politics of Difference', *Cultural Anthropology*, 7(1): 6–23.

Hastrup, Kirsten and Fog Olwig, Karen (1997), 'Introduction', in Karen Fog Olwig and Kirsten Hastrup (eds), *Siting Culture: The Shifting Anthropological Object*, pp.1–16. London and New York: Routledge.

Herzfeld, Michael (1997), *Cultural Intimacy: Social Poetics in the Nation-State*. New York and London: Routledge.

Kearney, M. (1995), 'The Local and The Global: The Anthropology of Globalization and Transnationalism', *Ann. Rev. Anthropol.*, 24:547–65.

Langdale, John (1985), 'Electronic Funds Transfer and the Internationalisation of the Banking and Finance Industry', *Geoforum*, 16:1–13.

Lash, Scott and Urry, John (1994), *Economies of Signs and Spaces*, London, Thousand Oaks; New Delhi: Sage Publications.

Luke, Timothy W. (1995), 'New World Order or Neo-world Orders: Power, Politics and Ideology in Informationalizing Glocalities', in Mike Featherstone, Scott Lash and Roland Robertson (eds), *Global Modernities*, pp. 91–107.

Mayer, Phillip (1961), *Townsmen or Tribesmen*. Capetown: Oxford University Press.

Mitchell, J. Clyde (1969), 'Urbanization, Detribalization, Stabilization and Urban Commitment in Southern Africa: 1968', in Paul Meadows and Ephraim H. Mizruchi (eds), *Urbanism, Urbanization and Change*. Reading, Mass.: Addison-Wesley.

Olwig, Karen Fog (1997), 'Cultural Sites: Sustaining a Home in a Deterritorialized World', in Karen Fog Olwig and Kirsten Hastrup (eds), *Siting Culture: The Shifting Anthropological Object*, pp. 17–38. London and New York: Routledge.

Rapaport, Richard (1996), 'Bangalore', *Wired*, February: 112–70.

Rosaldo, Renato (1989), *Culture and Truth: The Remaking of Social Analysis*. Boston: Beacon Press.

Rouse, Roger (1995), 'Questions of Identity: Personhood and Collectivity in Transnational Migration to the United States', *Critique of Anthropology*, 15(4):351–80.

Salt, John (1992a), 'Migration Processes among the Highly Skilled in Europe', *International Migration Review*, XXVI(2):484–505.

—— (1992b), 'The Future of International Labor Migration'. *International Migration Review*, XXVI(4):1077–111.

Sarup, Madan (1994), ' Home and Identity', in George Robertson, Melinda Nash, Lisa Tickner, Jon Bird, Barry Curtis and Tim Putnam (eds), *Travellers' Tales: Narratives of Home and Displacement*, pp. 93–104. London and New York: Routledge.

Sassen, Saskia (1988), *The Mobility of Labor and Capital: A Study in International Investment and Labor Flow*. New York: Cambridge University Press.

—— (1991), *The Global City: New York, London, Tokyo*. Princeton, NJ: Princeton University Press.

—— (1994), *Cities in a World Economy*. London: Thousand Oaks; New Delhi: Pine Forge Press

(1996), 'Whose City Is It? Globalization and the Formation of New Claims', *Public Culture*, 8(2):205–23.

Shah, Ryhaan (ed.)(1995), *Cayman Islands Yearbook 95 & Business Directory*. Grand Cayman: Cayman Free Press.

Szanton Blanc, Cristina, Basch, Linda and Glick Schiller, Nina (1995), 'Transnationalism, Nation-States and Culture', *Current Anthropology*, 36(4):683–6.

Waters, Malcolm (1995), *Globalization*, London and New York: Routledge.

Watson, James (ed.) (1977), *Between Two Cultures*, Oxford: Basil Blackwell.
Wilson, Rob and Dissanayake, Wimal (1996), 'Introduction: Tracking the Global/Local', in Rob Wilson and Wimal Dissanayake (eds), *Global/Local; Cultural Production and the Transnational Imaginary*, pp. 1–18. Durham and London: Duke University Press.

Coming Home to a Dream: A Study of the Immigrant Discourse of 'Anglo-Saxons' in Israel

Nigel Rapport

Introduction

Deep in the Negev desert lies the Israeli new town of Mitzpe Ramon. And in Mitzpe Ramon's modernistic, state-sponsored Visitors' Centre and Museum, between exhibits of the town's pioneering past and projected future, hangs this (English) sign:

MITZPE RAMON AS AN IMAGE OF THE STATE OF ISRAEL
MITZPE RAMON IS LIKE THE STATE OF ISRAEL IN MINIATURE.
— IN ITS SIZE
— IN ITS STATUS IN THE REGION
— IN ITS SPIRIT
MITZPE RAMON IS SMALL AND ISOLATED
LIKE THE STATE OF ISRAEL.
ITS BEGINNINGS, LIKE THOSE OF THE STATE OF ISRAEL,
CAME OF A FAITH THAT THE DESERT CAN BECOME
A FLOWERING GARDEN.
ITS EVERYDAY LIFE, LIKE THAT OF ISRAEL, TENDS TO
DISSOLVE
THE DREAM AND DELAY ITS REALIZATION.
SOME BECOME TIRED
SOME DESPAIR AND LEAVE

SOME LACK PATIENCE
SOME LACK STRENGTH
SOME THIS . . . SOME THAT.
BUT AS IN ISRAEL, SO IN MITZPE RAMON:
THERE ARE THOSE WHO ARE CAPTIVATED
BY THE SPELL OF THE PLACE
THERE ARE THOSE WHO ARE INTOXICATED
BY THE MOUNTAIN AIR AND WIDE OPEN SPACES
AND THERE ARE THOSE WHO SENSE UNBORN POTENTIAL.

MITZPE RAMON IS A REFLECTION OF ISRAEL
HARDSHIP AND BEAUTY IN ONE.

Here is the development town represented as microcosm of the developing state.

Since its creation, in 1948, the modern-day State of Israel, for purposes of defence as well as development, has functioned as a highly centralized organism. Not least amongst its concerns has been language: the language of its citizens; the language of its self-descriptions. For when 'Next year in Jerusalem', from being a ubiquitous phrase of prayerful longing of generations of Diasporic Jews – longing for a talismanic dream-future; a centre to their lives, at once physical and spiritual, to call 'home' – becomes a present-day reality, dramatic measures are in order for a new routinizing of the everyday. Otherwise, the dream-future might remain 'matter out of place' from which speakers expect presently to awake (as Hobsbawm has observed, notions of 'home' move us perhaps most powerfully as absence or negation (1991:63)). Thus, since 1948, with its official policy to welcome the repatriation on Israeli soil of the entire, global Jewish family, the institutions of the Israeli state have gone to some length properly and 'officially' to define the country's new beginning and to provide normative imagery for its citizens' daily discourse.

Not that such discursive measures are unusual. Anthropologically we are well aware of officers of centralistic polities seeking to impose official images and ideology on the manifold areas and arenas of their state domain, so as to focus citizens (and visitors) on one view of past and present, and one line of future development. Indeed, in such imagery, it has been widely argued, is to be found an important vehicle of state control, an essential fount of state authority and power. Compassed by the formulae of official public discourse, citizens are often said to find it impossible to express themselves 'accurately', to articulate 'true' needs and interests, to think beyond predefinitions that obfuscate social reality, that serve merely to bolster the hegemony of the state (Mueller 1970:103–6; Zaslavsky 1982:82–5; Goldschlaeger 1985:165).

But what of the circumstances of such discourse when the integrity of the nation-state can today be found to be under threat from perhaps unprecedented movements of populations, from people who determine to choose the terms of their citizenship from amongst an increasingly wide and 'compressed' array of discursive practices, thus laying claim to 'creolized' meanings and identities significantly distinct from those predefined by conventional practice within the state (Paine 1992; Hannerz 1987)? How does the imposition of verbal imagery fare when, as Marx puts it (1980), we find nation-states no longer regardable as single entities within geographically definable boundaries but rather as increasingly transitory sites for interaction between individuals and communities: between series of partially overlapping, open social aggregates that differ widely from one another, whose various boundaries vary between situations, and whose ultimate extent is global? To what extent does the state version of a new beginning, of the institutionalized dream-become-reality, actually colour its new citizens' daily lives? How, in short, does the official discourse translate into individual constructions of immigrant identity?

These are the questions I treat. I do so through a case-study of David Feinberg and Rachel Silberstein, two recent Jewish immigrants from the United States who came to live in Mitzpe Ramon at roughly the same time as I did (cf. Rapport 1996; 1997). Both have chosen to make definite breaks with their American pasts and to build new homes for themselves in the Holy Land. Indeed, in moving to Mitzpe Ramon and not a more established or successful settlement, they have become not just *olim chadashim* ['new immigrants'] but *chalutzim*: 'pioneers' within the pioneering state. But in what way do their conceptions of their new home-lives in Mitzpe Ramon relate to official, administrative ones? For the state, as we have heard, immigration to Mitzpe Ramon is synonymous with membership of the renewed Israeli family. Being at home in the new town is imagined as one of the institutional routes (running alongside the Ministry of Absorption, the army, the *kibbutz*, the *moshav*, the *Histadrut* labour union) to assuming the identity of the 'renewed' Jew: 'redeemed' from generations of Diaspora. For David and Rachel, as we shall see, making new homes in Mitzpe Ramon entails importing and preserving what they take to be the distilled essences of their American pasts. They come to be at home in Israel and in Mitzpe Ramon only to the extent that they feel they are retaining their distinct American, individual, even Diasporic identities – and by coming to terms with the paradox this represents.[1]

The Setting

American Jews who immigrate to Israeli new towns are something of a rarity. They are unusual, firstly, in immigrating at all. The idea of making *aliyah* ['ascending to the Holy Land'] has not been central to American Zionism, which has more entailed political and economic support for the Jewish State; and less than 1 per cent of American Jewry has immigrated since 1948. Secondly, they are unusual because once in Israel, 75 per cent of American immigrants head for established urban locations, or else for *kibbutzim* and *moshavim* ['communalist and collectivist villages'] (18 per cent). Only 7 per cent, at most, settle in 'development towns' (cf. Avruch 1981:53–6; Isaacs 1966; Gitelman 1982). And yet a development town is certainly what Mitzpe Ramon represents.

The general condition of these Israeli new towns has been roundly portrayed.[2] Here are some thirty settlements, planted over fifteen years in peripheral and/or strategic parts of the country (the Galilee, the Negev) and away from the heavily-concentrated coastal strip in the west. Established by government statute rather than arising out of local demand, they were largely financed from the national development budget (by the international Jewish Agency). Since, they have been remote-controlled by competing and politically partisan Government ministries, and their local functionaries, more in accordance with heterogeneous external conceptions and policies than with internal conditions. Not surprisingly, many (most?) of these 'development towns' have found great difficulty in maintaining a social core, attracting a rural hinterland or attaining economic take-off.

The new-town of Mitzpe Ramon has suffered the history and stigma of its set. It was founded in 1954, with the strong support of the Ministry of Defence, and soon acquired a complete infrastructure (shops, industrial zones, apartment blocks, schools, synagogues, clinic, local and national government offices); also some few thousand new Moroccan immigrants as citizens.[3] However, with only army bases and self-contained *kibbutzim*

---

1. Notions of home, it is interesting to note, are often defined by a sense of circularity, not to say paradox: 'a place of origin returned to' (Hollander 1991:34; cf. also Hobsbawm 1991:65).

2. For example Cohen 1970; Deshen 1970; Aronoff 1973; Marx 1976; Efrat 1984.

3. Local and national government censuses are unable to agree on exact statistics of population growth and decline.

for company, and lying one-third of the way between Beer-Sheva (a town of 100,000 on the Negev desert's northern edge) and Eilat (a town of 40,000 on the southern tip), Mitzpe Ramon was isolated. Moreover, when, in 1967, a new paved road between Beer-Sheva and Eilat took a different route (via another new town), Mitzpe Ramon lost even the company of passing traffic – and its main source of income, aside from some light industry and gypsum and clay mining – and people left in droves. The population total sank below 1,500, and the only incomers were a few score 'Black Hebrews': part of an impoverished revitalization sect of American negroes from Chicago and Detroit (via Liberia) who lived largely on welfare (cf. Singer 1979). With empty, often vandalized factories and flats, the atmosphere in Mitzpe Ramon was generally found to be depressive. Distant from the main Israeli markets, entrepreneurs put no trust in the longevity of compensatory Government subsidies for new businesses. Nor did they have faith in the diligence of a primarily Moroccan workforce.[4] In outside Israeli eyes, Mitzpe Ramon became 'the real Wild West'; 'a badly designed, thrown-up, concrete mass'; populated by work-shy, working-class and violent layabouts who had 'no vision of a better future', and no way to reach it even if they had; 'not nice people', in short, 'and not the sort of place you would want to take your wife to', unless of course you liked being 'knee-deep in the mire'.[5]

Nevertheless, in the hope of attracting new settlers, the Government advertised further 'development-zone' dispensations (on income tax, on rental prices, on mortgage terms). Bureaucrats with local faces gradually replaced outside appointees. And in the late 1980s the population total began to show growth.[6] For, notwithstanding its problems, on the panoramic brim of Ramon Crater (an enormous wind-gouged excavation) and at 850 metres above sea-level, Mitzpe Ramon did possess an aesthetically very singular location. Hence, artists were encouraged to colonize, asthmatics too; the local High School also launched an art-focused programme for gifted students who wished to board. Tourists began to be more professionally catered for, not only in the aforementioned Visitors' Centre but also in a youth hostel, restaurant

4. Although the largest immigrant group to have arrived in Israel since 1948, the Moroccans are not traditionally regarded as having made the most successful or committed of migrations (cf. Klaff 1981:57).

5. Anthropological fieldwork in Mitzpe Ramon was carried out by participant observation in 1989. Names are pseudonyms; when anonymous, the reported speech is that of informants met outside the town.

6. The large influx of Soviet immigrants to Israel of the 1990s is beyond the ethnographic scope of the present piece.

and gardens. After the Palestinian *intifada* took hold further north, 400,000 tourists were known to flit through Mitzpe Ramon in one year; a new Ramon Crater Nature Park complex was planned, which might cater for a million. Moreover, while these latter figures remained pipe dreams, that of about 35 English-speaking Jews, mostly Americans, who became newly resident in the town was not.

Most American immigrants to Israel are under thirty, single, female, religiously observant, and have invested heavily in an ethnic Jewish identity whilst in the United States (Gitelman 1982:63–4; Avruch 1981:58). They also tend to be well-to-do, and hence neither attracted to new towns by the carrot of government subventions nor prone to being bullied there by bureaucratic sticks; for, if dissatisfied, they can always return 'States-side'. Those who have now come to Mitzpe Ramon might be expected to possess rather different sociological profiles, then, and this indeed turns out to be the case. For they are not young; many are not single, or particularly religiously observant; some are 'mixed' couples (*oleh* and *sabra* ['immigrant and Israeli-born'], that is); and more than a few are entering upon retirement. Furthermore, for all there does seem to be a financial incentive: in Mitzpe Ramon they can buy a retirement villa or rent apartments and make do on a pension in ways that would be precluded elsewhere. In Mitzpe Ramon, as Prager puts it with regard to other elderly 'long-distance movers', they can journey towards self-development without economic hassle, and 'let it all hang out' (1985).

Moreover, in Mitzpe Ramon it is less a Jewish identity in which these new immigrants can be seen to invest than an American one. Such, indeed, was the case for David Feinberg, who moved there with his wife Mirium on the occasion of his retirement at the end of 1988, and for Rachel Silberstein, who came then too, at the formal (and financial) settlement of her divorce; and it is upon these two individuals that I shall now concentrate. Both David and Rachel remained Americans not just in their talk, in the 'patriotic' posturings of their 'mother-country imagery' (Gold and Paine 1984:2,4) and in their choice of English-language, American-run settings to display and exchange such imagery, but, significantly, in the way they went about substantiating their future national (Israeli) identities through recreating the cognitive and physical environments of their past (US) ones.[7]

David and Rachel also remained Americans in the everyday categorizations of their Israeli neighbours in Mitzpe Ramon. For the latter, at least,

7. Cf. Thomas and Znaniecki (1984:239ff.) for a corresponding argument on the behaviour of Polish immigrants earlier in the century in the USA.

they were (in a neat terminological inversion) 'Anglo-Saxon Israelis' – which was how I came to meet them.

The Immigrants

Flying into Tel Aviv's Ben-Gurion airport in 1988 (*en route* to a new post at Ben-Gurion University), I was met by a representative of the British Immigrants' Society; he recognized me because of the blue-and-white badge I had been told to wear: 'I'm Coming Home.' In a jiffy I was past the passport queue and proceeding upstairs to Immigration. 'Don't worry', he assured me, 'but when we get up there there'll be half-a-dozen Russians on one side of you and half-a-dozen Ethiopians on the other, not knowing what's hit 'em. We've got them all up there tonight! But we'll soon have you through.' True to his word, I was the first to see 'his friend behind the computer', receive my immigration papers and identity numbers, and be heading down the road towards the Negev desert.

In Mitzpe Ramon I discovered it was not my Britishness that was so salient, but the fact that I spoke English. First, I was allocated my particular flat by the man from the Building Ministry because he remembered there was an English girl living in the block for me to talk to. Then, the café owner was to conclude: 'Well there are a few English-speakers moved in here recently . . .', in assessment of my chances of liking the town and settling. 'Aha! Anglo-Saxi', I was next to hear from a group of off-duty soldiers whom I met at the gym. Finally, from the Local Council woman who vetted my application to become a resident of the town I learnt: 'There are Hebrew lessons put on for Anglo-Saxons like you; 10 till 12, every Sunday.'

Obviously, fellow English-speakers were regarded as my natural allies; and turning up to the Hebrew class I found that the 'Anglo-Saxons' thought so too. The class was a small one – ten people at most in any one week – but David and Rachel were two of the more regular members. Soon we were meeting and chatting, albeit in English, in the streets or out shopping or over coffee. Comparing our histories before *aliyah* and planning our futures after it were the staple forms of discourse.

Here, in reported speech, is my composite of David's and Rachel's own accounts:

David Feinberg is 65. He and his wife Mirium moved to Israel a few years ago. At first they lived in immigrant Absorption Centres, then they rented accommodation in Beer-Sheva, and then last year, when a friend found them and himself affordable houses to buy, they moved to Mitzpe

Ramon. Furthermore, by getting the deposit down and all the paper work done when he was still aged 64½ – despite all the obstructions the Building Ministry put in his way, like refusing to speak English, claiming there were no houses there for sale, or no Americans living nearby, and saying his mortgage was from the wrong bank – David managed to get an interest-free loan from the Israeli government.

In the USA David was a pollution engineer, and at one time ran his own contracting business. Then it was bought out by a conglomerate and he moved into local government. It was an opportune time because local government was just coming under civil service regulation; suddenly David found himself to be the highest technically-qualified official in the county. After three months of having his nose rubbed in the dirt as a general dogsbody, he was now head man, with his own budget and staff! And he soon had them eating humble pie. In fact for nine years he forced through anti-pollution legislation that made his county of two million people the most advanced in the state, in the USA, in the world – with him as probably its most successful pollution officer! Until his own age caught up with him.

David and Mirium had been considering *aliyah* a number of times. First, before 1948, then in 1952–3. But in those days they never had any money. They had four sons to rear and their only capital was sunk in the house. And the Jewish Agency told them it would be foolish to move, since they would be coming to a place where they'd be lucky to have a roof over their heads, lucky to have a table; because all Jewish Agency money was going to the likes of the Iraqis, getting knifed in Baghdad and needing to emigrate fast. So they left the move till David retired.

Some folks retire to Arizona, but Israel is just as convenient; more so, because the weather is the same, while you don't need a car to get around. All the same, David thought to bring the old Volvo and shipped it over for $4,000. But when they heard about the $8,000 import tax, they decided to ship it back again for their son. The only way people afford a big car here is to have it company-owned, which David finds totally iniquitous. The Government says: 'Look how we're taxing the big man', while really he's getting it all through his benefits (benefits can add up to half a man's income here, and all non-taxed)! Meantime the Government taxes any little 'Moshe' who wants to go on holiday: $150 exit tax every time you leave the country! Only the Soviet Union had an exit tax once, then the Israelis thought they'd join them – just to make the Soviets feel better. Now the Soviets have dropped theirs and the Israelis are the only ones. It's disgusting! But then this isn't a real government, David feels. In fact, Israel's not a real state! It's just a jumble of rules, operating on a catch-as-catch-can basis. Slap on a tax here, a tax there; give a benefit here, a hand-out there. The Israeli government is worse than . . . Kenya! It's like Rumania. When he and Mirium first arrived with their dog, they had every 'Mickey Mouse' form going: inoculation papers falling out of their pockets. And then nobody even asked to see one! The place, in short, is a hotch-potch of laws and benefits; with no real consumer organizations that do anything besides protect the jobs of their members. And laws never do any good anyhow. Jews are too clever for a start, always looking for ways round them. Slap on a law or a tax, and a Jew'll find a loophole. It's always in an open economy that Jews do best. Like Iraq, or Prague. Whereas the Israeli Government is always trying to take from you, and your Israeli neighbour is just out to gouge you. As if your loss was their gain. But really, no Jew should treat another like that, however they used to behave toward *Goyim* [Gentiles] in the *Galut* [Diaspora].

Another problem is that most Israelis are now Orientals: used to living as second-class citizens under Arabs. So they come to Israel, learn Hebrew easily (because its a related language) and get an easy government job. But they have no experience of democracy; it is, after all, a long and difficult process to learn. Meanwhile the English-speakers aren't taught Hebrew properly and mostly stay out of politics because they don't know the local issues and can't understand what's going on. It is as if after two thousand years living among *Goyim* the Jews bring all the worst things they learnt from them to Israel; they're so smart in the *Galut* then they come here and act dumb. Which is a shame, because, as one rabbi said, 'This may not be much of a country but it's the only one we've got.' Boiling-point will probably be reached when there's an American economic crisis, meaning less support for Israel, meaning the Israeli army will be starved of its share and there'll be a military take-over and dictatorship like in other Middle Eastern countries. Then they'll all park outside the American Embassy and demand to be flown home. And it'll happen before the year 2000.

Frankly, David's sorry he came. He never thought Mirium would actually agree to leave her Cleveland suburb. Now it seems they've got to adjust and at least try and live like Israelis. But he can't even seem to balance his cheque-book. For the first time in his life he needs counselling on how to make ends meet! Still, the bureaucracy here doesn't faze him. Nor the fact that it makes Israelis corrupt from top to base: from rabbis to workers. Because bureaucrats are the same the world over and he knows all about them. They'll give out as little information as possible and do as little as they can. But what the corrupt cannot stand is publicity and exposure, so you just have to threaten to supply it. Remind them that in this way any problem of yours that they find too small or beneath their dignity you will gladly make bigger. Show them you won't be taken for a sucker. You are not some Oriental, prepared to bang on the table, return day after day, and finally get violent or pay *baksheesh*. You will simply type a letter to their superior or the government minister responsible and say that if something isn't done, and soon, then American agencies will hear. As it is, he has petitioned his friends back home to stop donating to the Jewish National Fund because little from their cheques reaches here; what gets past some bureaucratic fat-cats in the States ends up paying fat-cat salaries here.

David keeps improving his Mitzpe villa too, because his children can always keep it on and benefit after he's gone. He's built an outhouse and insulated the living-room, and he's busy landscaping the back yard. He employed some Black Hebrews on the house, since they're cheap and work like dogs, and they're pretty skilled too. He paid them the same rate as the local contractors do, but then he paid up without keeping them waiting for ages, so they were really grateful. In fact, David is considering opening his own business, because local businessmen could do with being taught a thing or two about customer-care. They take on a contract, demand money up front and then disappear for months; finally you get subcontractors coming round demanding more money to finish the job! (That's what happened to that Englishman, Levy, trying to get his house painted.) So David could buy a truck, employ a few Black Hebrews, and offer his services for any haulage, building or decorating work needing doing. He's sure people would appreciate an efficient and reliable job for a change!

For the foreseeable future, then, Mitzpe is where David's staying. The town is pretty self-sufficient, and apart from lacking a good hardware store, the shops and merchandizing are impressive. A town of around 2,500 in the States wouldn't have three supermarkets and more stores . . . it's lucky the Israelis like their food!

Rachel Silberstein is 49. She lived in Israel for a few years, in absorption centres and a number of settlements (most recently Beer-Sheva), before making the move to Mitzpe Ramon. Camping in the youth hostel, she found the desert town beautiful, and not like other new towns. She had always found deserts inspiring, and Mitzpe seemed a great place for alternative energy, for meditation and yoga. In fact, Rachel imagined that the town could act as an alternative energy centre for people she knew spread right around the country needing just such a focus. They could caucus in Mitzpe and recharge their mental batteries – not to mention those of her ageing Afghan hound!

In the USA Rachel had been a ceramicist. But she could see ceramics there would take her little further and she wanted to journey elsewhere. So she came to Israel. She had already come on various short volunteer programmes over the years; but the $3,000 she got in her final divorce settlement seemed like the perfect incentive to immigrate. One year seemed a natural, organic period of time to see if the place was right for her, and she could leave herself enough money to get home if not. Folks in the States said she must either be crazy or else idealistic to come. Perhaps so. But it was a personal journey she needed to make; she had been brought up in the Sates to be moral on the one hand and a Jew on the other: here she had the opportunity to put the two together.

Sadly, Rachel has found that the two do not fit. And already the decision to immigrate seems a weird one; she should have stayed in the USA and used the $3,000 to set up a business somewhere she knew the ropes. Now she is financially in a ditch. Besides this, she has experienced a shattering of illusions. Not that she would have known it without coming, but there is so much mental illness here. The psychic garbage-dump of Judaism, lurking beneath the surface for two thousand years of Diaspora, has finally been uncovered. It's not certifiable madness as such, rather that people do things and say things that simply cause pain, both in their own lives and those of others. Like all the beatings and killings by the settlers and the army in the West Bank. It's like the early days of fascism.

Rachel was a bit frightened to say something like that at first, but then she read in the paper how some Tel Aviv professor had said the same in a public lecture. The trouble stems from the repression that dominated the primitive Oriental societies these people have mostly come from. Their tribalism violently repressed their natural individualism, breeding closed minds and antagonisms. Now they need educating. Because these are people who never went through the Industrial Revolution, were never liberated from their traditional communities, and never reached constitutional government and the better, freer thought it inculcates. So one of the outcomes you see is young kids with lots of energy but torn between the traditional and the modern. They ask her about the USA, searching for they don't know what. Their individuality yearns to come out, but it is pressed beneath army discipline, and so it explodes on the West Bank. But it's not only the young. Almost all Israelis have mental blackspots that you simply have to learn to steer clear of because they refuse to consider them: she could put her discussions with right-wingers to music!

What a shame they cannot build something better from the energy that the blackspot burns up. So here they are doing nasty nationalistic things, and seeing them in Biblical terms, when nationalism is such a backward part of the human psyche that Rachel had hoped it was disappearing. The Government is putting her into the position of oppressor just by living here, and that's something she won't stand for. In fact, being here she doesn't even feel Jewish any more: just Human.

In the States, Judaism was something Rachel had hankered after. Because she felt deprived of it. But now she can see it was like losing a father, say, whom you may not have liked anyway. Now she has worked it out of her system, and if she were to go back, this experience would go with her. Meantime, over here she's quite pleased to be classed an American, not an Israeli. She liked the big family feeling here at first, but not now: everybody expecting to know personal things about you. At least in the USA they leave you alone; and looking back she appreciates the American blanket spread lightly over great difference, and she misses the respect accorded in Western democracies to ideological positions that you may personally dislike. If only she'd followed her first hunch in Israel that she'd be happier living among the Arabs on the West Bank. As it is, she always has better conversations nowadays with the Arabs than the Jews: with the Palestinians you can just be normal somehow, and have normal relationships.

But being here is a learning experience; in fact, the whole country is an experiment, that's the only way to see it, and she is not ready to leave yet. The thought of starting afresh is too daunting for the present; and anyway she couldn't afford to. Moreover, she feels that only a Jew could come here and understand what goes on, and maybe do something about it. It's very strange. There are all these different types in Israel and yet, through some common genetic or mental circuiting or something, Rachel feels that she's similar to them all: similar behaviour, similar reactions. So she can start chatting to some stranger at a bus-stop – an old Moroccan man, say – and feel an instant chemistry. So although the terrible inefficiency of the place gets to her, now she is here she may as well get to grips with the bureaucracy and make some sort of a future. The trouble is that she has to gear herself up for each bureaucratic encounter; and then you can keep going for six months and never see the end. It obeys a logic of its own that bears no correlation to your efforts; you push and push and get no movement, till one day it's easy. It's because the clerks don't like anyone being successful independently of them – such as through their own business sense.

Sometimes Rachel aches to write a book about all her experiences here, to share them. And she wants to get into ideas more, period. She'd like to go to Graduate School and study Political Science: study what it takes to make the democratic personality, someone who respects democracy. Also she'd like to do something political; she may not be able to affect Russia or Northern Ireland, but here there's something relevant she can do. Traditionally, English-speakers may have retreated from involvement with a political system they disliked, but now she sees they are doing more, like sponsoring non-partisan lists in the newspapers of who to vote for to get things run more efficiently. So she intends doing her bit too. Like lobbying against the Exit Tax, not because of the money, but because of the nasty image it gives of the country and the additional case of individual repression it entails. Also she intends writing to the President and the Secretary of State and the New York Times, asking them not to support further a violent Israeli state; adding her voice to the Alternative American Jewish Lobby. Because democracy is more important than a Jewish state, and there are anyway enough Jewish institutions to carry on.

For the present, what's encouraging is that Rachel finds to her surprise that even folks who have been here a while (and not necessarily Anglo-Saxons) are not automatically any more enamoured of the general mentality than she is. They agree that only if you've known nothing else could you be satisfied with the way Israel is. More and more Rachel finds that experiences here are like that: not one thing or another; not clear-cut like elsewhere. And that's a new experience too.

So now Rachel has unpacked the kilns she had shipped over, and used the packing cases to make book shelves in her flat. She could even consider investing in a villa in Mitzpe if the town took off. In the meantime, she ships pottery back to a US agent for sale; just so long as the bureaucrats who hand out her unemployment cheques don't look too closely!

The Immigrant Discourse: I

What is immediately striking in David's and Rachel's accounts are the morphological similarities in story-line between the two – detailed differences notwithstanding. For example, David and Rachel both report considering *aliyah* for a number of years and making pilot-trips. Ultimately, the promptings of changes of life presented opportune personal and economic moments: retirement and divorce. The to-ing and fro-ing did not stop after immigration, however, and there were returns to the USA for settling further plans of finance and transfer, as well as a few years' repeated movement around Israel. Most recently both lived in Beer-Sheva, before jumping off into the desert proper. But having now resided in Mitzpe Ramon about six months, both feel great ambivalence about their decision. For one thing, there is the inefficient and inscrutable bureaucracy. Then there are the obstacles put in the way of free enterprise; also the intractable economic situation, the disrespect for democracy, and the generally alien manners of the Oriental majority. Both can imagine returning States-side, but, bemoaning the Israeli Exit Tax, both claim immediate departure to be financially impossible. So they set about making some sort of lives for themselves, including reconstructing physical homes replete with furnishings and pets, using what economic opportunities the Israeli state has to offer for the purpose: interest-free loans and unemployment cheques. These homes, moreover, consist, at least in part, of reconstituting links with their American pasts: US statesmen and newspapers; US charities and kinsmen. Estranged from many Israelis, they each emphasize their Americanness and find new salience in the American values of pluralism and efficiency. Finally, taking cognizance of local commercial openings, both imagine setting themselves up again in business.

Furthermore, it was not long after their arrival in Mitzpe Ramon that both chose to institutionalize these formal similarities. For when another retired American couple from the Hebrew class, Ruth and Gerald, mooted the opening of their own local branch of the AACI (the Association of Americans and Canadians in Israel), both David and Rachel were pleased to attend the inaugural party-cum-business meeting. Significantly, it was this translation of the verbal imagery of Americana into collective action that brought to the fore the detailed differences between them.

The Immigrant Association

The AACI is a nation-wide organization founded in 1951, with Israeli governmental backing. It counsels new immigrants about their rights and duties, fosters ties among English-speaking Jews in Israel and represents their interests. It works to improve their quality of life, and by extension the standard of living in Israel as a whole, and maintains links with family and friends in North America, encouraging further *aliyah* (although anyone from an English-speaking background can join, the vast majority are Americans). The AACI also publishes regular regional *Newsletters* containing branch reports, gossip, Biblical commentary, news from the 'old country', and upcoming local events: Young Adult or Senior get-togethers; trips to the Sea of Galilee; holidays at synagogue and holocaust sites in Poland. Recently there had been a column in the *Southern Region Newsletter* about Mitzpe Ramon. The group of English-speaking 'pioneers' in Mitzpe Ramon, it said, that 'clean, beautiful, healthy community for people with ideals', was 'on its way'; so why not 'come and develop the Negev' with them. Now, 'Ruth and Gerald' invited all English-speakers in the area to an opening meeting of the Mitzpe Ramon AACI in a rented room at the town Cultural Centre.

The meeting was attended by about twenty-five people, including David and Rachel. Ruth began by explaining that the AACI was one of the most important and successful lobbies in Israel. She had, in fact, a collection of AACI informational pamphlets for people to digest, and also AACI petitions to sign. For example, did folks know that there was to be a new one-shekel tax levied on every kilogram package of old clothing entering the country from abroad? That may not be a lot, Ruth conceded, but previously it had been free. The meeting was not slow to express its dismay: 'If a parcel is 20 kilograms, that's 20 shekels!' Judy Lerman calculated, 'That's a lot!' 'It's *schnorrering* ['begging']', David Feinberg agreed. 'Any excuse and this country will *schnorrer*. It's disgusting! And the money won't do any good.' David was vitriolic in his condemnation, standing up and wagging an accompanying finger. In fact, while Rachel was silent for much of the evening, David was often on his feet, prancing round the room and letting off steam, joining in the general criticism of the state of affairs in Israel and Mitzpe Ramon.

Besides 'the country', the culprit most often named was 'the Eastern' or 'Levantine mentality'. These were people content to put up their hands and say: 'What can I do?', and so do nothing. It was exactly the same as *mañana* in Mexico, and it wasn't good enough. Those present had to introduce some Western efficiency into the place, as well as demonstrating the efficacy of lobbying; show the Israelis how things can be done, now, and to timetable, and not just be left in the hands of others. Another thing, it was agreed, the Eastern Mentality said was: 'I deserve everything because I'm here, living in Israel and Mitzpe Ramon. Give it me.' Well, those present shouldn't become part of that. They had to show that things could be done differently. It wasn't that Westerners couldn't learn a thing or two from Orientals – like living a more relaxed life – it was just that Westerners could introduce a better way of going after things yourself. And here again David added his contribution. He had nothing against the Orientals as people – when he attended the Sephardi synagogue in town, he got on fine – but they had to be shown.

After one of David's outbursts, Arnold Gold, an elderly man from London, was heard to nominate David quietly as prospective AACI

Bingo-caller. Then, another Londoner, Len Levy, said more loudly that they were hearing an awful lot about what the town and country should do for the AACI but little about what it could give them; he, for one, had not come to Israel to live apart, in another ghetto. But jumping out of his seat, a gesticulating David was quick in his rebuff: he had no ghetto mentality either, but when bureaucrats began playing fair with them, that would be soon enough to do likewise. When they gave their services courteously and treated everyone alike, then maybe the lobbying could stop. Anyhow, changes effected by the AACI lobby helped everyone, David concluded, and the meeting tended to agree.

It was not long after this meeting that Rachel left Mitzpe Ramon. At least, she did not give up her apartment – as a new immigrant, rent was only costing her twelve shekels per month – but she stopped attending Hebrew class and found a room in east (Arab) Jerusalem, where she proceeded to spend much of her time. Holed up in Mitzpe Ramon, she had grown lonely, bored and depressed. Even after she struck up relations with a local Hungarian divorcee she realized that Mitzpe Ramon, by itself, was not the place to grow that she had hoped for. But by shuttling to Jerusalem and back she could get the best out of both. There she could learn Arabic, mix in the Women's Network, join 'Peace Now' demonstrations and expeditions to the West Bank, and meet Palestinians involved in liaison. Then she could return weekly to Mitzpe Ramon, relax and 'space out'; she might be a political animal, but for her sanity she still needed to keep in touch with the earth.

David thought Rachel was quite misguided, and had latched on to a hopeless cause. And he told her so in no uncertain terms whenever she was back in Mitzpe Ramon and they met out walking their dogs:

'The world was full of lost causes. Plan to erect statues to commemorate Ibo massacred in Nigeria and that would be a good lost cause; the other tribes wouldn't let you, no one else would care, but you could go on trying anyway. Rachel's learning Arabic and wanting to work with the Arabs towards peace was a similar case. Because Arab culture was just not constructive. The world could pass it by and it would not care. They had lived here all those years and all they could make was one town: Ramallah. And this Palestinian issue was merely political. If you had asked a Palestinian living here in the 1930s what he was, he would probably have replied, 'Syrian'; back then it was the Jews who might have answered, 'Palestinian'. Even today the Palestinians were not united or decided amongst themselves, so how were you going to talk to them? No! You only went through life once, so why work on a lost cause? And if Rachel wanted a good cause then why not try to unite the Jews? They came from these diverse cultures – Indian, Syrian, Yemeni, Iraqi – and now all were here. Barriers were dropping, true, but there was still far to go, so why didn't she work on that? Okay, progress would be slow, and it might take a hundred and fifty or two hundred years to complete, but change accelerated once it had begun, and it was amazing what one man could do. Like the effect that he had had, one man, in getting people interested in conservation and anti-pollution in the States . . .'

However, it seemed to David that Rachel wouldn't hear: it almost felt as if she had moved away altogether.

But Rachel had not. Rather, like David, she had found a way of routinizing a new life for herself in Israel and in Mitzpe Ramon in the image of her old; indeed, if she could just 'get into civil rights' in Beer-Sheva, then Rachel even planned to live in Mitzpe Ramon again full-time.

In addition to the similarities of story-line in their accounts of immigration, their common America-mediated discourses on Israel, then, both David and Rachel had relocated their old American behaviours: David, the search for an economically secure retirement; Rachel, the search for self-development outside an economic rat race. However seemingly makeshift, and however different from their dreamt-of imaginings, both were 'at home'.

The Immigrant Discourse: II

Essentially, routinizing new identities for themselves in Mitzpe Ramon had involved David and Rachel in the relocation of their old ones. At the very least, old American identities provided important foundations towards the construction of their Israeli ones; at most, their old identities had simply been imported to new milieux. Each may have had to make a new house and new friends on the other side of the globe, but really they had settled back into old local worlds of experience.

Much of this was claimed in their verbal accounting. David, then, had come up against bureaucrats in the US, and threatened and cajoled them into compliance, and he was sure he could do the same here: bureaucrats were the same the world over. He had dealt with Blacks in the US, and he could do so here – employing a few Black Hebrews on the cheap, and not allowing the *mañana* attitude of the Moroccans to interfere with his work schedules. In the States he and seven other businessmen had formed a joint corporation so that the financial losses of any of them could be written off through corporate taxes or liquidation loopholes, and if a few people were to come in with him on his truck idea he could imagine doing the same here. He soon fixed up a house and garden whenever they moved in the States, and there was no reason this place should be any different. With the stores and the synagogue and his circle of friends close by, Mitzpe Ramon was not so far from retiring to Arizona; more convenient, in fact, without a car.

Rachel had searched in the USA for a clearer understanding of that eternal spark that had set Jews apart since Mount Sinai, and here she was – still searching. She had lived for some years in the American Deep South, where Black servants went home from White mansions to over-sized families and shacks, and she made a point after that of not cutting herself off from the underprivileged; mixing with poor Moroccans, chatting to Arabs met on buses, she would make the same moves here. In the States she got mental energy from mixing with educated, free-thinking, politically committed artists and liberals, usually men, and now she would seek out the same types. All the while she would support herself through her pottery, as she had done since she was 24, inspired still by the desert. Living here, she would even extend the personal pathways for herself that she discovered journeying round the States.

In many respects, David and Rachel have moved geographically and socially but not cognitively. Indeed, with their repeated trips to the USA over the past years, and their maintained contact with family and friends, even their geographical and social moves are only partial. Nor do David and Rachel seem alone in this. There were always tales around Mitzpe Ramon of American immigrants who had 'gone States-side' and may not be back – or not for a while, or not before an education is completed or a sick relative has recovered or died. And Ruth and Gerald (of the AACI) flew back periodically so that he, an industrial psychologist, could return the results of commissioned demographic research to firms in Phoenix and Albuquerque. Officially, they might have retired; cognitively they had simply moved house slightly more radically than their earlier move from Chicago to Boulder when they had had a family to rear.

In short, in constructing homes for themselves in Israel it is old notions of American identity that these new immigrants come to relegitimate. Indeed, these notions become linchpins of their local selves, explaining how David and Rachel and the rest can envisage being Jews in Israel but still apart from the Orientals. They are here with a mission: to use Americanism in order to save the country from becoming just another backward Middle Eastern ('Mickey Mouse') state; they will take up the 'burden' of democracy and stay. As Avruch put it: 'Having come to Israel as Jews, the *olim* find themselves confronting it as Americans';

here, 'only by being better Americans can they be good Jews' (1981: 159,171).

The further paradox is that this appears to be by no means a distinctly American phenomenon in Israel. Notwithstanding the wealth of American immigrants, their influential links with powerful networks and personages in the USA and their ability to move 'States-side' and back more or less at will, there is evidence of individuals from many different immigrant groups discoursing on Israeli futures for themselves and constructing local identities by highlighting their Diasporic Jewish pasts.[8] Furthermore, in studies since the late 1960s, immigrant groups have not only maintained what viable ethnic identities they may have brought to the country (if any), but manifested new awarenesses and vitality (cf. Smooha 1978; Weingrod 1979). As Weingrod concludes: 'cultural assimilation and heightened ethnicity are quite compatible trends; in fact, their linkage may be inevitable' (1985:x). Except that, as Paine puts it (1989), it is not 'assimilation' that each particular immigrant group would appear to intend so much as a variety of mutually exclusive constitutings of what 'common Jewishness' in the 'becoming' nation is to entail – even if not all immigrants have the clout of the *Anglo-Saxim* to bring this about. Here is immigrant identity overturning the Israeli melting-pot (and existing independently of state discourses) rather than being dished up from it.

The Immigrant Identity

David, Rachel and I always spoke in English amongst ourselves in Mitzpe Ramon. It was implicitly agreed that we couldn't say what we wanted to in Hebrew. Not only did we not have the vocabulary, but the Anglo-Saxon world remained too fresh in our minds for us to refrain from using its words as a toothing-stone towards current evaluations and comparisons.

But this was not wholly the case. A Danish immigrant in Hebrew class occasionally insisted on struggling along with me in Hebrew, and David and Rachel had already lived in Israel for a few years, and continued to conduct conversations with various erstwhile nationalities in Hebrew. Clearly, David, Rachel and I could not say what we wanted to in Hebrew because it had to be said in English. Talking in English about our 'dreams' of Israel and our reactions to being in Israel, we shared common notions of past and future expectations.

---

8. For example 'In Iran I was a Jew, in Israel I'm an Iranian' (Goldstein 1985:254); 'In Morocco I was a Jew, here I am a Moroccan' (Goldberg 1985:181).

But this was not really the case, either. My expectations, moving from Britain for a job, were not David's and Rachel's, moving from the USA for personal and Zionistic fulfilment; and David's and Rachel's reactions to Mitzpe Ramon and Israel were no more closely aligned. It is more likely, then, that what we shared, besides a common categorization by non-English-speakers as *Anglo-Saxim*, was a common feeling that by conversing together in English we could maintain identities, memories, sentiments and ideals we might otherwise lose. Our regular talks about coming to and being in Israel were really about continuing an elsewhere and the identities that had belonged there. Our discursive imagery was a home-from-home; in fact, a home in itself (cf. Rapport 1987:170–1).

As a form of home, moreover, this may be increasingly common, according to Berger. He argues that after migration from an 'original' home – one that perhaps was seen as occupying the physical centre of the world – the migrant tends to improvise a makeshift shelter out of routine behaviours. The new home comes to be represented by a set of habitual practices: by 'words, jokes, opinions, gestures, actions, even the way one wears a hat' (1984:64). For Bachelard, likewise, the human imagination always builds 'walls' of impalpable shadows, comforting itself with the illusion of protection, and so carries 'the notion of home' into any 'really inhabited space', whether cognitive or physical. Thus it is that 'we ever bring our *lares* with us' (1994:5; and cf. Rykwert 1991:54). Rachel even said something of the kind to me: physical domicile notwithstanding, 'home was something she carried round in her head'. This did not strike me as particularly unusual either; it seemed a typically Jewish image: the wandering Jew, perennially opposed to the time and place of current residence and society. It was a truism I had often heard from continental Jews in Britain.

But in Israel, maybe I should have been struck by its irony. For here were David, Rachel and I 'returning home' to *Ha'Aretz* ['The Land'], and talking as though we were still 'wandering'. We remained at home in the old verbal routines of criticizing and distancing ourselves from the present. So it did not matter that the places we had come from and the expectations brought were *de facto* so different, because the sharedness of our association and discourse was rooted not so much in solidarity over things left behind – that was a more private matter – as in constructing a future based on common opposition to what we had together wandered into. We became at home in Israel, as we would in any other nation-state, by staying cognitively apart (cf. Fallers 1974:10; Marx 1983:142).

Hence, there was the easy negotiation amongst ourselves of an 'immigrant discourse' with common verbal imagery. Moreover, in mapping out a wider possible community in Mitzpe Ramon and Israel to be part of in future, there was a pleasurable recognition and seeking-out by David and by Rachel of features of this imagery in others they met: 'Even folks who have been here a while – twenty, thirty years – aren't necessarily taken in by the mentality of the place, you know. When you talk to them you can see they're equally ambivalent about being here' (Rachel); 'I'm not disgusted by the Jews here; I'm a Zionist. They might jack the prices and make you haggle, but you know, some new little shops opened last year, wanting a share of the market, and prices came down' (David).

Being an Israeli, for David, for Rachel and for me, meant maintaining the discourse of an 'Anglo-Saxon Jew' and eschewing that of the Israeli state – however officious the latter might be in prescribing particular procedures of *aliyah* and absorption. And what sounded to me truistic in the Diaspora becomes, inside Israel, a more interesting phenomenon: a country of migrants who come home to their dream of a homeland by remaining on its normative margins; determined to live by their wits and negotiate ways around the institutional, they remain wandering outsiders and 'transnationals' (Gonzalez 1992). Nor does time and assimilation to local routines necessarily weaken the sense in which relations between individual immigrants and immigrant groups and the state are opposi-tional, schismogenetic; the opposite might even be argued, as we have heard. At the same time as David, Rachel and I routinize homes for ourselves in immigrant discourses, so we find ourselves part of a popula-tion equally intent upon individual negotiations and individual settlements with the seemingly centralist and essentialist institutions of the Israeli state.

In short, despite their having travelled the institutional route from Absorption Centre through Hebrew class and new town to becoming Israeli, the 'sense of unborn potential' that 'intoxicated' these new Mitzpe Ramon residents, David and Rachel, did not reflect the official state imagery of its Visitors' Centre; barely was it coterminous even with state structures or boundaries. Instead they expressed themselves in an American imagery whose commonalities allowed fellow *Anglo-Saxim* to initiate interaction, map out communities and, above all, plan to remain the individual migrants they were: pollution engineer and ceramicist, scourge of the corrupt and champion of the repressed. David and Rachel had not moved out of 'America' at their changes of life, merely to a margin. Hence, it was out of a preservation of the essential and central imagery of their old selves that their new immigrant identities were to be constructed.[9]

9. For their help with this chapter, my thanks to Emanuel Marx, Don Handelman, Gideon Kressel, Moshe Schwartz, Marilyn Strathern, Allison James, Andrew Dawson and Anthony Cohen.

References

Aronoff, M. J. (1973), 'Development Towns in Israel', in M. Curtis and M. Chertoff (eds), *Israel: Social Structure and Change*, New Brunswick: Transaction.

Avruch, K. (1981), *American Immigrants in Israel*, Chicago: University of Chicago Press.

Bachelard, G. (1994[1958]), *The Poetics of Space*, Boston: Beacon.

Berger, J. (1984), *And Our Faces, My Heart, Brief as Photos*, London: Writers & Readers.

Cohen, E. (1970), 'Development Towns – The Social Dynamics of "Planted" Communities in Israel', in S. Eisenstadt, R. Bar-Yosef and C. Adler (eds), *Integration and Development in Israel*, Jerusalem: Israel University Press.

Deshen, S. (1970), *Immigrant Voters in Israel*, Manchester: Manchester University Press.

Efrat, E. (1984), *Urbanization in Israel*, London: Croom Helm.

Fallers, L. (1974), *The Social Anthropology of the Nation-State*, New York: Aldine.

Gitelman, Z. (1982), *Becoming Israelis*, New York: Praeger.

Gold, G. and Paine, R. (1984), 'Introduction', in G. Gold (ed.), *Minorities and Mother-Country Imagery*, St. John's: ISER Press.

Goldberg, H. (1985), 'Historical and Cultural Dimensions of Ethnic Phenomena in Israel', in A. Weingrod (ed.), *Studies in Israeli Ethnicity*, New York: Gordon & Breach.

Goldschlaeger, A. (1985), 'On Ideological Discourse', *Semiotica*, 54 (1/2).

Goldstein, J. (1985), 'Iranian Ethnicity in Israel: The Performance of Identity', in A. Weingrod (ed.), *Studies in Israeli Ethnicity*, New York: Gordon & Breach.

Gonzalez, N. (1992), *Dollar, Dove and Eagle*, Ann Arbor: University of Michigan Press.

Hannerz, U. (1987), 'The World in Creolization', *Africa*, 57 (4).

Hobsbawm, E. (1991), 'Introduction', in A. Mack (ed.), *Home: A Place in the World, Social Research* (special edition) 58(1): 63–8.

Hollander, J. (1991), 'It All Depends', in A. Mack (ed.), *Home: A Place in the World, Social Research* (special edition) 58(1): 31–49.

Isaacs, H. (1966), *American Jews in Israel*, New York: Day.

Klaff, V. (1981), 'Residence and Immigration in Israel: A Mosaic of Segmented Groups', in E. Krausz (ed.), *Studies in Israeli Society Vol.I*, New Brunswick: Transaction.

Marx, E. (1976), *The Social Context of Violent Behaviour*, London: Routledge & Kegan Paul.

—— (1980), 'On the Anthropological Study of Nations', in E. Marx (ed.), *A Composite Portrait of Israel*, London: Academic.

—— (1983), 'Review of "American Immigrants in Israel" by K. Avruch', *Jewish Journal of Sociology*, XXV (2).

Mueller, C. (1970), 'Notes on the Repression of Communicative Behaviour', in H.-P. Dreitzel (ed.), *Recent Sociology No. 2*, London: Collier-Macmillan.

Paine, R. (1989), 'Israel: Jewish Identity and Competition over "Tradition"', in E. Tonkin, M. McDonald and M. Chapman (eds), *History and Ethnicity*, London: Routledge.

―― (1992), 'The Marabar Caves, 1920–2020', in S. Wallman (ed.), *Contemporary Futures*, London: Routledge.

Prager, E. (1985), 'Components of Personal Adjustment of Long-Distance, Elderly Movers', *Journal of Cross-Cultural Gerontology*, I(1).

Rapport, N. J. (1987), *Talking Violence. An Anthropological Interpretation of Conversation in the City*, St John's: ISER Press.

―― (1996), 'Edifying Anthropology. Culture as Conversation: Representation as Conversation', in A. James, J. Hockey and A. Dawson (eds), *After Writing Culture*, London: Routledge.

―― (1997), 'The "Contrarieties" of Israel. An essay on the cognitive importance and the creative promise of both/and', *Journal of the Royal Anthropological Institute* (N.S.) 3(4): 653–72.

Rykwert, J. (1991), 'House and Home', in A. Mack (ed.), *Home: A Place in the World, Social Research* (special edition) 58(1): 51–62.

Singer, C. M. (1979), 'Saints of the Kingdom: Group Emergence, Individual Affiliation, and Social Change among the Black Hebrews of Israel', unpublished Ph.D. Thesis, University of Utah.

Smooha, S. (1978), *Israel: Pluralism and Conflict*, Berkeley: University of California Press.

Thomas, W. I. and Znaniecki, F. (1984[1918]), *The Polish Peasant in Europe and America*, Urbana: University of Illinois Press.

Weingrod, A. (1979), 'Recent Trends in Israeli Ethnicity', *Ethnic and Racial Studies*, II.

―― (1985), 'Introduction', in A. Weingrod (ed.), *Studies in Israeli Ethnicity: After the Ingathering*, New York: Gordon & Breach.

Zaslavsky, V. (1982), *The Neo-Stalinist State*, New York: Sharpe.

Homeless at Home: Narrations of Post-Yugoslav Identities

Stef Jansen

My name is Offred. I have another name, which nobody uses now because it's forbidden. I tell myself it doesn't matter, your name is like your telephone number, useful only to others; but what I tell myself is wrong, it does matter.

Margaret Atwood: *The Handmaid's Tale*

'I am from Zagreb,' you said and perhaps it is the only right answer, to be a Citizen. But not now. Not here.

Slavenka Drakulić – *Letter to her Daughter* (Drakulić, 1993)

To Begin With — 'Home' at Both Ends of the War

In *Migrancy, Culture, Identity* Iain Chambers distinguishes between 'travel' and 'migrancy' (Chambers 1994:5). Travel, he argues, implies an itinerary from a fixed point of departure to an equally stable point of arrival, whereas migrancy 'involves a movement in which neither the points of departure nor those of arrival are immutable or certain'. For a migrant, therefore, 'the promise of a homecoming – completing the story, domesticating the detour – becomes an impossibility'. In this chapter, I intend to translate Chambers's eloquent sketch into a different kind of prose: the grim story of the millions who lost their physical and/or metaphorical homes in the republics of former Yugoslavia. For these involuntary migrants, the notion of an impossible homecoming takes on a sharp edge in a number of ways.

In the Dayton Agreements, the result of the talks that supposedly brought peace in the region in December 1995, it is stipulated that all refugees have the right to return to their homes. However, this abolition of the impossibility of homecoming, endorsed by the politicians who are primarily responsible for the war and who build their power on it, has little equivalent in everyday life in former Yugoslavia. Their houses may have been taken by others and they themselves have been expelled from their own houses; they may have been destroyed; or it may simply be impossible to reach them. If we move from the bricks-and-mortar reality of the house to the metaphorical reality of 'home' on which I will focus in this text, the picture of a possible homecoming in former Yugoslavia becomes even more blurred. The term repatriation includes a reference to 'a return' and to 'a fatherland', and is therefore inadequate for a great number of people who had to flee from the war.

In many ways, the war that tore Yugoslavia apart was precisely a war about the notion of 'home', and this notion was there at the beginning and at the end of the war. Bammer draws attention to the analogy between the concept of 'home' and that of 'nation': both are constructed, and in both instances the act of telling the story of it creates the 'we' that belongs to it (Bammer 1992). What took place in former Yugoslavia was a conflict about the right to a home in the name of different 'we's'. Conflicting visions of 'home' provided the basis for a bloody conflict, and, as a result, the meaning of 'home' underwent drastic changes for all inhabitants of the republics of former Yugoslavia.

Life Narratives and Yugo-Narratives: The Case of the Witches

'I'm going home, I think as the plane takes off above the Atlantic (. . .) Going back to my country – is it still called Yugoslavia? – this time feels different, more difficult than ever before: the word "home" sticks in my throat, as if I would choke on it if I tried to say it out loud' (Slavenka Drakulić in April 1991, two months before the outbreak of the war).

On 11 December 1992 the Croatian magazine *Globus* published an anonymous yet virulent attack on the personal lives and the political ideas of a number of the country's female intellectuals. The targets of the article, subtitled 'The Witches of Rio', were women in their forties, known for their critical stance towards the dominant nationalist discourses, who at the time had attended a literary conference in Rio de Janeiro.[1] These 'profiteers of communism and postcommunism' were said to have 'serious problems with their own ethnical, ethical, human, intellectual and political

1. Rada Iveković, Dubravka Ugrešić, Slavenka Drakulić, Vesna Kesić and Jelena Lovrić.

identity'. This mental defect was related mainly to two things: they are feminists (even though not all of them explicitly call themselves feminists) and three of them are or have been married to Serbs, as the result of 'a systematic political choice' and not because of love. In her defence of the women in question, Svetlana Slapšak observed that:

> It has to be the case that these well-known Croatian writers got married for political reasons, as part of a conspiracy against Croatia. As opposed to the rest of the Croats, who were weeping in the chains of slavery, living in the trenches, and never ever wanted to be Party members, these witches lived in houses and they travelled, even to Beograd [Belgrade] and Ljubljana (1993:122).

In what follows I would like to focus on the narratives of what Dubravka Ugrešić has called, thereby including herself, 'privileged refugees' from former Yugoslavia (1995:19). I will refer to publications by three women writers from former Yugoslavia, two of whom belonged to the so-called 'witches of Rio', Slavenka Drakulić and Dubravka Ugrešić. The third author whose work will be looked at is Svetlana Slapšak, with a Serbian background but living in Slovenia, who declared her solidarity with the 'witches'. The texts in question are mainly autobiographical and could be located in the twilight zone between fictional short stories, journalistic articles, open letters, diary fragments, political statements and theoretical essays.[2] All of them have been written during the war that brought an end to Yugoslavia, and a great majority of them bear some relation to that conflict. If Minh-ha is right in suggesting that writers of a diaspora are condemned to write autobiographical work, then it might also be a typical war genre, particularly associated with women (Minh-ha 1994:10; Ugrešić 1995:10–11).

Without wanting to obliterate the differences between these three writers, it seems logical to draw attention to their commonalities. Before I do so, however, I want to make it clear that this is not a biographical exercise – instead, I will rely on the texts written by these women as a starting-point for a discussion of possible perceptions of home constructed by non-nationalist former Yugoslavs. Obviously, this is a very partial

2. Slavenka Drakulić (1993), *Balkan Express* (trans. M. Soljan), London: Hutchinson; Dubravka Ugrešić (1995), *De cultuur van de leugens* (trans. R. Schuyt), Amsterdam: Nijgh en Van Ditmar; Dubravka Ugrešić (1993), *Nationaliteit: geen* (trans. R. Schuyt), Amsterdam: Nijgh en Van Ditmar; Svetlana Slapšak (1993) *Joegoslavië, weet je nog?* (trans. R. Dokter), Amsterdam: Jan Mets.

approach: I will only look at a set of very specific cases, and thereby limit the scope to narrative aspects of identity formation. But let me first briefly sketch some coordinates on which the authors in question are positioned.[3] All three women were born shortly after the Second World War, and have careers as urban intellectuals. Both Dubravka Ugrešić and Svetlana Slapšak are university lecturers (Literature, Philosophy, Women's Studies), and both have published a number of novels. Slavenka Drakulić is a feminist activist, a journalist and writer. All three authors share a very critical stance towards the current nationalist discourses in the former Yugoslav republics, and seem to embrace a certain form of cosmopolitanism. Ugrešić and Drakulić have Croatian state citizenship but live abroad, whereas Slapšak has a Serbian passport but lives and works in Slovenia.

Let me make one thing absolutely clear: not in the slightest do these texts provide a representative view on the war and on nationalism in former Yugoslavia. I am aware that we are talking about a specific minority of people 'who will not be contained within the *Heim* of the national culture and its unisonant discourse, but are themselves the marks of a shifting boundary that alienates the frontiers of the modern nation' (Bhabha 1994: 164). In this way I hope to go some way along the lines of what James Clifford suggested when he argued that 'one needs to focus on hybrid, cosmopolitan experiences as much as on rooted, native ones' (Clifford 1992:101). This, then, should allow us to look at the crossroads of the two, for 'both are constitutive of what will count as cultural experience' (ibid.). I am thus looking at a specific category of cases that could be termed 'anomalous' in the present nationalist discursive structure – from this point of view, these women are Bauman's 'strangers', who constitute a permanent threat for the discursive closure attempted by the nationalisms in former Yugoslavia (Bauman 1990:143–69, 1992:687; Sarup 1994:101).

But can we learn about these issues from writings? In an article about anthropology in Asia, Sweeney argued that 'Western anthropologists spend much time reading everything written by other Western anthropologists about the Asian society they intend to study, but often devote little attention to what that society writes about itself' (1989:99–100). It is, of course, impossible to find out what a society writes about itself, and, with Sweeney, I would certainly not want to replace fieldwork ethnography with the study of literature *tout court*. However, I believe that specific writings of specific people can give us an insight into the

3. These data were valid at the time of writing the final version of this text – November 1997.

society from which they emerge – and, of course, into the perspectives of the writer. For this purpose novels, autobiographical 'faction', and open letters differ from social scientific work mainly in conventional features: the context in which they came about, the intention behind them, the expected response, the institutional relation between writer, text and reader (Lamarque 1990:134–5). What interests me, then, is the way in which the authors of the texts that served as the basis for this article engage in a (re)formulation of their personal life narratives and those of the places they live in. Ganguly, in her study of members of the Indian diaspora in the US, argued that the past becomes increasingly important for people whose perspective on the present is unusually unstable as a result of enforced displacement (1992:29–30). She makes the point that 'the stories people tell about their pasts have more to do with the continuing shoring up of self-understanding than with historical "truths"'. This exercise in self-understanding through narrative will be at the focus of what follows.

The Narration of Yugoslavia as 'Home': Definitions of Time

In a letter to her daughter, written in April 1992, Slavenka Drakulić recalls what it meant to her to marry a man of a Serbian background:

> I was aware of the fact that he was from a Serbian family while I was from a Croatian one, but it didn't mean anything to me, one way or the other. World War II was long over when the two of us were born and throughout my life it seemed to me that everyone was trying to escape its shadow, to forget and just live their lives. Your father and I never even discussed the different nationality of our families. Not because it was forbidden, but because it was unimportant to the majority of our generation. It wasn't an issue (Drakulić 1993:129).

In what follows she explicitly draws the connection between her personal experience of nationality and the official pan-Yugoslav discourse on identity. Embedded in a thick layer of irony, she argues that:

> Maybe it was a consequence of the repression of the communist regime, of the brainwashing of our education system, the plan to create an artificial 'Yugoslav' nation – the fact is that in the 1980 census 1.5 million declared themselves Yugoslav, people of a non-existent nation, and interestingly enough, they were all born after the War and approximately thirty years old (1993:129).

It is, I think, significant that in both cases there is a reference to the Second World War. In communist Yugoslavia, the assumption that 'real' history started with the Titoist victory over fascism served as an ideological cornerstone of the regime. Excessive celebration of the merits of the Partisan heroes often substituted for serious education about the past and provided an affirmation of the moral superiority of the Partisan forces in the war, and therefore of the legitimacy of the regime that was built on it. Ernesto Laclau has shown how revolutionary governments seek to establish themselves as the only source of political positivity – an endeavour that leads them to present the revolution and its consequences as a necessary whole, thereby attempting to conceal the contingency of their own rise to power (Laclau 1990:68–9; see also Gross 1985:65ff.). Yugoslavia was not different: Tito's regime aimed at the imposition of an authorized cultural representation of the past, of a discursively closed version of history.

Apart from containing the past in simplistic categories, the communist regime also seriously impeded a sense of the future in political terms. This is not to say that Yugoslavia did not inscribe itself in the great historical narratives of Progress. When writing about her primary school reading books, Dubravka Ugrešić offers a colourful description of the optimism they evoked: all Yugoslavs together *en route* to a better future (1995:19–27). However, tied to this narrative of a bright future was a one-party political discourse: the communists would be in power for ever and, for that matter, it seemed impossible that Tito would ever die. Critics in the late 1970s panicked as it increasingly looked as if the man actually was immortal, and after Tito's death in 1980 one would recall the slogan in which this ideology was epitomized: after Tito, Tito!

Everyday Life and the Yugoslav Cultural Space

In this climate anti-regime attitudes easily translated themselves into an aversion from politics, which characterized large parts of the Yugoslav cultural élite. Drakulić argues that the fact that civil society failed to develop a strong alternative to war is linked to the ideological control of the future by the regime. 'If there is any excuse it is in the fact that we were deprived of the sense of future. This was the worst thing that communism did to people' (1993:136).

However, there were a number of very important differences between Titoist Yugoslavia and Eastern Bloc countries. Of all communist regimes Yugoslavia was the only one to grant its citizens the right to travel freely;

there was a wide range of home-made consumer products, a steady influx of Western goods, and a large degree of cultural freedom, albeit it with a taboo on nationalist statements (Ugrešić 1995:48–51). Although the country went through severe economic crises, Yugoslavia was not the scene of people queuing up for bread or meat, as many former Yugoslavs are keen to point out (see for example Ugrešić 1995:21, 46; 1993:74; Drakulić 1993:50). Note the sharp cynical angle when Ugrešić derides Western misconceptions of living standards and technological development in Yugoslavia, even during the war:

> I've heard of sympathetic foreigners who were moved by the suffering of war and who then sent an enormous amount of irons that worked on coal to a refugee camp. It didn't cross their minds that the savage tribes living here, have had electricity since ages. But maybe, the irons were for those who don't have electricity, like the citizens of Sarajevo, so they can die in nicely ironed clothes (1995:115).

In another article, called Yugo-Americana, Ugrešić describes how after Yugoslavia's break with Stalin in 1948, American popular culture became increasingly accessible: books, films, comics, toys and all kinds of consumer goods:

> In this way, America became part of our daily life. (. . .) The first post-war translations of American books were full of footnotes. Everything had to be explained, what a juke-box was, marijuana, jeans. These footnotes (such as: 'juke box: a machine which makes music when a coin is inserted') disappeared quickly, because with astonishing speed all these unknown things became a part of daily life (1995:71–2).

If daily life is the site of the construction of 'home', we can see how Yugoslavia was the discursive background against which different cultural frameworks were invoked in the creation of a sense of belonging. Apart from patterns uniquely associated with their own republic, people drew on Western discursive practices and on the inter-republican Yugoslav diversity. In such a climate it became possible and attractive for many people to imagine the federation as a cultural space with a distinct Yugoslav character. It has been convincingly argued, I think, that this appropriation of cultural flows on a global scale does not necessarily lead to a homogeneous global culture (Appadurai 1990; 1995).

When trying to explain the fact that, for all its authoritarian short-comings, a great number of people positively identified with Titoist

Yugoslavia as their homeland, Drakulić invokes the notion of a 'contract with the government'. Especially in the 1960s and the 1970s, the pan-Yugoslav urban, intellectual and cultural scene in particular was aware of the fact that they lived under a 'liberal' form of communism, and also of the fact that they were situated in between East and West Europe in political, economic and cultural terms. Drakulić argues that they were prepared to pay the price of limited political freedom because, to put it very straightforwardly, they were comfortable, they felt 'at home' in Yugoslavia (1993:135). Many people living in the cities owned a house at the seaside or in the mountains, often in another republic, and it was possible to receive pensions all over Yugoslav territory. Academics were constantly on the move between universities in different republics, often living in two flats. Interrepublican contacts were especially important for intellectuals, as they assured a steady flow of information, and access to publishing and audiences. For example, for those critical of the regime, it was common practice to escape government control in one republic by publishing in another (Slapšak, 1993:101). Many works of East European dissident literature were translated first into Serbo-Croatian and officially published in Yugoslavia, and only then in the West (1993:43). Students would compare different application conditions of schools and colleges, and craftsmen and traders started businesses where the market seemed most favourable (1993:20–1).

In education there was a strong emphasis on the multi-ethnicity of Yugoslavia: its rich diversity was, often in idyllic terms, celebrated in songs, poems, and theatre, and in language lessons pupils learnt the Latin and the Cyrillic alphabets (1993:24). It is against this background that we can understand Ugrešić's contention that:

> Yugoslav culture was the common domain of different cultures and literary traditions which interacted with each other. In practice, this meant that a Yugoslav writer had to know both the Cyrillic and the Latinic alphabet; it meant you lived in Zagreb and had a publisher in Beograd; it meant your books were printed in Sarajevo, and they were read in Ljubljana, Skopje and Priština. In practice, it meant you lived in different cultures and you experienced them as part of yourself (1995:51).

In this last comment, Ugrešić refers to the Yugoslav cultural space in a twofold way, which I would suggest shows how Yugoslavia served as a typical double narrative of 'home' for a number of people. On the one hand, it constituted the diverse cultural framework in which one positioned oneself; and on the other hand, as the other side of the same coin, these cultures were 'experienced as part of oneself', and as such provided a polysemic and dynamic reservoir of discursive material for the construction of one's identity, precisely because of their diverse and open character.

Belonging at Different Levels — Official Yugoslav Identity

During and after the war, the issue of a Yugoslav sense of belonging has taken on a strongly controversial character and has become a major issue of political antagonism. It is likely, therefore, that the question will remain as to to what extent this idea of a Yugoslav 'home' had taken root in people's minds and hearts. One indication can be found in the censuses; but as we shall see, this has to be qualified. The option 'Yugoslav, nationally undetermined' in the censuses has always remained a rather marginal phenomenon: in 1971, 'Yugoslavs' accounted for 1.3 per cent of the population; in 1981, this was 5.4 per cent (Sekulić et al. 1994:95; Lendvai 1991:253). However, strong regional and social differences distorted the picture: for instance, in 1981 7.9 per cent of the Bosnian population declared itself Yugoslav, whereas only 1.3 per cent did so in Slovenia (Garde 1992:116). Identification as 'Yugoslav' flourished in particular in mixed families, in military circles, and in an all-Yugoslav academic and cultural scene.

However, there is a further twist to the story, for the category of 'Yugoslavs' was presented as having 'no nationality' (Hodson et al. 1994:1542). Yugoslav socialist patriotism, it was argued, was not an alternative form of nationalism. According to the regime, instead of an exclusivist discourse negating the differences between the constituting national groups, it was an all-embracing patriotism, which subsumed the component national identities. It was emphasized that people could identify both with one of the South Slav nations and with Yugoslavia as a whole. As Tito expressed it during the war: 'The term National Liberation Struggle would be a mere phrase and even a deception if it were not invested with both an all-Yugoslav and national meaning for each people individually' (quoted in Cohen 1995:23). It would be wrong then, I think, to equate the census data on 'Yugoslav identity' with the sense of belonging that people felt towards Yugoslavia. For many, it was perfectly possible to feel an affinity to both the republican and the federal level, and of course to a whole range of other discourses.

This is not to deny the fact that for others the Yugoslav idea was irrelevant, especially with increasing decentralization from the mid-1970s onwards, or even offensive, particularly with the rise of nationalism in the 1980s. In line with these developments, the present political climate in the former Yugoslav republics has deemed this pan-Yugoslav mode of cultural representation illegitimate. As we shall see below, in all republics the war was accompanied by a discursive internal war against what is derisively called 'Yugo-nostalgia'. The main perpetrators of this latter-day inquisition will not rest until any sense of Yugoslav belonging is confined to history as one of the great lies of Titoist communism.[4] In this context it is important to note that to the pan-Yugoslav cultural framework as described above, war and nationalist violence was 'alien'. For many people, it simply did not belong to the conceivable possibilities in their life-world. To pick up Slavenka Drakulić's point at the beginning of this section: for them the notion of a nationalist war resonated with old-fashioned narratives of the Second World War, long since covered with the dust of times immemorial, and mainly known from propaganda in speeches, school-books and films.

Broken Narratives of 'Home in Yugoslavia'

The disintegration of Yugoslavia was realized not only through the destruction of lives, villages and cities. On another level, it constituted a break in a number of narratives, such as the post-holocaust 'never again' belief in civilization, liberal democratic postcommunist euphoria, the political narrative of Titoist 'brotherhood and unity', etc. At this stage I want to explore one particular dimension of this discursive break: the interplay between the private narratives of the above-mentioned writers who felt/feel a sense of belonging to Yugoslavia and the demise of that pan-Yugoslav narrative. This will involve a closer look at the dynamics of continuity and discontinuity, at fixity and movement, at dwelling and travelling at both levels. For, in Minh-ha's words, identity '[l]ies at the intersection of dwelling and travelling and is a claim of continuity within discontinuity, and vice-versa' (1994:14).

Narratives of Before and After

The discrediting of old frameworks of reference and a formerly self-evident sequence of events by the war and the nationalist discourses have brought about a breaking-point both in the grand narrative of Yugoslavia

4. This process is not identical in the different post-Yugoslav states, but under its different and even opposed shapes (as in the case of the new F R Yugoslavia and Croatia) lies a similar desire to deny legitimacy retroactively to the former Yugoslav discourses of identity.

and in the narration of individual identities. A main thread through the studied texts is the experience of an irreparable split in the narratives of the writer's life. As a result of the break-up of Yugoslavia, meaning now derives its quality from its location in one of two moments, separated by a wide gap: before or after (Drakulić 1993:128). The dramatic changes that accompanied this temporal and spatial reorganization are evoked by Ugrešić:

> A country disappeared, and it was replaced by a number of other countries – a whole fifty year period disappeared. Whether good or bad, right or wrong, it was the period in which we lived: these were the letters and words we had learned, the books we had read, the objects that were ours, the films we watched, the streets in which we walked. Suddenly everything had to change: address books, the language and our names, our identity . . . Everything changed with astonishing speed into old garbage, but nobody had found the opportunity to make a catalogue of it all, and put the right labels on (1993:13).

In this last comment it becomes clear that the process is not a neutral temporal division, but that it is laden with value judgements: before, i.e. life in Titoist Yugoslavia, has become associated exclusively with negative meanings. In the words of Slavenka Drakulić:

> [O]n the eve of independence I feel ambiguous. I feel robbed of my past, my childhood, my education, my memories and sentiments, as if my whole life has been wrong, one big mistake, a lie and nothing else. I'm a loser, indeed we are all losers at the moment. The Croatian 'new democracy' hasn't brought us anything yet but promises to believe in. The cost is high: renunciation of the whole past and sacrifice of the present (1993:57–8).

A little further Drakulić makes it clear that she is longing to feel at home in postcommunist Croatia: 'I hope I will love my new country' (1993:58). However, elsewhere she describes her fear that constructing a home isn't always easy, and that it 'would take another lifetime to find my place in a foreign world' (1993:33).

For many inhabitants of the former Yugoslav republics, the construction of a sense of home between new borders is further complicated by legal obstacles. Svetlana Slapšak has been married to a Slovene for several decades, and she commuted between Ljubljana and Belgrade. When returning from France in the summer of 1992, she found herself obliged to buy a visa at the border in order to go back to the place where she had lived (albeit not exclusively) for a quarter of a century (1993:67).

Throughout the former Yugoslav territory, problems concerning state citizenship and residence status have affected hundreds of thousands. One could view these regulations as a sort of second-line bureaucratic ethnic cleansing, and it is not surprising, therefore, that the main target consists of the unacceptable anomaly for the establishment of nation-states: mixed families. Moreover, the break-up of Yugoslavia puts into an entirely different perspective the lives of the generation that fought with the Partisans and lived their adult life under Tito. Drakulić recounts how, only now, confronted with the historical 'futility of his life, frittered away by history', she can feel close to her father, who had believed in the Yugoslav communist project (1993:73).

Homeless at Home

In a number of ways the situation of the writers discussed here is very different from that of 'non-privileged' refugees: during the writing of these books Slavenka Drakulić and Dubravka Ugrešić lived partly in Zagreb, which is where they used to live before. However, even here one could argue that there is a situation of an 'impossible homecoming', for home is not home any more: the Yugoslavia that existed before doesn't exist any more. Here, the 'homeland that was left, forever lost, survives only in traces and memories, but the returned exile becomes a Janus-faced "translated person", a migrant with a cross-border hybrid identity' (Robertson *et al.* 1994:3). 'Yugoslavia' has come to signify a longing, and returning is impossible, for this would involve 'not a spatial but a temporal journey', such as is described by Pollock in her article on her birthplace Africa (1994:83). This feeling of homelessness at home is described at length by Ugrešić:

> I shudder at the phantom spectre of my old fatherland, where I have become a stranger, and which doesn't even exist any more. I shudder at my new country, where I'll be a stranger and where I still have to apply for citizenship, because I lost that of my old fatherland. I will have to prove that I've been born there, even though I have been born there, that I speak the language of my country, even though it's my mother tongue. I shudder at my old-new fatherland, where I'll enter as if I am an immigrant (1993:145–6).

Svetlana Slapšak points out how in Croatia a term became widely used during the war: 'Yugozombies'. She remarks that it was picked up in other republics shortly afterwards, which ironically testifies to the fact that the new states still have cultural ties (1993:17). Yugozombies are the living dead of Yugoslavia: they have not discarded their Yugoslav past, or at least not completely. Therefore, by their very existence they pose a threat to the new national spirit. It is possible, I think, to distinguish a time- and a space-dimension in the living/dead character of the Yugo-zombie.

An important corollary of the condemnation of the Titoist period is a collective enthusiasm for amnesia. Especially in Croatia and Slovenia, immediately after the declarations of independence by the new regimes, there was an attempt to do away with everything Yugoslav. This accounts for the numerous corrections of the past that were established by the nationalist governments: streets, squares, buildings were renamed, new school-books were written, museums and libraries were cleansed of Yugoslav elements.[5]

> A war has been waged against the past, in the name of the present. And a war against the present, in the name of the future. The war has devoured our future in the name of a new future. (. . .) The self-appointed rulers of life and death have re-established the co-ordinates of left and right, of just and unjust, and of true and false (Ugrešić, 1995:12–13).

Elsewhere, Ugrešić connects these politics of time with mechanisms of memory and forgetting:

> [S]pace is being created for a new (and this time, really new), bright (and this time truly bright) future (and this time really a future). The terror of memory has its counterpart in the terror of forgetting. Both processes are indispensable for the creation of a new state of events and a new truth. The terror of memory is a strategy which restores the (apparently uninterrupted) continuity of national identity, whereas the terror of forgetting is a strategy to wipe out Yugoslav identity and the possibility to restore it – afterwards (1995:113).

Naturally, the tension of time on the level of the great narratives of the new republics has its counterpart in, and can exist as another half of, people's everyday life experiences. The tipp-ex of national correctness also reigned in the smaller narratives of individual and family histories. This theme constitutes an important part of the writings discussed in this chapter. For example, Drakulić left Croatia when Zagreb came under threat, and she describes how only as a refugee she realized that her past wasn't hers any more:

5. Ugrešić 1995:80ff., 1993:154ff.; Drakulić 1993:74–5, 85.

That first Sunday in Ljubljana was empty and white like a sheet of paper waiting for me to write something on it: new words, a new beginning. But I couldn't. (. . .) I knew I had been deprived of the future, but I could bear it. But until that moment I wasn't aware that I had been deprived of the past too. Of my past I had only memories and I knew they would acquire the sepia colour of a distant, undistinguished event, then slowly dissolve, disappear in the soft forgetfulness that time would bring as a relief, leading me to doubt that I had ever lived that part of my life (1993:32).

This questioning of the reality of the past links in with a wider sense of temporal disorientation. The revival of certain discourses of the Second World War seems to exist independently from the historical logic that gave rise to it: 'The hand that holds up the knife remembers the virulent hate, but it doesn't remember the reason or the objective' (Ugrešić 1993: 57). This is what Ugrešić describes with a metaphor of a phantom ship:

[I]n this age of insanity, the Balkans sail through their own history like a phantom ship. I've got the feeling that we enter some Bermuda triangle of time and disappear in magnetic oblivion. I don't know where I am any more: in a future or in a past of myself. A real reality does not exist any more (1993:57).

What this means in everyday situations is illustrated by Slapšak's story 'Trains', where she recounts how she was sharing a compartment with young Serbs from Knin in 1991. The boys were discussing the tragic fate of their grandparents in the hands of the Croatian fascists in the Second World War, and, more importantly, the need for revenge on the Croats of today (1993:161). Slapšak, whose own grandfather was killed by the Ustaše, fails to understand their obsession with the war and the anachronistic atmosphere of revenge that permeates the discussion.

Apart from a temporal sense of disorientation, an upsetting of the chronological order of the narratives in question, there is also a break in the spatial order. When referring to 'a world in movement', we have to analyse at least two levels: people are travelling (physically and mentally), but even when they stay at home they can find themselves displaced, for borders are travelling as well. Earlier I referred to the feeling of homeless-ness at home, which finds just one possible expression in the narratives discussed here: the impossible homecoming of these writers in what replaced the all-Yugoslav cultural background they identified with. Balkan historian Ivo Banac argues that 'the history of the Balkans is the history of migrations, not just of peoples, but of lands' (quoted in Bennett

1995:16). Thus, when asked where she's from, Dubravka Ugrešić answers: 'From Zagreb.' But where is that? And Ugrešić has to admit 'Yes, where is it? In Croatia, a country that doesn't exist yet. And where's that? In Yugoslavia, a country that doesn't exist any more' (1993:15).

Maybe it is necessary here to clarify the position of the new 'small' Yugoslavia. The republics of Serbia (including the formerly autonomous provinces of Vojvodina and Kosova/o) and Montenegro are united in a new federation and claim to be the successor state of Former Yugoslavia. This is not the place to discuss the power politics behind that claim; but it contrasts sharply with the fact that many people in that new Yugoslavia who say they 'feel Yugoslav' would often immediately add that they are referring to the 'old' Yugoslavia. This seems to illustrate the point made by Edward Said: 'Borders and barriers which enclose us within the safety of familiar territory can also become prisons, and are often defended beyond reason or necessity' (quoted in Chambers 1994:2). These reflections throw a critical light on questions of responsibility in the latest war. Svetlana Slapšak bitterly denounces the proclaimed Yugoslavism of Milošević and his allies: 'Who is more committed to Yugoslavia, those who had to abandon a normal life in order not to kill other Yugoslavs, or those who, even though they still call themselves Yugoslavs, killed others, some of whom were still citizens of the same country?' (1993:19).

Nationalism and the Ill-fitting Shirt

Not only did the nationalist discourse put enormous pressure on what could be talked about, it also issued restrictions on how people could locate themselves in the world. In her first week after she left Zagreb, Drakulić had a discussion with a man in Ljubljana. Talking to him, she understood that 'it was the war speaking through our mouths, accusing us, reducing us to two opposing sides, forcing us to justify ourselves' (1993:33). Virtually all the texts discussed here testify to this tendency towards national homogenization.[6] The authors deplore the loss of significance, and often even the de-legitimization of other forms of identification, such as their gender, their occupation, their sense of belonging to Yugoslavia, their individual feelings and beliefs, etc. For example, when feminists all over former Yugoslavia protested against the systematic rape of large groups of women in Bosnia, they were soon

6. Which again seems to point to the interdependence of globalization and national cultural compression as two sides of same coin (Featherstone 1990; Appadurai 1990: 307–8).

reminded that this should be seen as violence against a nation, not a sex. In Serbia the government went so far as to issue a law stating that rape of Serbian women by Albanians should be punished more severely than sexual violence the other way round and than 'intra-ethnic' rape (Slapšak 1993:73).

In the different republics, a discourse of what we could call 'national correctness' was imposed: criticism of the dominant nationalist discourses was condemned with standard phrases such as 'pathological hate of the people' or 'treason to the nation' (Slapšak 1993:110). Again, in this discursive framework where nationality is the most important qualification of a person, people in mixed families are victimized, as can be seen in the above-mentioned letter of Slavenka Drakulić to her daughter:

> The tragedy and the paradox of this situation now is that you will have to decide, to take his or my side, to become Croat or Serb, to take on and suffer his and my 'guilt' of marrying the 'wrong' nationality. In the war there is no middle position. All of a sudden, you as Croat or Serb, become responsible for what all other Croats or Serbs are doing. You are reduced to a single nationality – almost sentenced to it, since nationality in the war brings a danger of being killed just because of it (1993:130).

In a piece called 'Overcome by Nationhood', the same author clarifies the homogenizing pressure of nationalism on her identity with reference to a metaphor of '[A]n ill-fitting shirt. You might not like the colour, and the cloth might itch. But there is no escape; there is nothing else to wear' (1993:51). Elsewhere, Drakulić shows how it does not leave out the children:

> The demons in us have already made people perceive themselves as nothing but parts of the national being. 'The Serbs must be slaughtered,' says a twelve-year-old child from my neighbourhood playing with the bread-knife. His mother slaps his face, while the other grown-ups around the table lower their eyes, aware that they are to blame for his words (1993:9).

The case of nationalism in the former Yugoslav republics is yet another illustration of the anthropological teaching that the 'inside' of a national identity has to be approached through its boundaries with an 'outside'. Bauman for instance refers to Ricoeur's distinction between two dimensions of identity: *la mêmeté* (identity with itself over time) and *l'ipséité* (drawing boundaries that separate the self from the others). In order to understand nationalism, he argues, we have to see how the latter precedes and conditions the former (Ricoeur 1990:148–50; Bauman 1992:677). This throws light on the great enthusiasm displayed by the new nationalist regimes for the practice of labelling others, and thereby homogenizing their 'own people'. The nation must be imagined as limited: if nationalism as a discourse creates, structures and maintains a national identity, it can only do so by simultaneously conceiving the existence of other national identities. In this context, Bhabha quotes Balibar in saying that 'the racial/ cultural identity of "true nationals" remains invisible but is inferred from (. . .) the quasi-hallucinatory visibility of the "false nationals"' and that the fact that 'the "false" are too visible will never guarantee that the "true" are visible enough' (Bhabha 1996:55–6). When the Croatian president Tudjman asserted that 'we have established a state and now we will decide who are its citizens', he simultaneously made it clear that others would not enjoy full citizenship (Lutard 1993). Dubravka Ugrešić draws attention to this labelling of outsiders in 'Priests and Parrots':

> It started with a careful, secret stock-taking of the differences between the diverse population groups, which were gradually emphasised more and more strongly from then on. Eventually this led to straightforward and overt discrimination. How else can one mark one's own cattle, how else could one distinguish one's own herd from the other's? (1995:52–3).

Linked with the dominant place attributed to nationality, another main theme in the texts is what they present as a wider process of the collectivization of identity. Slavenka Drakulić tells how she feels orphaned, because the war robbed her of 'the only real possession I had acquired in my life, my individuality' (1993:51). Similarly, Svetlana Slapšak recounts how she felt she had to escape the oppressive climate in the Serbian dissident intelligentsia, when the large majority of those who were dissidents under Titoism lined up behind the Milošević nationalist reformation programme (1993:63–4). An equally frightening picture is presented by Ugrešić, who comments on the perceived need for homogenization in Croatia under the influence of threats from outside and the will to build a positive image in the world (1995:105ff.). At the same time, as a result of an ironic twist in history, many former Yugoslavs have unwillingly acquired another collective pan-Yugoslav identity: that of refugees from the Balkans (Drakulić 1993:35–41; Ugrešić 1993:145, 1995:46–7). Of course, there is also another side to the story; earlier I referred to the awareness of the uniqueness of the Yugoslav cultural configuration and the reluctance of Yugoslavs to be categorized as Eastern European by the West. Dubravka Ugrešić points out how the collective identity of 'East European Writer' is now eagerly adopted by some authors, who, in order to accumulate cultural capital when facing Western publishers, even make up a history of suffering under Titoist censorship (1993:93, 1995:112).

Reconstructions of the Normal: Patterns of Continuity

When looking at the construction of 'home' in former Yugoslavia, it is not sufficient to highlight the ways in which narratives on different levels were distorted and broken. In what follows I will explore some patterns of continuity that seem to prevail at the same time, as another side of the same coin. The first one is the paradoxical but undeniable fact that the present situation mirrors certain aspects of the Titoist period, despite, or actually because of, the dramatic attempts to differentiate the post-communist societies from that time. I am not referring to the obvious continuities, such as the occupation of influential positions by the same persons (prime example: Slobodan Milošević), or the copying of Tito's style and megalomaniac habits (prime example: Franjo Tudjman). Instead, I mean that, like communism, the dominant discourses of today are build around a 'new start' – and precisely in this desire to do away with what was before, they are not different from the revolutionary Yugoslav narrative.

> People live without the past, both collective and individual. This has been the prescribed way of life for the past forty-five years under communism, when it was assumed that history began in 1941, with the War and the Revolution. The new history of the state of Croatia also begins with war and revolution and with eradicating the memory of forty-five years under communism. Obviously, this is what we have been used to. It is terrible that this is what we are supposed to get used to again (Drakulić 1993:73).

The correction of the past is seen as an urgent and necessary task, to be carried out, again, by 'the people', who are defined this time by national rather than class standards. The important differences between the present nationalisms and the Titoist discourse are to be found in the content of these corrections, and not in the practice of attempting to establish this discursive closure.

Equally striking is the attempt to preserve a certain continuity, a sense of spatial and temporal orientation, in the narratives of everyday life displayed in the texts of the three women. They tell us about sometimes dramatic efforts to cling to normality, even as war creeps into the details of life. Drakulić describes how she bought new wallpaper shortly after the outbreak of war in Slovenia, and knowing very well that the fighting might soon render her purchase a sign of hopeless *naïveté*. However, she argues, it is precisely this knowledge that made her buy it at that very moment: an act of faith in the future (1993:25). Svetlana Slapšak's story about the significance of a simple little black dress is an illustration of how she also turns to everyday objects in order to preserve control over the narratives of personal identity. The little black dress, she argues, is an explicitly European urban phenomenon – it is not typical for any national culture, and therefore, it subverts nationalist discourses through its simplicity (1993:150–3).

Of course, the discourses of violence and homogenization do not dominate all aspects of life to the same extent, nor all at once. At first, the war is seen as something distant, something alien, something unhomely that will not affect one's own life if it is kept out of the place, the network, the meanings that constitute 'home'. Even when it turns out to be irreversible, when the conflict has invaded everyday life, Drakulić comments that she 'hesitate(s) to use the word war, which has recently become tamed and domesticated in our vocabulary like a domestic animal, almost a pet' (1993:34–5). Note that, etymologically, the term 'domestic(ated)' refers to 'home' – and it is the fact that the word 'war' has found itself a place, even at home, that makes the author reluctant to use it. It is therefore not surprising to see this notion reappear when Drakulić reports on her visit – as a journalist – to the front line: she finds it hard 'coming to terms with the fact that the front is less than an hour's drive from my home' (1993:62).

Attempts to keep the war out of the narratives of 'home' are realized through a number of strategies in everyday life. In the background, a general form of cultural anaesthesia seems to take root: the barbarism of the conflict is attributed to madness, is seen as a symptom of a world that is completely different from one's own.[7] Television, by far the most

7. It was in Alan Feldman's article (1994) that I first came across the term 'cultural anaesthesia'. This reminded me of a scene in Aleksandar Tišma's *The Use of Man*, with Sep Lenart, who worked as an executioner in the Nazi camps, and his Jewish brother-in-law Robert Kroner. Drunk and hysterical, Lenart recounts how he executed large groups of Jews like an automaton, and he expresses his paranoia that 'there's still more of that scum around and that it will never be possible to liquidate them all'. Kroner does not believe him and clings to the idea that Lenart must be mad, because 'if he is not insane, if anything at all in his whole story was true, then the world would be insane, and that was something Kroner could not accept, because he still felt part of the world'(1990:76).

important propaganda instrument in all the republics of former Yugo-slavia, plays an important role in this process. It brings the war home, but at the same time allows a 'feeling of detachment' through which the war can be kept at a distance:

> All last year war was a distant rumour, something one managed to obscure or ignore – something happening to other people, to people in Knin or Slavonia on the outskirts of the republic, but never to us in the centre, in Zagreb. We were busy with our private lives, with love, careers and a new car. War was threatening us, but not directly, as if we were somehow protected by that flickering TV screen which gave us a feeling of detachment – we might just as well have been in Paris or Budapest (Drakulić 1993:18).

Television is also important in that it feeds the hunger for news that is so typical during wartime. Slavenka Drakulić argues that the war has made all the people involved news-addicts: 'I can talk about one thing only, because everything else seems inappropriate, because everything personal has been wiped out, and endless news, news, news . . .' (1993:8). In this way, a society dominated by war also leads to new configurations of normality: endless communiqués on TV; patriotic songs, gadgets, and books; people stocking up food and so on (1993:18ff.).

Earlier I referred to the dependence of nationalist discourses on processes of re-interpretation of the past, especially the forty-five years of communism, and the enthusiasm of the majority of the population when it comes to realizing this in everyday life. Paradoxically, the post-communist climate has also led to a re-interpretation of Yugoslav reality from another point of view: maybe it is only now, in retrospect, that one can understand the pan-Yugoslav configuration in its fullness. In her discussion of the significance of popular music, Slapšak argues that 'Today the former Yugo-rock is re-interpreted: now we really listen to it as emigrants. It has become a symbol of a time which is definitively over.' She goes on to praise the music made by Goran Bregović for Kusturica's film *Arizona Dream*. This soundtrack is a typical example of postmodern eclecticism: it draws on Serbian, Macedonian, Bosnian and Gypsy tradi-tions, but also uses newly composed folk music, contemporary music like that of Philip Glass and Astor Piazolla, etc. On top of it all, there is the voice of rock 'n' roll animal Iggy Pop:

> A world had to be lost so that others can get to know about what it has been. (. . .) Goran Bregović has used his acquaintance with the margins in order to give a new chance to a world that has disappeared. If Yugo-rock has now

succeeded in becoming a creative margin, a contact between diversities, nothing has been lost. Apart from numerous lives. Therefore, this music can only be music of human compassion, of wandering, of re-investigating guilt, a music of forgiving (1993:173–4).

Writing and Nomadic Identity

It is clear that some of the texts discussed in this chapter are self-conscious stories of identity: they read like manifestos of individuality against oppressive homogenizing discourses of nationalism. However, even in the other contributions, mainly snapshots of their everyday lives, these writers seem to engage in the narration of an identity. The very act of writing itself functions as a strategy to ensure a form of continuity: after all, these women are writers, and 'for a number of writers in exile, the true home is to be found not in houses but in writing' (Minh-ha 1994:16). In this sense, the writings have served as a kind of refuge, which allows the writers to 'pull themselves at once closer and further away from it [sc.'home'] by telling stories' (Minh-ha 1994:10). These authors write themselves a position in the world – it is a way to locate themselves in relation to the discourses that structure the post-Yugoslav societies. Similarly to the idea of 'travel', the notion of 'home' draws most of its significance from its function as a metaphor. The concept of 'home' is linked to that of identity, in that it is about 'the story we tell of ourselves . . . which is also the story others tell of us' (Sarup 1994:94). Narrative mediates our journey through life, for in Chambers's words, 'To write is, of course, to travel' (1994:10). Similarly Michel de Certeau argues that 'every story is a travel story, a spatial practice' (1990:171). Here we have a journey of introspection, in which the authors dissect their lives in order to reintegrate them into an intelligible narrative in retrospect (see Curtis and Pajaczkowska 1994:212; Rasmussen 1996:165; Ricoeur 1990:167–93).

As we have seen, the writers in question had developed an identity with many characteristics that could be termed 'nomadic'. They travelled frequently, and they felt at home in those travels. However, there was a background against which they did this: Yugoslavia. It seems that precisely the diverse and open character of that cultural framework made Yugoslavia suitable to serve as a 'home'. With the break-up of the federation, the Yugoslav nomads were robbed of the cultural space that was 'home' to them; but this doesn't mean the end of their nomadic narratives. On the contrary, finding themselves in exile, they develop the nomadic aspects of identity that were there already; but this time the disappearance of home leaves them little choice (Slapšak, 1993:175). Ugrešić expresses this as follows: 'I didn't know then that the image of someone who's been dropped in an empty house would eventually be replaced by a permanent feeling of homelessness' (1993:10).

Paradoxically, writing, then, seems to allow the authors to construct a partial sense of continuity, of identity with themselves, precisely through aspects of fragmentation and hybridity. Unable to find themselves at peace with the discourses of nationalism, these women adhere to an always incomplete nomad identity.

> I haven't been to my flat in Beograd for one and a half years now. My mother often comes and visits me in Slovenia: she then stays for a month or two. I meet my friends from Beograd in Ljubljana, Paris, Wien, Berlin or Amsterdam. (Slapšak 1993:66).

> Even though I have the Croatian nationality now, every time someone asks me what or who I am, I repeat my mother's words: 'at the moment I don't know who or what I am any more'. Sometimes I suddenly think of it, and then I say: 'I am a post-Yugoslav, a gypsy'(Ugrešić 1995:14).

Recent literature on notions of nomadism and cosmopolitanism has, I think, often an overly rosy tone, with its references to 'dwelling as mobile habitat' (Chambers 1994:4) and 'a willingness to engage with the Other' (Hannerz 1990:239). Clifford talks of the 'travel myth', with its Victorian bourgeois overtones and its privileging of a specific white, male, rich subject characterized by security and freedom (Clifford 1992:105–7). He makes a case against a relativist nomadology that does not take into account the obvious fact that the most dramatic movements made by people on the planet are not made out of free will (1992:114–5).[8] Throughout this chapter I have attempted to make it clear that, although the possibility of nomadic narratives can constitute a liberating and an enriching opening of discourses, it can also, even in the case of 'privileged refugees', be at least partly imposed, and can be accompanied by insecurity and injustice. It is therefore not surprising that Dubravka Ugrešić's vision of 'home' in the transit areas of an airport has a somewhat desperate undertone:

---

8. Over 20 million refugees worldwide in 1994 (De Viafoon, Temanummer Vluchtelingen 1994,19:3).

The way from one plane to another, from gate to gate, from flight to flight, is a way of inner freedom. (. . .) I like it here. I am a human maggot. I will build my nest here, in a place that belongs to nobody. I will wander from sector A to sector B, from sector B to sector C. (. . .) During the day I will be carried by the passenger conveyor, as if I'm a traveller; at night I will find a place in one of the seats and, half-asleep, I will wait for a flight that will never be announced. (. . .) I will live in the artificial light of the airport as an example of the postmodern species, in a transit phase, in an ideal shelter, in purgatory, in an emotionally sterile room (1995:146).

This fragment seems to fit in with what Augé wrote on *non-lieux* (non-places). Examples of *non-lieux* are shopping malls, train stations and airport terminals – spaces that epitomize the space–time compression in what he calls *la surmodernité* (1992:100–7).

If we refrain from essentializing 'nomadism' and allow for a number of reservations, I believe it is instructive to think of life as a journey even for those whose lives are dominated by fixity and locality. 'We are all exiles whose return is always deferred' (Robertson *et al.* 1994:4). However, it is crucial to a discussion of globalization and de-territorialization of identity that, even within this late modern, globalized and hybrid sphere of identity, there is a constant dialogue at work between movement and fixity, between dynamism and stasis. And of course, every dialogue is permeated by inequality and power relations, so that every identity remains not only internally contested, but also subject to questioning or undermining by other narratives. I have attempted to highlight the problematic relations between different narratives on different levels of post-Yugoslav reality. Clearly, the writers in question have a certain freedom to locate themselves and the stories of their lives within the sphere of identity; but at the same time a number of other very powerful narratives can limit this freedom severely. According to de Certeau, writing is one of the most powerful mythical practices of modern times (1990:198ff.). This, I would suggest, explains its ambiguous character: stories on different levels in former Yugoslavia constitute a vehicle for oppressive homogenization and for otherness to break through the dominant discourses. A look at the ways in which three former Yugoslav writers explore this space in their texts suggests that identities truly are 'untold stories', but that one often has limited freedom in telling them.

References

Anon (*Globus*) (1992), 'Hrvatske Feministice siluju Hrvatsku', *Globus*, 11/12/ 1992, pp. 41–2.

Appadurai, A.(1990), 'Disjuncture and Difference in the Global Cultural Economy', in M. Featherstone (ed.), *Global Culture: Nationalism, Globalisation, Modernity*, London: Sage.

—— (1995), 'The production of Locality', in R. Fardon (ed.), *Counterworks: Managing the Diversity of Knowledge*, London: Routledge.

Atwood, M. (1990), *The Handmaid's Tale*, London: Vintage.

Augé, M. (1992), *Non-lieux: introduction a une anthropologie de la surmodernité*, Paris: Seuil.

Bammer, A. (1992), 'Editorial', *New Formations*, Issue 17: The Question of 'Home'.

Bauman, Z. (1990), 'Modernity and Ambivalence', in M. Featherstone (ed.) *Global Culture: Nationalism, Globalisation and Modernity*, London: Sage.

—— (1992), 'Soil, Blood and Identity', *Sociological Review*, 40(4): 675–701.

Bennett, C. (1995), *Yugoslavia's Bloody Collapse: Causes, Course and Consequences*, London: Hurst and Co.

Bhabha, H. K. (1994), 'Dissemination: Time, Narrative and the Margins of the Modern Nation', in H. K. Bhabha, *The Location of Culture*, London: Routledge.

—— (1996), 'Culture's In-Between', in S. Hall and P. duGay (eds), *Questions of Cultural Identity*, London: Sage.

Certeau, M. de (1990 [1980]), *L'invention du quotidien: 1. arts de faire*, Paris: Gallimard Folio Essais.

Chambers, I. (1994), *Migrancy, Culture, Identity*, London: Routledge.

Clifford, J. (1992), 'Traveling Cultures', in L. Grossberg, C. Nelson and P. A. Treichler (eds), *Cultural Studies*, London: Routledge.

Cohen, L. (1995), *Broken Bonds: the Disintegration of Yugoslavia and Balkan Politics in Transition*, Boulder: Westview.

Curtis, B. and Pajaczkowska, C. (1994), 'Getting There: Travel, Time and Narrative' in G. Robertson *et al.* (eds), *Travellers' Tales: Narratives of Home and Displacement*, London: Routledge.

Drakulić, S. (1993), *Balkan Express* (trans. M. Soljan), London: Hutchinson.

Feldman, A. (1994) 'On Cultural Anaesthesia: From Desert Storm to Rodney King', *American Ethnologist*, 21(2): 404–18.

Ganguly, K. (1992), 'Migrant Identities: Personal Memory and the Construction of Selfhood', *Cultural Studies*, 6:1.

Garde, P. (1992), *Vie et mort de la Yougoslaviel*, Paris: Fayard.

Gross, D. (1985), 'Temporality and the Modern State', *Theory & Society*, 14(1): 53–82.

Hannerz, U. (1990), 'Cosmopolitans and Locals in World Culture', in M. Featherstone,(ed.), *Global Culture*, London: Sage.

Hodson, R., Sekulić, D. and Massey, G. (1994) 'National Tolerance in Former Yugoslavia', *American Journal of Sociology*, 99(6):1334–58.

Laclau, E. (1990) *New Reflections on the Revolution in Our Time*, London: Verso.

Lamarque, P. (1990) 'Narrative and Invention: The Limits of Fictionality', in C.

Nash (ed.), *Narrative in Culture: The Use of Story-telling in the Sciences, Philosophy and Literature*, London: Routledge.

Lendvai, P. (1991), 'Yugoslavia without Yugoslavs: The Roots of the Crisis', *International Affairs*, 67(2): 251–62.

Lutard, C. (1993), 'Dérive autoritaire en Croatie et en Serbie', *Le Monde Diplomatique*.

Minh-ha, T. (1994), 'Other than myself / my other self', in G. Robertson *et al.* (eds), *Travellers' Tales: Narratives of Home and Displacement*, London: Routledge.

Pollock, G. (1994), 'Territories of Desire: Reconsiderations of an African Child-hood', in G. Robertson *et al.* (eds), *Travellers' Tales: Narratives of Home and Displacement*, London: Routledge.

Rasmussen, D. (1996), 'Rethinking Subjectivity: Narrative Identity and the Self', in Kearney, R. (ed.), *Paul Ricoeur: The Hermeneutics of Action*, London: Sage.

Ricoeur, P. (1990), *Soi-même comme un autre*, Paris: Editions du Soleil.

Robertson, G. *et al.* (eds) (1990), *Travellers' Tales: Narratives of Home and Displacement*, London: Routledge.

Sarup, M. (1994), 'Home and Identity', in G. Robertson *et al.* (eds), *Travellers' Tales: Narratives of Home and Displacement*, London: Routledge.

Sekulić, D., Hodson, R. and Massey, G. (1994), 'Who Were the Yugoslavs? Failed Sources of a Common Identity in the Former Yugoslavia', *American Socio-logical Review*, 59(1):83–97.

Slapšak, S. (1993), *Joegoslavie weet je nog?* (trans. R. Dokter), Amsterdam: Jan Mets.

Sweeney, A. (1989), 'The Malay Novelist: Social Analyst or Informant? Or Neither?', in *Review of Indonesian and Malaysian Affairs*, 23: 96–126.

Tišma, A. (1990 [1976]), *Het Gebruik van de Mens*, Amsterdam: Meulenhoff.

Ugrešić, D. (1995), *De Cultuur van de Leugens* (trans. R. Schuyt), Amsterdam: Nijgh & Van Ditmar.

Ugrešić, D. (1993), *Nationaliteit: geen* (trans. R. Schuyt), Amsterdam: Nijgh & Van Ditmar.

4

The Metaphor of 'Home' in Czech Nationalist Discourse

Ladislav Holy

Although all nationalisms share common features, each of them has also its own particular characteristics, determined by the historically specific context in which the nationalist ideology emerged and the specific circumstances in which it persists. Czech nationalism, like many aspects of Czech historical consciousness (Rak 1994), crystalized during the period of conscious nation-building, referred to by the Czechs as the national revival (*národní obrození*) and started at the end of the eighteenth century. Its ideology was closely connected to the way in which the Czech nation became conceptualized – particularly in the first half of the nineteenth century – as a linguistic community that was asserting its identity against the German-speaking population of the historical Bohemian kingdom, also referred to as the lands of the Bohemian Crown or, simply, as the Czech lands (Bohemia, Moravia and Silesia). Apart from its strong linguistic orientation, which has been constantly noted by virtually all students of Czech nationalism, its most striking – but in the existing scholarly writing much less emphasized – feature is its fascination with, and celebration of, the beauty of the Czech countryside and its close equation between homeland (*vlast*) and home (*domov*). This close analogy between 'homeland' and 'home', on which I am going to concentrate in this chapter, is closely linked with the sharp distinction that the Czechs draw between patriotism and nationalism.

Patriotism and Nationalism

For the Czechs, patriotism is a positive attitude to, or the awareness of belonging to, one's homeland (*vlast*). Most of them define it as a love of

111

one's homeland that manifests itself in the willingness to do something positive for it. This can range from one's contribution to the development of national culture to a cultured lifestyle that respects national customs and traditions. Even people who did not claim strong patriotic feelings and said, for example, that they would never fight for their country, maintained that patriotism was a desirable attitude. As some of them argued, it has to be because love itself is a positive feeling, and so, of course, is love of one's country. But above all, patriotism is a positive attitude, because it expresses love for one's country without engendering animosity, hatred and a feeling of superiority towards other nations.

The latter sentiments are characteristic of nationalism, which most of my Czech informants described as immoderate, fanatical or exaggerated patriotism – as patriotism gone too far. According to them, nationalism stresses the exceptional qualities of a particular nation and belittles the qualities of other nations; it is thus an attitude that considers one's own nation to be superior to those of others. It is an expression of a negative attitude, and often of open hostility to other nations, and it manifests itself in intolerance towards other nations, in the pursuit of national interests at their expense and in the denial of their rights. Whilst patriotism is solely inward-looking, and is thus tolerant of other nations, nationalism is always outward-looking. It is a hatred of other nations that typically leads to violence committed in the name of one's own nation on others.

When trying to convey their understanding of nationalism, most Czechs with whom I discussed the subject gave a definition that was a paraphrase in their own words of Schumpeter's definition of nationalism as an 'affirmative awareness of national character, together with an aggressive spirit of superiority' (Schumpeter 1951: 211) or of Ferrero's definition of it as an 'active, often aggressive and violent, national or nationality-oriented politics and movements' (Ferrero 1995: 205). All people I spoke to condemned nationalism as a negative and undesirable attitude, and most of them expressed the view that while Czechs, or at least most Czechs, were patriots, they were certainly not nationalists. These views were reflected in a survey conducted in the Czech republic in autumn 1990, in which 52 per cent of respondents expressed the opinion that the Czechs did not possess any strong awareness of themselves as a nation (*Aktuálne problémy Cesko-Slovenska*, November 1990: 26).

Opinions like this give rise to the often expressed view that Czech nationalism does not exist or, if it does, emerges only as a reaction to Slovak nationalism and its openly expressed anti-Czech sentiments. The perceived lack of Czech national awareness is to a great extent the result of the facts that the Czechs have been the dominant nation in the

Czechoslovak republic and that in 1945 and 1946, when the German population of Bohemia, Moravia and Silesia was transferred to Germany, they became – if we discount the gypsies – effectively the sole inhabitants of the Czech lands. Czechhood is not felt to be under threat and does not need to be openly asserted. Nationalism is something that plagues others – Slovaks, Serbs, Croats and various nations of the former Soviet Union; but not the Czechs. Denial of Czech nationalism is part of the construction of a positive image of the Czech nation, for nationalism, whether as a militant movement or as heightened national feelings, has unambiguously negative connotations.

Only a few students of nationalism have paid systematic attention to the differences between patriotism and nationalism in their analyses (Snyder 1976; Janowitz 1983; Kosterman and Feshbach 1989; Bar-Tal 1993; Connor 1993, 1994: 196–7; Eller and Coughlan 1993; Billig 1995: 55–8). One of the main reasons why the analytical distinction between patriotism and nationalism has been underplayed probably stems from the fact that the sharp conceptual separation that the Czechs are able to draw between them is far from being a universal feature of what may be called the construction of national sentiments. To appreciate how such a separation is generated, it is useful to bear in mind that two opposed models of the nation underlie the notion of national identity. Historically, these two opposed models emerged as the result of different developments in France and Germany in the second half of the eighteenth and the beginning of the nineteenth century. One model emerged in the French revolution of 1789. It is a model of a unified and indivisible collectivity that crystallized in a struggle aimed at overcoming the previous divisions of class, religion and regional and ethnic differences. Building on the ideas of Rousseau and Herder, a different model emerged in Germany, particularly in the atmosphere of the Napoleonic wars in 1806–15. It was consciously formulated in opposition to the French model, and it conceptualized the nation as a non-political but linguistic and cultural entity. Both conceptions of the nation grew out of different historical conditions, of a unified French nation-state on the one hand and the political fragmentation of the German-speaking population on the other hand. The German historian Friedrich Meinecke (1907) characterized the two opposed models of the nation as *Staatsnation* (the state nation) and *Kulturnation* (the cultural nation). Kohn (1955, 1967) and Plamenatz (1973) similarly differentiated between the Western concept of the nation conceptualized as an association of people living in a common territory under the same government and laws, and the Eastern concept of a nation as an organic ethnically based community. In Kohn's view the Western model of the nation was the product of the middle classes, who came to power particularly in France. Britain and America at the end of the eighteenth century. The Eastern model was the product of the intellectuals, who led the resistance to Napoleon in the countries east of the Rhine.

Smith characterizes the 'Western' civic-territorial model of the nation as 'historic territory, legal-political community, legal-political equality of members, and civic culture and ideology' (1991: 11; 1986: 134–7). Historically, this model emerged as a 'consequence of prior economic, social, cultural and political developments. Unity defined in terms of the nation followed facts established by firm administrative, legal and cultural institutions' (Csepeli 1992: 235). Given the importance of the legal-political component in the 'Western' model of the nation, the national ideology that this conceptualization of the nation produced was to be 'centred around the idea of the nation defined in terms of *state*' (ibid.).

The distinguishing features of the 'Eastern' ethnic-genealogical model of the nation are 'its emphasis on a community of birth and native culture' and its elements are 'genealogy and presumed descent ties, popular mobilization, vernacular languages, customs and traditions' (Smith 1991: 12; 1986: 137–8). The national ideology that this model of the nation produced could be said to be 'centred around the idea of the nation defined in terms of *culture*' (Csepeli 1992: 235). Historically, this model emerged as a result of formulating national unity in the absence of 'adequate economic, social, political and cultural foundations. Here the notion of the nation came before the establishment of the relevant national institutions; the emerging national ideology had to refer more actively to such elements of the ethnocentric heritage as descent, cultural values and norms' (ibid.).

Although the two opposed models of the nation and the ensuing types of nationalism played their role in different historical periods in both Western and Eastern Europe, particular national ideologies differ in the extent to which they follow one or the other ideal type. The civic-territorial conceptualization of the nation was not altogether absent among the Czech intellectuals of the nineteenth century (Koralka 1988: 30); but the conscious building of the modern Czech nation during the period of the national revival at the end of the eighteenth and the beginning of the nineteenth centuries was informed by the ethnic-cultural model of the nation. Since then, this conceptualization of the nation has been perpetuated through the teaching of history in schools and through literature, art and the popularization of various branches of scholarship such as ethnography, history, art history, literary criticism and linguistics, which investigate, and so in fact create (Smith 1986: 148, 200–8) national culture and traditions. Whilst the civic-territorial model of the nation conceptually subsumes state, in the ethnic-cultural model, the nation and state are conceptually separated. The Czech nation has been constructed as having existed without its own state, and the political goal of Czech nationalism, which came gradually to the fore in the second half of the nineteenth century, was at first the renewal of Czech statehood within the federated Habsburg empire and later the creation of an independent Czech nation-state. The two opposed models of the nation not only give rise to different types of nationalism (Smith 1991: 82–3), but also to different conceptualizations of the main functions of the state. The argument of Czech political nationalism of the nineteenth century was that the nations language and culture could be preserved only if the nation had its own state. The main function of the state was thus defined as the protection of the nation's cultural heritage; the state was needed to protect the nation's vital interests and to guarantee its continuous existence as a distinct cultural entity.

In the Western model, the nation, state and country (which the nation inhabits and over which the state exercises its authority) can be talked about and conceptualized in terms of each other. In the Eastern model, they always remain separate entities, which may give rise to various specific configurations: a nation without a state (Czechs in the nineteenth century), a nation without a homeland (Diasporic Jews/Palestinians), a common homeland of two or more nations (Israelis/Palestinians), a multi-national state (Belgium), a nation state.

Patriotism and Nationalism in Historical Perspective

Nationalism – whether of the Western or of the Eastern variety – is a phenomenon of modernity. Patriotism, on the other hand, is probably a sentiment of considerable antiquity, and rooted in the Graeco-Roman and Judaeo-Christian traditions of Western thought (Huizinga 1940; Viroli 1995). It is a sentiment that was certainly not absent from Bohemian society before the period of conscious nation-building that began at the end of the eighteenth century.

The main carrier of patriotism at this time was the Bohemian nobility, who used it to defend political and economic privileges threatened by the centralizing efforts of the Austrian Monarchy and the reforms of Joseph II (particularly the abolishment of serfdom). Resistance to these reforms manifested itself in efforts by the nobility to maintain the status of the Lands of the Bohemian Crown, in which it was the dominant political force; and it generated its own local patriotism (*Landes-patriotismus*). The aristocrats were patriots in that their objective was the maintenance of the Bohemian Crown as a sovereign political entity within the Austrian Monarchy. They needed support for their political aims, and the fostering of the image of Bohemia as a unique country, with its own history, tradition, customs and language, was in their immediate interest. Hence the sponsorship of many of them of the study of Bohemian antiquities, history, ethnography and natural history, and of the Czech language (even if most of the aristocrats were themselves German-speaking).

The nobility emphasized Bohemian statehood, the historical traditions of the Bohemian state and the specificity of the Czech lands (Bohemia, Moravia and Silesia) within the Austrian Monarchy. For the regional patriotism, (*Landespatriotismus*) of the Bohemian nobility it was quite irrelevant whether any particular nobleman spoke Czech or German, or possibly even Italian or French. In fact, both Czech and German were widely spoken by the population of the Czech lands at large. The strong presence of the German-speaking population dates back to the Middle Ages, and is not the result of a military expansion but of a peaceful colonization instigated by the Bohemian kings. Their subjects – Boemi – spoke Czech and German (*böhmisch und deutsch*). Only in the eighteenth century were the *Deutschböhmen* (i.e. German-speaking Bohemians) terminologically distinguished from the *Stockböhmen* (i.e. 'home-grown' Bohemians). In the nineteenth century, the latter started to be described (in German) as 'Czechen' or 'Tschechen'. They have always called themselves *Cesi* and Bohemia *Cechy*.

The German-speaking inhabitants constituted some 37 per cent of the population of Bohemia, 25 per cent in Moravia and 50 per cent in Silesia in the first half of the nineteenth century. Peasants in the interior of Bohemia spoke Czech, in the border areas, German. Bourgeoisie, aristocracy and intellectuals spoke German, albeit the aristocracy often conversed in French, and at the beginning of the nineteenth century Latin was still the main literary language of the intellectuals. The town-poor in the interior spoke Czech corrupted by numerous Germanisms. As a consequence of the Josephinian reforms of public administration inspired by the rational ideas of the Enlightenment – which manifested themselves most profoundly through the compulsory conduct of all official business of the Austrian Monarchy in German – fluency in German became the necessary condition for social advancement (Podiven 1991: 66, 73).

An enlightened state school system in the eighteenth century provided elementary education for all its citizens in their native languages. Education in secondary and vocational schools as well as university education was in German. Although the strongly centralized state did not deprive its inhabitants of their mother tongue, it insisted on creating a common language for its citizens in which the administration of public affairs could be efficiently conducted. Only during the Enlightenment can we thus talk about the increased Germanization of Bohemia and see the existence of the Czech-speaking population as eventually being threatened (Podiven 1991: 28).

I have mentioned regional patriotism as a sentiment espoused by the Bohemian nobility. Patriotism was, however, not the prerogative of this class only. The nationalist reading of Czech history sees the period of re-Catholicization of the seventeenth and eighteenth centuries as a period of 'darkness' and gradual Germanization threatening the very existence of the Czech nation. The consciously non-nationalist interpretation of this period sees it as a period of unprecedented cultural and spiritual flowering of the Czech nation during which the cultural development of Bohemia was once more in tune with that elsewhere in Europe, recovering after the disruption of the Reformation (Pynsent: 1994: 176). The country not only accepted cultural impulses from elsewhere but creatively trans-formed them into its own style, known as Czech Baroque – a style that has contributed to the contemporary image of Prague much more than any other and that has affected virtually every Czech town and village and the whole Czech countryside (in architecture, music, folk costumes, etc.) (Holy 1996: 124–5). The forcible re-Catholicization certainly did not mean Germanization. Administration and the institutions of the Catholic Church were supranational: Latin was the language of administration, and the Jesuits were preaching the Catholic faith in Czech. It was not until the need emerged in the enlightened absolutism of the Monarchy to unify the administration and language that we can meaningfully speak of conscious Germanization of the Czech Lands on the grounds of *raison d'état*. Only then comes the period of the retreat of Latin, of the establish-ment of German as the *lingua franca* and of the reduction of Czech to the speech of peasants (Podiven 1991: 40).

It is part of a critical re-evaluation of the Czech nationalist interpreta-tion of history to see strong elements of patriotism in the Baroque period (Pynsent 1994: 176; Pithart 1990: 44–5). Pithart puts it in the following way:

Regional legends and myths, local cults, especially those connected with St Mary, respect for the places of miracles, the sculptures of saints scattered throughout the countryside, all that linked the Baroque faith of a Czech peasant to a *specific* place, region, home and, through higher sacralisation, particularly in terms of the traditions of St Wencesalas and St Jan Nepomuk, and through the respect for Czech patrons, to the whole Czech country, to the Czech homeland. Patriotism is always a relation to a country, but not a direct relation to its totality: it is a locally motivated sentiment which has been created and becomes strengthened in a meaningful progression from the near to the far, from the intimately known to the imaginary, or more or less, abstract. Only, let us say, 'the sum of the regions of birth', 'the sum of homes' constructs the homeland in that patriotic sense which does not need to assert itself by being suspicious of 'our' imaginary and hostile to the imaginary 'alien'. Baroque religiosity is from this point of view always firmly emotionally anchored in a concrete landscape of the home. The home is here a sacred place of which we are proud for it is made special by beautiful churches, famous pilgrimages which bring together people from far away, miraculous paintings and venerated sculptures, famous events of the past (Pithart 1990: 44).

There were Baroque patriots who would have recognized their own sentiments in this description. The best known of them was the Jesuit priest Bohuslav Balbín (1621–88), the author of numerous histories and topographical, linguistic and natural-historical descriptions of the Bohemian kingdom, particularly *Miscellanea historica regni Bohemiae*, 1679–87 (Balbín 1986) and *Dissertatio apologetica pro lingua slavonica praecipue bohemica*, which was not published until at the beginning of the national revival in 1775 (Pynsent 1994: 176). Lesser figures falling into the category of Baroque patriots were various village chroniclers, of whom the best known is Jan Vavák of Milcice.

This Baroque patriotism became completely alien to the Czech nationalism of the nineteenth century, which often appears as if it were consciously opposed to any kind of emotional identification with a particular place or region and fully committed to the idea of Czechness epitomized by the Czech language. This overtly linguistic orientation of the Czech national revival has been constantly noted by all the students of this historical period (Macura 1983: 47–68). Inspired by Johann Gottfried Herder's ideas about the importance of language in the development of nations, the period of the national revival was a period of hectic linguistic activity. New Czech words were invented to enlarge Czech vocabulary; translations from foreign languages were done; the generally acknowledged leader of the revival, Josef Jungmann (1773–1847), compiled a large Czech–German dictionary in five volumes (1835–9) that stabilized Czech vocabulary and set the norm of the modern Czech literary language. The whole century was filled with a struggle for Czech schools, Czech theatres, Czech books and newspapers. Looking back at all this hectic activity, one has the distinct feeling that it did not matter that much what the revivalists actually wrote; the only thing that mattered was that they wrote it in Czech.

The opposition of the revivalists to territorial patriotism, or love of one's country, as not sufficient to promote the desirable national awareness, was explicit and most clearly stated by another leading revivalist, Jan Kollár (1793–1852): 'One can always find a mother-country again, if she were lost: but one can never, anywhere, find one's nation and language again' (1844; quoted in Pynsent 1994: 58–9). For Kollár, '[n]ationalism (creative love of goodness or specialness of one's nation) is a sign of high culture . . ., where patriotism (love of one's country) is typical of low culture' (Pynsent 1994: 58). He is worth quoting at length:

The mother-country herself is dead soil, an alien object, a non-human being [*Nicht-Mensch*]: the nation is our blood, life, spirit, subjectivity. Love of one's mother-country is something instinctual, a blind nature drive. Love of one's nation and nationality is more a product of reason and cultivation [*Bildung*]. One may find love of mother-country even in plants and animals. . . . The coarse savage clings to his wretched, reeking, stinking, smoke-filled hut and his inhospitable wilderness more than an educated man is attached to his country house and park. . . . One should beware of dull, intolerant, hate-filled patriotism; it is often merely an excuse for the blackest deeds; beyond his fellow-countrymen the patriot knows only enemies; patriotism often serves only for the ostensible justification of injured human rights and for misused violence against weaker neighbours or fellow countrymen who belong to other peoples. In writing this I do not on any account wish to damn love of one's mother country, but only to express a desire that love should abandon its Ancient character and assume the character of *Humanität*. . . . Anyone who scorns his nation, fails to honour and love its language, neglects its spirit and character, can in any case not be receptive to any true patriotism. The smaller must be subordinate to the greater, nobler, love of one's country to love of one's nation (1844; quoted from Pynsent 1994: 59).

Kollár expressed his rejection of emotional identification with a concrete place conceptualized as native homeland in the famous verses of his poem *Slávy dcera* (Sláva's Daughter) of 1824: 'Do not ascribe the holy name of homeland / to the region in which we dwell, / we carry the real homeland only in the heart . . .'. Elsewhere, he goes so far as to consider 'the tight love of the homeland' (*vlast*) to be 'the sin of mankind' (Pithart 1990: 45).

In the large cities of Prague or Brno, most activists of the national revival were first-generation immigrants into the city who probably never saw their nationalist sentiments as conflicting with their patriotism – their deep-seated love for their native villages and the regions from which they came, which in their totality constituted their homeland. For them, this homeland was a specific place, and not the vague metaphysical idea that Kollár had urged them to see it as. Their patriotism had changed from the Baroque patriotism Pithart describes; but more in the direction of patriotism as understood by Jungmann rather than Kollár. In line with Jungmann's idea that homeland is only that place where one speaks Czech (Pithart 1990: 45), their patriotism combined their love of their homeland with their love of the Czech language (and by extension of all things Czech).

The first verse of the Czech national anthem asserts that the 'Czech land' or country (*zeme ceská*) is 'my home' and the second, now hardly remembered verse, that my home is 'among the Czechs'. In the process of conceptualizing the homeland – the object of patriotic love – as 'home', the home ceased to be Bohemia and became 'the Czech land' or a place 'among the Czechs'.

It was this kind of patriotism that affected many of the cultural constructs of the period of the Czech national revival, and it is this kind of patriotism that is still a strong component of Czech national culture two hundred years after it first emerged.

Country as 'Home'

Historically, the first mention of the Czech land or country as 'home' dates back to 1834, when it was referred to as such in a song 'Where is my home?' (*Kde domov muj?*) sung during the last act of Josef Kajetán Tyl's play *Fidlovacka*, for which Frantisek Skroup wrote the music. Antonín Dvorák's (1841–1904) Overture op. 62, first performed in Prague in 1894, is called *My Home*. It originated as the overture to a play about Tyl's life, and is based on Tyl's song. The song was immensely popular during Dvorák's lifetime, and after Czechoslovakia's independence in 1918 it became the Czech national anthem in spite of Masaryk's doubts about its suitability, given the strong German minority, whose loyalty to the new state would hardly be likely to be fostered by its exclusively Czech patriotic tone.

One would like to believe that Tyl's song was chosen as the Czech national anthem because of Dvorák's use of it in his overture. However, I am not that sure, and it was probably the lasting popularity of Tyl's song itself that was decisive. It inspired the production of numerous variants as well as original compositions of songs describing the Czech country or homeland as home. 'I am at home only in Bohemia' (*v Cechách*) and 'I am at home only among the Czechs' says one of them, first published in a *Songbook for Czech Youth* in 1850 (Václavek and Smetana 1949: 236–7). Tyl's original song was published in over one hundred songbooks between 1849 and 1918 (Václavek and Smetana 1949), when it was officially adopted as the Czech national anthem.

When contemplating the question of how any particular nation con-structs its identity it appears often to be quite profitable to start by paying attention to what the national anthem specifically asserts. Pithart has already pointed to the Czechs' uncertainty about their identity (1990: 255), as manifested in the words of their national anthem. While the anthems of other nations assert, proclaim or boast about something, the Czech one begins with a question: Where is my home?

There are, in my opinion, three more aspects of the Czech national anthem that tell us probably more about Czechness than any kind of scholarly research can perhaps ever reveal.

First, the anthem originated as a song in a play that nowadays would be classified as a 'musical'. No Beethoven's 'Ode to Joy' or Haydn's 'Emperor' here as a national anthem, but a song popular with ordinary people, attesting, perhaps, better than anything else to the 'plebeian' character of the Czech nation so often emphasized by Czech intellectuals.

Second, it was sung by a *blind* violinist who himself could have never seen the beauty of the Czech countryside he sings about – this beauty is just simply asserted.

Third, the two most important things that the song establishes about the Czech land as my home are that it is *mine* (which means that it is *Czech*) and that it is *beautiful*. These two aspects of it have then subsequently been emphasized in all constructions of the Czech land as home. In what follows I want to consider each of them briefly, starting with the assertion of the outstanding beauty of the Czech land.

The emphasis on the beauty of the Czech land concentrates on the visual aspects of the homeland, and in its turn derives of course from the supremacy of sight in Western culture, with its roots in the ancient Greek and Christian traditions (Synnott 1993: 207). Standard adjectives that qualify Bohemia (*Cechy*) or the Czech land (*zeme ceská*) in song (including the national anthem) and poetry are 'beautiful' (*krásná*), 'the most beautiful' (*prekrasná*) and 'ennobling' (*spanilá*). Bohemia is a land of perpetual spring. Frequent references to 'spring flowers' (*jara kvet*) or 'May flowers' (*májové kvítí*) are metaphors of not only its beauty but also its youthful vigour. In art, the same idea is conveyed in the paintings of Josef Lada (1887–1957), best known as the illustrator of Hasek's *Good Soldier Schweik*. His pictures of quintessentially Czech villages dominated by their Baroque churches focus almost without exception on playing children.

The beauty of Bohemia is the beauty of paradise (*rajská krása*): 'paradise most pleasing to you' (*nejmilejsí tobe ráj*), 'the paradise unique in the world' (*ráj v svete jediny*), 'visually an earthly paradise' (*zemsky ráj to na pohled*), 'my home is in that paradise' (*v tom ráji domov muj*).

The link between the beautiful and the good on the one hand, and the ugly and the evil on the other hand, which can be traced back to classical Greek thought (Synnott 1993: 78) metamorphosed in Christianity into the equation of beauty with God and goodness (Synnott 1993: 83). Building on this mystique of beauty deeply rooted in European thought, the images of Bohemia in song and poetry transcend the distinction between earth and heaven: Bohemia is both 'an earthly paradise' (*zemsky ráj*) and 'a heavenly landscape' (*krajina nebeská*). Heaven, earth, paradise and the Czech country are all fused together in this imagery, making Bohemia 'a sacred land' (*posvátná zeme*), 'holy soil' (*puda svatá*), 'holy regions' (*svaté kraje*) or 'region pleasing to God' (*kraj bohumily*).

This sacralization of the homeland is yet another specific example of nationalism as a secular religion of modern society (Llobera 1994: 143–6). In its Czech version it leads to very debased poetry flogging to death a few standard metaphors. However, whatever the artistic qualities of the songs and poems through which the image of the exceptional beauty of Bohemia or the Czech land is perpetually constructed, the Czechs accept this image, without question, as an objective one. But even if most of them sincerely believe that Bohemia is the most beautiful country, or at least one of the most beautiful countries, in the world, they would be hard pressed to define the criteria by which the beauty of a country can be measured objectively. As already mentioned, in Czech nationalist discourse the beauty of Bohemia is simply ideologically asserted. It is also not localized. Bohemia is not beautiful because of its picturesque sandstone formations or numerous lakes and woods. In the nationalist discourse, it is the country as a *totality* that is construed as 'beautiful' and therefore as special (see Billig 1995: 75).

The way the Czech landscape is routinely depicted in literature, poetry and painting reflects the aesthetic criteria of natural beauty of the Romantic period in which the images of an exceptionally beautiful Bohemia first emerged. These images are often in stark contrast to reality. The image of the Sumava mountains (Böhmerwald) created by Czech patriotic writers of the nineteenth century like Bozena Nemcová (1820–

1862) or Alois Jirásek (1851–1930) is a case in point. Although Sumava's highest hill is only 1,457m, and Cerchov, the most famous of Sumava's hills, only 1,042m, their description of Sumava reads almost like a description of the Alps. Nemcová writes about 'peaks reaching into the clouds' and calls the local inhabitants 'mountain dwellers' (horalé). Jirásek describes Sumava as 'a huge buttress rising above the silent countryside and disappearing in clouds and darkness' and another description is of 'high mountains, occasional crevices, one rock on top of another, so that the top ones appear to stretch into the clouds'. Inspired by this imagery, the Czech writer Tereza Nováková searched in vain during her trip to Sumava in 1899 'for those bare and frightening slopes . . . expecting at least a sub-Alpine countryside . . . a very mountainous region, densely forested, rough and perpetually battered by winds'. She found instead an inviting region of meadows, fertile fields, ponds and welcoming hills (Maur 1988: 324–3).

Anderson's (1983) lasting contribution to the study of nationalism lies in his concept of the nation as an 'imagined community' stretching beyond the immediate experience of any of its particular members. However, as Billig has recently argued, '[a] nation is more than an imagined community of people, for a place – a homeland – also has to be imagined' (1995: 74). To imagine a 'country', means to imagine a bounded totality 'beyond the directly apprehended locality' and 'beyond immediate experience of place' (1995: 74). However, this bounded totality cannot be presented as an entity; only a partial image of it can be constructed and 'particular icons are produced to evoke the total entity' (Harvey 1996: 176). Pace Harvey, however, I would argue that how the total entity will be imagined does not depend on the icons that are selected, but that the selection of particular icons is determined by how the total entity is imagined. Not only are particulars inevitably selected to represent the whole country, but the process of their selection involves not only the inclusion of some of them but also the exclusion of others.

I have already described how when the Czechs imagine their homeland or home, they imagine it first of all as a place where one speaks Czech (for a more detailed discussion of the Czech conceptualization of the homeland see Holy 1996: 186–90). Historically, the Czechs have of course inhabited for centuries the same space as the German-speaking Bohemians, and thus they had to eliminate from that imagination anything that had not been 'Czech'. Home for them became only that space that was independent of German domination, and it was precisely this independence that was emphasized; the result was the emergence of specific regions, geographic features and places as icons of Czechness.

It was particularly the two regions of Bohemia in which the ethnic boundary corresponded with the frontier of the Bohemian kingdom that gradually became established as the icons of the Czech homeland during the period of the national revival of the nineteenth century. One of them is north-eastern Bohemia around the town of Náchod, which was brought into national consciousness through numerous novels by the nineteenth century realist and patriotic Czech writers describing the rebellions of Czech peasants against their 'German' overlords in the seventeenth and eighteenth centuries. The other one is the region around the town of Domazlice called Chodsko. Its inhabitants, called Chodové, have entered the national consciousness as guardians of the frontier of the Bohemian kingdom as the result of the popularity of the novel *Psohlavci* ('Dog-heads') by the patriotic Czech writer Alois Jirásek.

There were other reasons for selecting Domazlice as an icon of a wider Czech homeland. Apart from Náchod it was not only the sole town in the close neighbourhood of which the ethnic boundary corresponded with the state boundary, but also the only town in Bohemia that remained Czech-speaking in the first half of the nineteenth century. It was probably also significant that Chodsko preserved its own distinct folk culture long after folk culture had gradually disappeared in the rest of Bohemia and Western Moravia. The villages around Domazlice had already become the object of exceptional ethnographic interest before 1848 (Maur 1988: 338), and specific items of folk culture – folk costumes, pottery, embroidery, folk-songs and bagpipe music – gradually ceased to be seen as tokens of the folk culture of that particular region and came to represent Czech folk-culture as such. Many flats and houses in Bohemia that I visited would have a plate, a pot or a piece of embroidery from Chodsko on display.

Homeland and the National Theatre

In what follows, however, I am going to suggest that the building of the National Theatre in Prague can profitably be seen as the major contemp-orary model for and icon of the Czech homeland. Here, Domazlice and its surrounding Chodsko are not only commemorated by one of the foundation stones of the theatre but also by the painting of the view of Domazlice in the presidential box and by two of the fourteen lunettes from the cycle 'Homeland' (*Vlast*): 'Domazlice' and 'Guard at the frontier', which depicts two guardians of a border pass. No other place in Bohemia, not even Prague, is that frequently represented in the pictorial decoration of the theatre building.

The present-day reduction of the homeland to the Czech-speaking areas of the Czech land manifests itself clearly in the differing emphasis that the two main Bohemian rivers – the Vltava (Moldau) and the Labe (Elbe) – receive in poetry, music and painting. Of these two rivers, it is the Vltava that is habitually invoked as an icon of the Czech homeland (for example, one movement of Smetana's symphonic poem *My Country* is called 'Vltava'). The Labe could not have achieved this status. Its source lies in the Krkonose mountains, the inhabitants of which were mostly German-speaking; only its upper reaches are in Bohemia; and for most of its length it runs through Germany. It is hence clearly a river that the Czechs cannot claim as their own. But the source of the Vltava is in Sumava – which itself is one of the icons of the Czech homeland – and it flows only through Czech-speaking areas before its confluence with the Labe. Prague, the capital of the country and again an important icon of the Czech homeland, is located on the Vltava.

The construction of the homeland as the Czech-speaking areas of Bohemia and Moravia is most clearly visible in the origin of the foundation stones of the National Theatre, opened in Prague in 1881. In line with the cult of mountains in the culture of the national revival (Macura 1983: 215–17) most of the stones that were built into the foundations of the theatre building during the official ceremonial inauguration of its construction in 1868 had been hewn from hills – notably hills from the Sumava range of mountains, which has been the traditional boundary between the Czech- and German-speaking populations and the historical south-western frontier of the Bohemian kingdom (for example the hills of Práchen, Boubín, or Svatobor), or hills that are associated with particular legends, themselves invented only in the nineteenth century and describing various mythological events of the pre-Christian and early Christian eras (for example the hills of Radhost, Ríp, or Blanik). Others came from sites associated with particular events of Czech history (for example Domazlice, Vysehrad, Branka), and particularly from sites connected with the Hussite movement of the fifteenth century, which the protagonists of the national revival considered to be the most glorious period of Czech history (for example Zizkov, Trocnov, Chrast). The Committee for the Establishing of the National Theatre exercised only a limited control over the selection of suitable stones. In principle, the stones should have come from 'memorable sites' of Bohemia and Moravia, and the Committee did succeed in rejecting as unsuitable, for example, a stone from Pribyslav, the place of death of Jan Zizka, the military leader of the Hussite troops, arguing that it would be a reminder of Zizka's premature death (Rybarík 1983: 181, n.8). But the strength of the patriotic sentiments and the number of active patriots in particular localities, as well as their economic means, clearly played their role in deciding whether or not they would ship a stone from their locality to Prague. Branka, site of the council meeting to elect the Archbishop of Prague in 1068, and a battlefield of the Prussian–Austrian war of 1866 (Rybarík 1983: 201, n.109) would in the context of Czech history hardly count as a 'memorable' site, and the inclusion of this particular stone attests more to the activities of local patriots than to the historical significance of Branka. The same can be said about the stone from Hostyn, the site of the Mongol invasion of Moravia in 1241. Nevertheless, whatever the particular reason for their selection as icons of the homeland, the sites from which the stones originate clearly fall into three distinct clusters that correspond to the three areas of Bohemia and Moravia that were predominantly or exclusively Czech-speaking: Sumava and in particular the area around Domazlice; central and north-eastern Bohemia; and eastern Moravia.

The men involved in the construction and decoration of the National Theatre were fully aware of its symbolic significance. The patriots from Hostyn, apart from shipping a stone to Prague, brought with them to the ceremonial laying of the theatre's foundations a barrel of water that was used to mix the mortar with which the foundation stone plate was put into place (Rybarík 1983: 182). This is surely an action that goes beyond the demands of practical rationality, although its precise intended symbolic significance may retrospectively be difficult to interpret. The official speech that was published before the ceremony, when probably only seven foundation stones were expected, says: 'Seven rocks are fusing here, in the womb of the soil consecrated to the nation to form one mighty foundation of our national temple, which no human anger will ever be able to ruin' (Rybarík 1983: 183). I would go so far as to suggest that the building of the National Theatre can be seen as a model of the Czech homeland: the foundation stones, the actual physical tokens of the chosen icons, appropriately under the ground in the basement of the building, and the pictorial representations of the same icons, appropriately above the ground on the different floors of the building.

Although the icons of the homeland were selected on the basis of criteria that sometimes had little to do with the chosen icons' representativeness, they have become fixed in this model, and owing to the popularity of the National Theatre have determined the way in which generations of Czechs have imagined their homeland. Any time they visit the National Theatre – and there are hardly any Czechs who have never done so – they are forcefully reminded of how they should envisage their homeland.

Home and the Rural Homeland

In the Czech nationalist discourse, the imagination of Bohemia as home relies heavily on hills, rivers and other natural features as icons of the homeland, and emphasizes the beauty of the landscape. This selection has been primarily determined by the fact that Czech high culture – which was being created during the national revival – was not being created as something to replace the peasant culture through general education. On the contrary, as in all the societies that Hroch (1985) classifies as 'small', the peasant culture was the source of the newly created high culture. As a result, the peasant environment – the countryside, landscape and villages – became sacralized and venerated. The towns could not have been : they were German or Germanized. The only exception is Prague, which, however, became a symbol not of the humble origins of the modern Czech nation rooted in the village and countryside, but of the regal glory of the Czech nation and its past political greatness, which would again be achieved in the future when the Czech nation would again have its own state.

The emphasis on the rural idyll and the beauty of the countryside is usually associated with social and political conservatism, and on the face of it the Czech images of the countryside are not that different from those prevalent in England. The images of the lanes, hedgerows, moors, heaths and downs, wooded dales and streams, village greens, church spires and elm trees are presented not only as a 'refuge from the tensions and ugliness of modern urban society' and

a defensive turning away from the realities and challenges of the present; but one that at the same time has been incorporated into a national mythology mobilised at times of political tension to figure some essense of true English-ness, an ideal for which it's worth killing foreigners and pulverising their less leisured and civilised landscapes (Potts 1989:160).

In the popular literature of the Second World War,

the England which was evoked as the country being fought for and defended against fascism was one of oak-beamed pubs, punting on the Cam, and the image of cool summer evenings in country lanes or on velvet smooth lawns. The literature evoked the rural; it was largely the films which reminded people that there were cities to be defended (Worpole 1989: 138).

The Metaphor of 'Home'

But there are differences in the way in which England and the Czech
lands are imagined as particular places. The vogue for celebrating England
and Englishness that reached a peak in the 1930s produced titles like
The Landscape of England (1932), *The Beauty of England* (1933) and
The Beauty of Britain (1935) (Potts 1989). The Czech equivalents are
Krajinou domova ('Through the Landscape of Home', 1986) or *Jakou
barvu má domov* ('What Colour is Home', 1988), the latter not being, as
the title might suggest, a manual for interior decorators, but both being
collections of landscape photographs. Both England and the Czech lands
are presented as beautiful, but only the Czech lands are presented as home,
a word that evokes not only the particular place where one and one's
family live, but the whole country.

Most Czechs with whom I spoke found it difficult not to talk about
homeland and home in terms of each other, in spite of the fact that in
Czech, unlike English, there is no semantic relationship between the two
terms (homeland: *vlast*, home: *domov*). They often expressed the meaning
of 'homeland' by not differentiating semantically between 'home' and
'homeland', and by frequently stating that their homeland was not only
where they felt at home, but also *was* their home. 'Home' is not an
intangible entity, but always and foremost a specific space (Douglas
1991); the proper question is not '*What* is your home?' but '*Where* is
your home?' For most Czechs home is the place where they were born
and brought up or, alternatively, the place in which they established their
own families and had their children. In relation to the 'proper' home
understood in this way, the homeland is the familiar space stretching
beyond its boundaries, and is a 'home' in the wider sense of the term.
One woman, who stressed that her homeland was formed by her family
and friends and was not merely a territorial concept, expressed it in
the following way: ' My home is in this country. I see my homeland as
that territory in which I have my home; the centre of that territory is my
home.'

In Western folk conceptualization, 'home' is invariably imagined as
space inhabited by people bound together by ties of familial kinship:
'home' is where a family lives (Schneider 1968: 45–50; Douglas 1991).
This folk imagery has informed virtually all existing sociological
and anthropological discussion of 'home'. Following in this tradition,
Mary Douglas points out that, as relics of nineteenth-century romantic
enthusiasm, 'both home and community are able to draw upon the
same mysterious supply of loyal support . . . thanks to a kind of mystic

solidarity home and small local community are supposed to be able to overcome the forces of fission that tear larger groups apart' (Douglas 1991: 288).

It does not matter to what extent the notion of home as being able to overcome the forces of fission can be seen as a valid empirical generalization and to what extent it has to be seen merely as a 'folk' myth. Even if it is the latter it is still part of the actors' imagery with which we are concerned here, and in that respect it is precisely the assumed solidarity of those who inhabit the same home that provides us with an answer to the obvious question that arises here, namely that of why the space inhabited by a collectivity of people who imagine themselves to be a nation should be conceptualized as home. The answer suggests itself if we take our cue again from Mary Douglas (1991: 288), and pay attention to strategies that people adopt when they want to create solidarity. In this specific case, when they construct as home the space that they inhabit as a nation, they resort to a discursive strategy aimed at promoting the desired solidarity among the nation's members. Whatever their other diverse interests may be and whatever the social, political, religious or economic differences among them, their solidarity as the nation's members springs from their all recognizing the same space as their home and from all of them inhabiting that home.

This imagery turns home into a powerful metaphor. As home is first of all a place where a family lives, constructing the country as the home of the nation implies the image of the nation as a family: a collectivity whose members are bound together by primordial ties stronger than those established as a result of any kind of practical expediency, whether economic, political or whatever. Family implies ties of status rather than those of contract.

The concept of home enables the Czechs not only to imagine the nation as a family writ large but to imagine it as such without talking about it as sharing blood and soil or as a community of people linked together through common ancestry. In fact they never talk about it in this way, for all these various images, in which nationhood may be, and often is, expressed, are already all subsumed by the encompassing metaphor of home. The metaphor thus generates first of all two basic categories of people. These are on the one hand those who share the same home or who have the right to claim a certain space as their home, who are typically imagined as a family. On the other hand are all those who do not share the same home or do not have the right to a certain specific place as their home: in relation to those included within the boundary of the home, they are strangers.

The concept of home generates yet other categories to which hardly any attention has been paid so far in the few scattered comments on home that can be gleaned from the existing sociological and anthropological writing. These categories are made up of those who cross the boundary of home from the outside, and they include those who have been specifically invited to do so on a temporary basis (guests); those who do not count a specific space as their home, but may live there to carry out their work (servants); uninvited intruders (burglars); those who stay on a contractual basis in somebody else's home and enjoy to a specified extent the privileges of belonging (lodgers); and those who have moved without permission into somebody else's home and treat it as their own (squatters).

Home and 'Foreignness'

Their imagery of homeland as home and their conceptualization of the Czech lands as their home enables the Czechs to categorize foreigners in a way that is analogous to these various categories. It is this categorization that then ultimately shapes the Czechs' attitude to foreigners temporarily or permanently living among them.

I regret to say that I lack detailed ethnographic data with which to back up my following general observations on the Czechs' attitude to foreigners as analogous to the various categories into which specific individuals can be assigned according to the way in which they cross the boundary between home and non-home. The analogy that I postulate here is the result of my own understanding of the generally prevailing attitudes of Czechs to specific categories of foreigners. It is an understanding gained from numerous discussions with my informants (the topics of which have not always necessarily been Czech nationalism or patriotism), as well as from my own personal knowledge of Czech culture resulting from my own socialization. To what extent the analogies I suggest are explicit or implicit among the Czechs themselves and to what extent they inform the various discourses in which the Czechs are engaged would certainly merit further investigation through empiral field research. Methodologically, such research should be, if nothing else, able to show what kind of insights into the actors' understanding can be reached by pursuing as far as they will go the implications of core cultural metaphors and what role such metaphors play in shaping the actors' cognitive processes.

The analogy between specific categories into which people can be assigned according to the way in which they cross the boundary of someone else's home and specific categories of foreigners that the Czechs express most explicitly is the analogy between burglars and foreigners who invaded their country. This includes the Germans, who occupied Czechoslovakia in 1939, and the Soviets and their Warsaw Pact allies, whose invasion in 1968 ended the brief period of liberalization known as the Prague Spring,

Historically, Germans have always been the most significant foreigners for the Czechs. However they might have been perceived beforehand, after the annexation of the Sudetenland by Germany following the Munich agreement of 1938 they clearly came to be seen as squatters. The annexation of the Sudetenland represented a dramatic change in the right of the Germans to residence there. Before the annexation, their right to live there could have been seen as the result of a specific contract into which they had entered with the rightful owners of that space centuries ago and thus as analogous to the right of lodgers or tenants. The annexation of the Sudetenland amounted to the Germans' denouncing the Czechs' right to it as to their home and appropriating it for themselves as their own, which in the popular perception was seen as analogous to squatting. As a result of this widely shared perception, most Czechs see as fully justified the forcible repatriation of the German population from Czechoslovakia to Germany in 1945 and 1946. The issue of this expulsion of some three million Germans was reopened by Václav Havel after he became president of the Czechoslovak republic. He questioned particularily the principle of collective guilt that motivated the expulsion of an ethnic group as a whole as a punishment for actions carried out before and during the war by particular members of it. He apologized for the atrocities committed by Czechs during the transfer of the German population. Most Czechs saw this as his biggest political blunder, and in the eyes of many it affected (temporarily) the tremendous popularity that he otherwise enjoyed. In 1993, according to a poll published in the Czech daily press, 76 per cent of Czechs approved of the 1945 transfer of the Sudeten Germans and considered the issue closed.

The role of squatters is nowadays ascribed by many Czechs to the Vietnamese who began arriving in Czecholslovakia in great numbers in the 1970s and 1980s as a result of the Czechoslovak government's agreement with the socialist government of Vietnam. According to this agreement, the Vietnamese came to Czechoslovakia to participate in a vocational, on-the-job training programme aimed at their acquiring qualifications necessary for the performance of various specialized jobs. In fact, they were employed as unskilled labour in various nationalized Czech industrial enterprises, equivalent to Germany's *Gastarbeiter*

(Kandert 1996). After the change of political system in Czechoslovakia in 1989, many of them did not return to Vietnam but continued to live in Czechoslovakia and later the Czech Republic, in spite of the fact that most of them were either made redundant as a result of the economic reform that immediately followed the change in political system or have resigned from the jobs they were originally hired to perform. Most of them are now engaged in petty trade or earn their living as small-scale private entrepreneurs. In terms of the analogy with specific categories of people generated by the concept of home they were originally perceived by many Czechs as servants hired to perform specific tasks in the Czech home, but are now seen as people who continue to stay in it without any longer honouring the contractual conditions under which they entered it. In terms of the analogy, this has turned them into squatters.

A special category of foreigners are tourists, millions of whom now visit the Czech Republic every year. They are not analogous to guests, for they arrive uninvited and, unlike guests, they choose what to consume and pay for their board and lodging and other services. The attitude towards them is ambivalent: on the one hand they bring in desired foreign currency and provide employment in the burgeoning service sector of the economy for people who would otherwise have to join the ranks of the unemployed. On the other hand, they bar the Czechs' access to various services and push their prices above the level that most locals can afford. The ambivalent attitude towards tourists stems from the fact that they bring into relief the difference between a home and a hotel, which is one habitually drawn by the actors themselves, and is routinely invoked in sociological and anthropological discussion to highlight the characteristic features of home (Douglas 1991: 297–8, 300). The ambivalence stems from the fact that the tourists treat as a hotel the same space that the Czechs see as their home, and from the fact that the tourists force the Czechs themselves to act as if they were hotel guests in the space that they conceptualize as their home. The tourists are a category of foreigners whose very presence blurs the difference between a home and a hotel, 'the mercenary, cold, luxurious counterpart against which the home is being measured' (Douglas 1991: 300).

As a result of the expulsion of the German minority from Czechoslovakia in 1945 the population of the Czech lands has become ethnically homogeneous for the first time in history. The only exception to this homogeneity is the gypsies, who nowadays are in many respects the Czechs' most significant Other and the source of much racial tension as well as – alongside the Vietnamese – the object of much racial hatred, which even permeates most of the university-educated section of Czech society. The gypsies have been living in the Czech lands for more than six hundred years: the oldest reference to their presence there appeared in the thirteenth century. Until the beginning of the Second World War, the gypsies roamed the countryside in their horse-drawn caravans and earned their livelihood as casual labourers, tinkers, acrobats or fortune-tellers, frequently augmenting their income by begging. After the Second World War, the government rigorously pursued a policy of forceful sedentarization of the gypsies, and of their integration with the Czechs, by dispersing and resettling them in the newly built housing estates throughout the country (and particularly in the houses that were left vacant after the expulsion of the Germans from the border areas of the Czech lands). As most gypsies earned their living as unskilled labourers, they have often been resettled in, or themselves gravitated to, the industrial towns of northern Bohemia and Moravia, some of which now contain vast gypsy ghettos as a consequence (Kandert 1996).

For most Czechs the gypsies represent the paradigmatic Other. However, they are not habitually seen as a category of inhabitants of or visitors to the Czech lands that is analogous to one of the categories into which individuals living outside one's home can be assigned according to the way in which they cross the home's boundary. In other words, they are hardly ever metaphorically imagined as burglars or as guests, servants, lodgers or squatters in the Czech home. This is due not so much to the ambiguity about whether or not they are part of the Czech nation: the Czechs' opinion clearly tends towards the view that they are not (Holy 1996: 64–5). It is rather due to the fact that, unlike all other foreigners, who can be seen as analogous to those who temporarily or permanently enter somebody else's home, the gypsies do not have a home of their own. If, as a last resort, the Germans could be removed from the Czech home and sent back to their own home in Germany and the Vietnamese could, at least theoretically, be treated in the same way if need be, the gypsies do not have a home of their own and somewhere else to go. They may not be seen as part of the nation that claims the Czech lands as its home, but they do, nevertheless, live there, unwelcome and embarrassing as they may be, for they do not have a right to a home elsewhere. The mixture of outright hatred, embarrassment, shame and guilt that underpins the Czechs' attitude towards them thus stems from the gypsies' ambivalent position in the system of symbolic classification generated by the equivalence that the Czechs make between homeland and home.

Conclusion

In this chapter I have aimed to show that the construction of homeland as home crystallized during the period of conscious nation-building that is referred to by the Czechs as the national revival and started at the end of the eighteenth century. The particular features of Czech nationalism, of which the imagination of homeland as home is one, as well as many aspects of Czech historical consciousness that were first articulated during the national revival (Rak 1994) were clearly linked to the way in which the Czech nation became conceptualized – particularily in the first half of the nineteenth century – as a linguistic community that was asserting its identity against the German-speaking population of the Czech lands.

The existence of particular cultural notions is of course not explained by pointing out their specific historical origin. They maintain their cultural salience not simply because they emerged at a specific time as a response to particular historical and political circumstances. They remain culturally salient in the present only in so far as they provide an effective response to present circumstances.

The images of the Czech land as a beautiful country and as home have remained salient cultural notions for almost two centuries following their first emergence. This is due mainly to the fact that they have effect-ively been mobilized to boost patriotic feelings in numerous situations perceived as national crises, particularly at times when patriotic feelings cannot be expressed in any other way. Thus, for example, a collection of poems composed in 1939 (Kropáč 1940) and entitled 'A beautiful country' (*Zeme krásná*) was published in 1940 during the German occupa-tion of Bohemia and Moravia. Without mentioning Czech history, the usual source of national pride and awareness, which would have been impossible at that time, it was nevertheless clearly aimed at boosting the patriotic feelings of the Czech population under German occupation. Similarly, the collections of landscape photographs accompanied by poems invoking the image of the Czech lands as home and celebrating the beauty of Bohemia and Moravia (like *Krajinou domova* or *Jakou barvu má domov*, which I mentioned before) boosted patriotic feelings during the 1968–89 period, which most Czechs saw as the time when they again lost their national sovereignty. The circulation of these books remained, of course, limited to the well-educated strata of the population. But all Czechs, not only the well-educated ones, have personal experience of foreigners living among them, and their attitude towards them perpetually re-creates the image of the Czech home and the conceptual equation of homeland with home that first emerged during the period of the national revival.

In everyday discourse, the conceptual equation of homeland and home is maintained through the frequent use of the expression *u nás*. Like its French equivalent, *chez nous*, it refers to any contextually defined in-group. Nevertheless, its primary and most frequently used referent is either one's home, in the strict sense of the term, or the locality in which one's home is situated. The Czechs, however, use it almost equally frequently to refer to their homeland, particularily when comparing the way of life, customary behaviour or manners current in the Czech land or lands with those usual abroad. The result is that the equation between homeland and home is perpetually reinforced through this everyday ordinary speech.

The emphasis on the beauty of the Czech land and the perception of that beautiful and sacred space as the Czechs' home is one of the characteristic features of Czech nationalism. This image of home is more than a core metaphor in much of the nationalist discourse. Because home is already a metaphor itself, it expresses all that would have to be expressed through further metaphorical elaborations. In that respect, it can be seen as a meta-metaphor, and its discursive power derives precisely from this.

References

Aktuálne problémy Cesko-slovenska: správa zo sociologického prieskumu, Bratislava: Centrum pre sociálnu analyzu.

Anderson, D. (1983), *Imagined Communities*, London: Verso.

Balbín, B. (1986), *Krásy a bohatství ceské zeme* (trans. of *Miscellanea historica regni Bohemiae* by H. Businská, ed. Z. Tichá), Prague: Panorama.

Bar-Tal, D. (1993), 'Patriotism as Fundamental Belief of Group Members', *Politics and the Individual*, 3: 45–62.

Billig, M. (1995), *Banal Nationalism*, London: Sage Publications.

Connor, W. (1993), 'Beyond Reason: The Nature of Ethno-national Bond', *Ethnic and Racial Studies*, 16: 373–89.

—— (1994), *Ethnonationalism: The Quest for Understanding*, Princeton, NJ: Princeton University Press.

Csepeli, G. (1992), 'National Identity in Post-communist Hungary', in K. Rupesinghe, P. King and O. Vorkunova (eds), *Ethnicity and Conflict in a Post-communist World*, New York: St Martin's Press.

Douglas, M. (1991), 'The Idea of a Home: A Kind of Space', *Social Research*, 58: 287–307.

Eller, J. D. and Coughlan, R. M. (1993), 'The Poverty of Primordialism: The Demystification of Ethnic Attachments', *Ethnic and Racial Studies*, 16: 181–202.

Ferrero, M. (1995), 'The Economics of Socialist Nationalism', in A. Breton, G. Galeotti, P. Salmon, and R. Wintrobe (eds), *Nationalism and Rationality,* Cambridge: Cambridge University Press.

Harvey, P. (1996), *Hybrids of Modernity: Anthropology, the Nation State and the Universal Exhibition*, London: Routledge.

Holy, L. (1996), *The Little Czech and the Great Czech Nation: National Identity and the Post-communist Transformation of Society*, Cambridge: Cambridge University Press.

Hroch, M. (1985), *Social Preconditions of National Revival in Europe*, Cambridge: Cambridge University Press.

Huizinga, J. (1940), 'Patriotism and Nationalism in European History', in J. Huizinga, *Man and Ideas*, Princeton, NJ: Princeton University Press.

Janowitz, M. (1983), *The Reconstruction of Patriotism*, Chicago: University of Chicago Press.

Kandert , J. (1996), 'Whites versus Blacks and Yellows: Constructors of a Picture of the Romanies, Vietnamese and Others in the Czech Republic after 1990', Paper delivered at the European Association of Social Anthropologists Conference in Barcelona.

Kohn, H. (1955), *Nationalism: its Meaning and History*, Princeton, NJ: Van Nostrand.

—— (1967), *The Idea of Nationalism*, 2nd edn, New York: Collier Macmillan.

Koralka, J. (1988), 'K pojetí národa v ceské spolecnosti 19. stoleti', in *Povedomi tradice v novedobé ceské kulture*. Prague: Národní galerie.

Kosterman, R. and Feshbach, S. (1989), 'Toward a Measure of Patriotic and Nationalist Attitudes', *Political Psychology*, 10: 257–74.

Kropác, F. (ed.) (1940), *Zeme krásná: sborník poesie z roku 1939*, Prague: Umelecká beseda.

Llobera, J. (1994), *The God of Modernity: The Development of Nationalism in Western Europe,* Oxford: Berg.

Macura, V. (1983), *Znameni zrodu: ceské obrozeni jako kulturní typ,* Prague: Ceskoslovensky spisovatel.

Maur, E. (1988), 'Poznámky k tradici a mytu boje s odvekym neprítelem', in *Povedomi tradice v novodobé ceské kulture*, Prague: Národní galerie.

Meinecke, F. (1907), *Weltbürgertum und Nationalstaat: Studien zur Genesis des deutschen Nationalstaates*, Munich and Berlin.

Pithart, P. (1990), *Dejiny a politika*, Prague: Prostor.

Plamenatz, J. (1973), 'Two types of Nationalism', in E. Kamenka (ed.), *Nationalism*, London: Arnold.

Podiven (P. Pithart, P. Príhoda, and M. Otáhal) (1991), *Cesi v dejinách nové doby*, Prague: Státni nakladatelstvi.

Potts, A. (1989), '"Constable country" between the wars', in R. Samuel (ed.), *Patriotism: The Making and Unmaking of British National Identity, Vol. III: National Fictions*, London: Routledge.

Pynsent, R.B. (1994), *Questions of Identity: Czech and Slovak Ideas of Nationality and Personality,* Budapest: Central European University Press.

Rak, J. (1994), *Byvali Cechové: ceské historické myty a steryotypy*, Prague: Nakladatelství H&H.

Rybarík, V. (1983), 'Základní kameny Národniho divadla v Praze', *Casopis Národniho musea — rada historická* 152, no. 3–4: 180–204.

Schneider, D. M. (1968), *American Kinship: A Cultural Account*, Chicago: University of Chicago Press.

Schumpeter, J. (1951), 'The Sociology of Imperialism', in J. Schumpeter, *The Economics and Sociology of Capitalism*, Princeton, NJ: Princeton University Press.

Smith, A. D. (1986), *The Ethnic Origin of Nations*, Oxford: Blackwell.

—— (1991), *National Identity*, London: Penguin.

Snyder, L. L. (1976), *Varieties of Nationalism: A Comparative Study*, Hisdale: Dryden Press.

Synnott, A. (1993), *The Body Social: Symbolism, Self and Society*, London: Routledge.

Václavek, R. and Smetana, B. (1949), *Cesky národni zpevník: písne ceské spolecnosti 19. století*, Prague: Svoboda.

Viroli, M. (1995), *For Love of Country: An Essay on Patriotism and Nationalism*, Oxford: Clarendon Press.

Worpole, K. (1989), 'Village School or Blackboard Jungle?', in R. Samuel (ed.), *Patriotism: The Making and Unmaking of British National Identity, Vol. III: National Fictions*, London: Routledge.

5

Imaging Children 'At Home', 'In the Family' and 'At School': Movement Between the Spatial and Temporal Markers of Childhood Identity in Britain

Allison James

Introduction

Lakoff and Johnson have argued that metaphor is 'pervasive in everyday life', structuring not only the language that we use but also our thoughts and actions (1980:3). Such a view transforms metaphor from mere description into a more active device that can both shape the ways in which we account for social action and provide us with strategic concepts to act with. It ascribes to metaphor a participative role in processes of imaging akin to those other cultural tropes – symbols and signs – that, taken together, not only reflect social experiences but also have a part to play in their constitution. The image is thus 'the result of an act of perception and construction which frames the world', for 'the meaning of the image gains its resonance in the practices and ways in which [an image] is viewed, in the discourses and ceremonial rituals which surround its use' (Featherstone and Wernick 1995: 4). An exploration of the process of imaging, therefore, promises to capture the play of these cultural tropes in the everyday social world that gives shape and meaning to people's lives.

This chapter addresses one particular set of these practices of enactment: the ways in which ideas of childhood dependency are imaged through images of the 'home' and the 'family' within Western discourse so as to render safe the potential for disorder that the identity status of 'child' potentiates.[1] That is to say 'home' and 'the family' are metaphoric means of stilling the potential disruption that our imaging of childhood movement leads us to fear. The argument presented therefore ranges freely between examining processes of metaphorization and those of symbolization to account for the seemingly ready ascription by parents, teachers and others of a constantly changing and malleable social identity to young children. Thus the 'images of childhood' to be discussed here are understood not simply in terms of an enveloping discourse, (though of course they are at one and the same time informed by such a discourse), but as a more dynamic process of imaging or image-making. Once these are untangled, our understanding of the ways in which 'childhood' can come to place a mantle of constraint upon children's daily experiences and sense of self is enhanced.[2]

This promise of childhood change is already identified by Schwartz (1976) in his location of childhood and youth as some of the primary cultural spaces through which social identities are explored. But to conceive of identities in the early part of the life-course as both fluid and changing is, of course, not new. It is premised, for example, in well-known scientific discourses of 'the child'. Traditional Piagetian developmental psychology and Freudian psychoanalysis both envisage childhood as the conceptual space within which the groundworks for future adult identities are located. A similar emphasis on the malleability of children and their embodiment of change is embraced by traditional socialization theory's emphasis on 'futurity' (Jenks 1996). This sets great store upon childhood as the period in the life-course when, through the socialization of children, the future shape of society is itself set out. In these renderings, or imaginings, childhood is thus literally characterized by change and movement (James et al. 1998).

However, the inherent plasticity envisaged for the child's nature in these kinds of accounts is also represented as potentially problematic.

1. Though not developing this idea here it is clear that by turns, the idea of 'the child' itself speaks to and helps constitute those of the 'home' and 'family' like a series of reflective mirrors.
2. Elsewhere (James 1995) I have described how children have to contend with images of childhood in their everyday lives. Here I focus on just one way in which those images come to be constructed and enacted through looking at the school as a site of construction and at that point in a child's school career when he/she enters school for the first time.

Within orthodox child psychology, for example, it is argued that a measured progression steadies the child's growing abilities and competencies through a sequential series of physical and psychological age-related stages. These order the child's potential for change. Thus it is that the child's changing identity in the social world is firmly represented as dependent upon developmental paths, a process that effectively 'naturalizes' a child's progression: those who exceed the expectations associated with their age group are said to be precociously forward in their achievements; those who fail may be stigmatized as backward or behind. Within this discourse, then, a child's changing intellect and physique, and consequent social participation, are only rendered comprehensible through controlling spatial metaphors conceptualized in relation to the temporal continuum of age.

Similarly, since at least the seventeenth century (Stone 1979), it has been suggested that children need careful social nurturing in the form of a caring control lest their potential for change run wild and their adulthood, and hence future adult society, be endangered. Whether it be the inherent evil in children noted by the Puritans, their instinctual innocence celebrated by Rousseau, or Locke's *tabula rasa*, children's malleability and potential for change is firmly represented in terms of risk (James et al.1998). Thus, traditional socialization theory, in arguing for the vulnerability of the child's present being, continually emphasizes the need to nurture, constrain and protect the child lest its future prospects as an adult be thwarted or damaged. In this way, the social institution of 'childhood' – that complex of material, social, moral and economic constraints that shapes children's' everyday lives – is held to place an important steadying hand upon a child's demands for access to the adult social world.

In sum, then, though dynamic images of movement and change may be said to be central to understandings of a child' s identity (whether in relation to some notion of a child's fundamental being or its 'need' for particular kinds of social care), these images are stilled through a heavy circumscription. In this sense, in both scientific and more popular discourses, the creative potential that 'the child' symbolizes is re-represented in terms of a twin dependency. The child is rendered dependent upon the progress and process of both its nature and its nurture, with any flux or unwarranted change risking demonization as potential deviance. Crises of identity in adulthood, whether of the mind or the social body, are conceived, in effect, as the products of unrestraint, of uncontrolled change. Thus, although the identity status of 'child' might literally embody movement, with common imaginings of 'the child speaking more often about its becoming than its present being', in Western discourse, ideas of childhood dependency work to naturalize and neutralize this promise of creativity (James *et al.* 1998). Indeed, it is this which makes the image of 'the child' the dominant metaphor for other dependent experiences (Hockey and James 1993).

Taking up just one of these childhood dependencies – questions of nurture – this chapter begins, therefore, by exploring the ways in which ideas of 'the home' and 'the family' have come, historically, to intermesh with those of 'the child' so as to construct a set of intertwined metaphors of dependency within contemporary British society. It then moves on to chart the practical and everyday outcomes of this metaphorization of dependency within one particular cultural setting – a reception class in an infants' school in central England – to ask what this entails for children's identities as children and their experiences of childhood. If, for example, 'home' is that conceptual and physical space where one best knows oneself, as this volume suggests, then the child might be said to be ideologically at home in the family. And yet children's everyday experiences of contemporary family life may bear little resemblance to commonplace renderings of happy, safe families upon which the child may unswervingly depend for responsible and protective nurturing; homes too may not be those metaphoric sentimental centrings for the heart and hearth; nor yet are children's experiences of social life necessarily those of a passive and obeisant dependency. As this chapter shows, it is through everyday encounters in the classroom that these differing images of 'child', 'home' and 'family' provide a dynamic and shifting characterization of particular children's identities as they begin to settle into life at school. And, in this, the child him/herself has an active part to play. Thus, this chapter concludes by asking how is it that images of dependency persist as spatial and temporal markers of children's identities when they are confounded in the everyday practices of teachers and parents, and what are the consequences of their persistence for children?

The Family at Home

The idea of the 'family' provides an important reference point for who we think we are. Ties of blood and those of marriage locate us in the present social world, whilst those of generation link us to a collective past and future. Yet these ties are not fixed and immutable. In Britain, and in many other European countries, ties of kinship can quickly go cold, increasingly lost or forgotten through inactivity or more purposefully dissolved (Strathern 1992; Edwards and Strathern 1996). For kinship ties to remain meaningful they require active maintenance through a continual reaffirmation, for, as Bernardes has indicated, time plays an important part in when people 'begin to regard themselves as members of "a family" and when they cease to use the term' (1986:601). What 'the family' is, he argues, largely depends upon what people think it is.

And yet, in everyday life the rhetoric of 'the family' looms large, social policy and political practice conferring upon it an ideological solidity: 1994 was, for example, designated as the 'year of the family'. However, what that might mean is not made explicit, so naturalized is the idea of 'the family' in our discourse. A traditional family ideology – a heterosexual couple with children and a division of labour whereby the wife and child are dependent upon the father – continues to dominate our thinking. This is despite its considerable inappropriateness for accounting for the contemporary forms of family life, which, as Simpson (1995) describes, may constitute unclear, rather than nuclear families.

That such a public family ideology does persist in the face of evidence to the contrary is, I suggest, a function of the metaphoric role that the idea of 'home' has had in normalizing and routinizing our understanding of family life as lived. In essence, the idea of 'home' effects a reconciliation between the various 'truths' of 'the family', fostering an ideological (if not practicable) resolution: within the European context 'home' has come to be recognized as the physical and emotional setting for people's personal and private lives. 'Home' is what contextualizes familial experiences (Allan and Crow 1989).

Emerging as a by-product of changing working practices – the shift from cottage industry to the factory system – the intensification of the privacy of the 'home' in the face of the public world of work during the nineteenth century ensured that it became a locus for the self – but a self, as Strathern notes, located in the family group (1992: 98–103). And the creation of family life – as I shall shortly argue, a life with children – became largely women's work at home, registering the conceptual shift from the family as a productive to a reproductive unit.

In these ways ideologies of 'family' and 'home' combined to lay the foundations for what Allan and Crow term 'the modern domestic ideal' (1989:1). Whether this twinning is literally cast in stone, as in the stately 'family seat' that symbolizes familial history amongst the British aristocracy, or visualized as more fluid – a home town to which a son or daughter might one day return – the conceptual links between 'family' and 'home' are mutually reinforcing. They have come to sustain one another, leading at least one observer to remark that in contemporary industrial societies 'the home is the family . . . [and] "home" and "family" are now virtually interchangeable terms' (Oakley, quoted in Allan and Crow 1989:2).

'Home' is thus both a conceptual and a physical space. It is an idea that guides our actions and, at the same time, a spatial context where identities are worked on. I turn now to examine just one of those – the child's identity: for it is in the family that the child is ideologically understood to be at home.

The Child at Home in the Family

In justifying this first assertion I introduce another: it is 'the child' who is conventionally held to constitute 'the family'. Parenting is what transforms the couple into a family – a shift that is also popularly held to make a house into a home. Both signal personal creativity: 'we're thinking of starting a family' and, by implication, making a 'home' (Finch and Hayes 1994). Notwithstanding the fact that adults may still feel a sense of belonging to their own natal families as grown-up sons and daughters, those who are 'childless' have traditionally been stigmatized. They have been, by turns, pitied for their infertility or singlehood or condemned for a perceived selfishness, nay, even social immorality, as Veevers (1980) has noted. No longer children themselves and yet without children themselves, their commitment to the idea of 'the family' has been questioned, and, by implication, so too has their commitment to social norms. Though still tied by kinship to the past, childless couples have been seen to have no future familial location, a social deviance the more marked in industrialized contexts where the wider extended family has a weaker ideological grip on the imagination than its nuclear cousin.

That advertising copy still popularly images 'the child' as being pivotal to concepts of 'family' and 'home' is testimony to this complex web of interconnections that, in Britain, had become firmed up by the end of the nineteenth century. The well-known, though by no means uncontroversial, history of the Western concept of childhood (see Aries 1979 [1962]; Pollock 1983; Wilson 1980) has documented, for example, the gradual centring of 'the child' within 'the family', so that by the late 1800s the family was no longer regarded simply as the site for reproduction. It had taken on responsibility for socializing (civilizing) the child within the increasingly privatized arena of the 'home'; the child for its part was becoming increasingly dependent upon the family and the home. In the case of Britain, this inward turn can be evidenced in the mass of child protection legislation that was passed during the nineteenth century. Enforced with increasing vigour, the laws were designed to protect those children whose parents were seen as irresponsible care-takers or whose homes were deemed unfit. Pinchbeck and Hewitt observe that 'nineteenth century legislation gradually imposed on the working class family a pattern of child dependence which the middle and upper classes had developed several generations before' (1973:651).

'Homes', 'families' and 'children' were subjected to increasing vigilance by the State, a process that, as noted elsewhere, meant that 'the concept of childhood dependency . . . developed as a feature of the emerging nuclear family and was justified through recourse to a cultural mythology which was developing simultaneously in relation to the child. . . . Children's social dependency was fast becoming a key feature both of the family and of childhood itself' (Hockey and James 1993:71).

In the late twentieth century, however, this ideological centring of a dependent child in the family home is becoming increasingly problematic.[3] For example, the extension of the social institution of childhood to encompass a greater part of the life-course (cf. Postman 1982), through the imposition of more extensive sets of moral, legal, social and economic constraints on children's independence, has been accompanied, at the same time, by an opposing view. There is growing acknowledgement of children's rights, and their roles as independent social actors, demonstrated in Britain, for example, in the passing of The Children Act in 1989.[4] More generally 'childhood' has become the focus for a range of often contradictory ethical and political debates, so that what may be regarded as one person's independent child may be another's evidence of neglect; what might seen as familial care may be experienced by the child as familial control. Thus within public and policy arenas recent questions have been raised about the new phenomenon of 'middle-class deprivation' experienced by children of professional parents who are left to fend for themselves at home (*Guardian*, 3 February 1997); about the extent to which welfare agencies should permeate the boundaries of the family home (Parton 1996); about how far, in the wake of the Bulger trial,[5] children or their parents are to be held criminally responsible for unlawful actions (James and Jenks 1996). The family/home/child matrix might remain, but in contemporary Britain its connections no longer seem so certainly unproblematic.

3. As discussed elsewhere (Hockey and James 1993), this dependency is neither an inevitable consequence of children's biology nor yet a reflection of some 'natural' state of childhood innocence. Rather, childhood as a period of dependency is a social construction with which Western children must contend.
4. However, the Act does not necessarily or unproblematically work to facilitate children's agency: see for example Alderson 1993.
5. This trial was of two young boys accused of the murder of a two-year-old in Britain in 1993.

That it is a commitment to childhood as a period of social dependency that underscores such worries can be seen in a parallel set of public concerns over those children who *are* seen as acting independently: children who work to contribute to family incomes; children who act as carers for those who should care for them at home; children who, leaving the family home, find homes on the street. Constituted as 'social problems', such children are said to have 'lost their childhood', precisely through their assumption of independent adult roles outside the boundaries of the home or beyond the confines of the family (Stephens 1995: 18–21). Such examples serve to highlight once more the ideological ties drawn by the idea of children's dependency between the concepts of childhood, family and home. However, that such questions are being raised repeatedly, and increasingly urgently, in the public domain is a sure sign of their new and contemporary fragility.

In everyday life the conceptual boundaries of 'home' and 'family' are constantly being threatened. Blurred through the changes in patterns of work wrought by technology (the office at home) or migrant work (the family and/or home fragmented in space and time), family life at home has begun to take on a greater fluidity. Wider shifts in social attitudes are beginning to de-privatize space within the home, making it difficult to know where the 'familial' home might begin or end or indeed whether it exists at all. Similarly, changes in work patterns – unemployment, expatriate work, commuting, migrant labour – are necessitating the continual re-creation of successional homes. In Britain economic recession in the 1990s has, for many bitten hard, literally severing families from their homes, a process envisaged as putting children 'at risk' (Clark 1996). As more than a faint echo, perhaps, of contemporary uprootings elsewhere in the world, family members, together or as individuals, may have to seek out temporary places of belonging, moving from one bed-and-breakfast hotel to another, from rented house to rented house, one city, two cities, many cities, one country passed through, perhaps a whole continent to explore.

Such changes in the home simply mirror the flux within families. Ever-increasing divorce rates and the emergence of reconstituted families embedded in complex webs of kinship may mean, for example, that children may not only have to find conceptual 'homes' in a number of different physical locations as outlined above (Clarke 1996), but they may also have to discover a sense of emotional belonging to successive sets of individuals as 'the family' changes: one father, then another, siblings, then half-siblings (Kosonen 1996). Indeed, 'family' breakdown may signal the break-up of the 'home', initiating for older children a period of homelessness, the street becoming conceptually a 'home' and other street children an alternative 'family' (cf. Hanssen 1996). The 'family' and the 'home' may thus no longer combine to constitute 'the child' as a naturalized dependant, a shift the more pertinent given contemporary awareness of the dangerous, rather than safe, places that 'family homes' can be. The 'discovery' of child sexual abuse (Jenks 1996) at the end of the twentieth century has meant that the symbolic boundaries of 'families' and 'homes' are increasingly being breached by interventions from the state, as police and social workers remove children to other places of safety. Somewhat ironically these are often 'children's homes', public spaces now embodying the safety and sanctity of private 'homes' for children without homes or whose own homes are said to fail to provide these comforts for the child.[6] If both 'family' and 'home' are thus in ideological flux, where does this leave children? Are they still seen as dependent ? If so, on what?

Evidential Contexts: The 'Schoolchild' at Home and in the Family

To begin to flesh out some of these concerns I return to a British primary school reception classroom in 1989 (cf. James 1993). The school was large, located in a mixed residential area in a Midlands town, catered for children from 3 to 9 years old, and had its own nursery unit attached to the main school. The reception class teachers, who were responsible for admitting children into the 'big' school at the age of 4 or 5, took pride in preparing children for school entry and were, themselves, asking these kinds of questions about families, children and homes. This is, I suggest, of great importance. First, it demonstrates that these particular discourses about the nurturing and socialization of children are firmly embedded in everyday understandings of 'the child' and of what 'childhood' should be. Second, how these questions were posed, explored and answered by the teachers had very practical outcomes for the children themselves: it positioned them along a continuum of social dependency that was at different times and in different spaces subject to different moral evaluations. And in this positioning the 'home' and the 'family' were employed as important symbolic markers of the child's identity as children moved from the home and family environment to that of the school.

---

6. Even more significant is the recent questioning in Britain of the ways in which children's homes are run through the revelation of abusive practices.

Two points are worth making at the outset. First, the identities which followed from the ascription of children to particular points along this continuum were not immutable; over a quite short space of time, children might be conceptually repositioned and their identities would subtly shift. Second, it is also important to note that particular kinds of families or home environments might be differentially judged by teaching staff in relation to particular individual children; sometimes what might have nominally been regarded by them as a 'good home' (stereotypically, lower middle to middle class, a clean and tidy house and parents interested in their child's education), was not necessarily considered to be 'good' for the child; equally the 'bad home' (stereotypically poor, working-class, dirty and untidy physical surroundings and parents who were not interested in their child's education) might not be seen to impact adversely upon the child. Taken together, then, these points serve to remind us that social identity is a strategic process, intentional as well as unintentional; it is about relationships of difference and similarity; it speaks to individual and collective or institutional power; but most of all it is a 'practical accomplishment . . . of the dialectical interplay of processes of internal and external definition' (Jenkins 1996: 25). The childhood identities that I shall reveal here are, then, the complex outcomes of situated practices that children encounter as they move between the family home and the school. These are the alternate identities of parental and school child (James and Prout 1996; Pollard and Filer 1996);[7] and in the following sections I describe four key phases in the child's early school experiences through which this movement between identities is accomplished.

Pre-school Visits

In the school where the research was carried out staff considered it to be beneficial that a home visit should be conducted before the children started school, a rhetoric of concern that was clearly stated in the school's philosophy. This stressed the importance of education for the whole child and of the shared responsibility that parents have for their child's schooling. In establishing this mutual care, the 'home visit' was seen as crucial, for, though situated in a mixed neighbourhood, the staff felt the school to be gaining an increasingly working-class profile. This was

---

7. 'Parental child' identity is here taken to mean that passive, dependent identity that is ascribed to children on the basis of his/her home and family background, while 'school child' is that identity that a child acquires through schooling. As such, the child his/herself contributes much more through his/her own actions and behaviour to this latter identity.

something that the head teacher and the staff saw as a potential difficulty. That this changing profile of the school should be seen as problematic and that the staff saw 'home' visits as a way to forestall danger already indicates the powerful conceptual links that are established in teachers' everyday practices between the concepts of the child, the home and the family and the ways in which each is manoeuvred to reflect the other.

First, it was significant that the teachers' visits were designated as 'home' visits, rather than 'family' visits, though clearly the expressed intention was not, in fact, to make judgements about the children's homes but to establish communication links between the school and its families. However, in the revealing tales staff later told about their visits it became clear that, in their view, the physical environment of the home *did* speak volumes about the family. By implication, then, the house and its family members were together taken to constitute the 'home' and were thought by the teaching staff to reveal much about the child who was about to enter their charge at school. Given the changing catchment area of the school, that such home visits were seen as being of increasing significance serves to underscore one particular aspect of this imaging process: it was assumed by the staff that children from poorer social environments would make poorer pupils and thus would need more help. Home visits, the staff thought, were one way in which to make contact, establish *rapport* and encourage parents to participate in their children's education. Thus the home and the family were imaged as constitutive of the child; the child's potential was deemed dependent upon its nurturing background.

However, such progressive educational ideologies, in practice, fell rather short of the mark. For the staff, home visits often simply confirmed their worst fears and underscored received stereotypes of particular local housing estates or neighbourhoods or provided information about a family that, hitherto, had been gleaned through gossip and hearsay. In this sense, then, the visits did not necessarily serve to open up a broader communication between the school and the family; they simply opened up the child to closer scrutiny. For example, after a visit had been made, conversational snippets revealed that the prospects for a child entering school were sedimented into a highly condensed image of the home and the family. The homes of 4-year-olds Jim and Kirsty provide us with some first examples:[8]

---

8. Here I acknowledge a debt to Rapport (1993). Presenting 'world-views' through the numbering of informants' statements is an economical and useful device.

1. Of her visit to Jim's house Mary, the teacher observed: '*It was dreadful. . . . complete with large, manky dog. There were rosettes all over the wall – her husband's dog is some kind of champion.*'
2. Kirsty's house, on the other hand, was '*plastered with photographs of the new baby and her mother's recent wedding. There were none of Kirsty and her elder sister.*'

These thumbnail sketches of two family living-rooms are revealing. They are inscribed with a series of value judgements that implicitly image the child as being in a potentially precarious or vulnerable position: Jim, it would seem, has to take second place to both his father and the family dog, while Kirsty and her sister may feel excluded from the reconstituted family in which they now reside. Through tone of voice, facial expression, exaggeration and metaphor ('. . . all over the wall'; 'plastered with photographs') both these accounts image experiences that, in the teachers' views, might make for a difficult or problematic schoolchild. Thus it is that the material circumstances of the 'home' are held to reflect upon the nature of family life; and the teachers reflect upon the effect this social and emotional environment will have had upon the child who is about to enter their care.

The physical surroundings of the home were also read by the staff for signs of parenting skills and hence as indications of the kinds of socialization processes to which the child would have been exposed. The account of a visit to Richard's home is particularly revealing:

3. '*The house was a tip. And I thought he* [Richard] *was dead. There was only a slight movement of the eyes when we left. He was draped over a chair . . . a vegetable.*'

Richard's inactivity was viewed by the staff with suspicion: this was likely to be a reflection of a mother's emotional, social and physical neglect, a neglect confirmed by the dirty and untidy home surroundings. Maxine's home visit, in the teachers' opinion, provided similar clues of potential future problems:

4. '*It was chaotic, with her running about and her mother saying nothing.*'

In the staff's opinion, the disorderly material appearance of the house mirrored an obvious lack of discipline and parental control: home and family combined in a potent image to identify Maxine as a potentially difficult or disruptive pupil.

Peter's house, by contrast, was described in somewhat different terms of disparagement:

5. *'It was stuffed full of stereos.'*

This pert observation, spoken sarcastically, eyebrows raised, imaged Peter more indirectly. Though absent as a referent, Peter is identified as a potential victim of his parents' disinclination to make material sacrifices for their child: in what was clearly not an affluent family, the staff feared that the parents would rather fill their house with stereos than possibly (probably) spend money or time on their children.

What, then, did the pre-school visits achieve? From the staff's point of view they served to highlight potential difficulties and to indicate which children might need extra help at school or for whom a regime of fairly strict discipline and control might be needed. These opinions rested on the unproblematic assumption of a fairly direct correspondence between the economic and social circumstances of the home and the educational achievement of the child – stereotypes that are routinely depicted in newspapers and on the television. The statistically established, though not undisputed, correlations between home background and educational achievement feed into a popular imagining of children's childhoods and, in these examples, enable the staff to image the educational prospects for specific children. Positioned as simply the dependent and passive outcome of particular home and family circumstances, at this point in time, the teachers rarely questioned their assumption that a particular kind of child represented the result of a particular nurturing style. Such a view, as Apple (1986) reveals, is the central platform on which all teachers encounter their pupils: 'We do not confront abstract "learners" in schools. Instead, we see specific classed, raced and gendered subjects, people whose biographies are intimately linked to the economic, political and ideological trajectories of their families and communities, to the political economies of their neighbourhoods' (Apple, cited in Pollard and Filer 1996: 6).

Thus it was that Jim, Kirsty, Richard, Maxine and Peter began their school careers in September with their identities already marked or signified by their belonging to particular homes and families.[9]

---

9. Not simply, or even, the unthinking articulation of cultural stereotypes, the drawing of these connections by the staff is but one example of what Giddens (1979) has referred to as the double hermeneutic of social science, through which social science plays a constitutive role in society itself through the dissemination of its knowledge.

The First Days

The first days at primary school are for many children an unsettling experience. If children have not attended nursery schools or spent much time apart from their mothers, the abrupt shift in social environment that schooling necessitates can be a difficult, and often a tearful, experience. Thus, parents were encouraged by the staff to bring their children directly into the classroom and not to leave them in the playground. They were asked to sit down with their child at a table so that together they could begin the task of writing the child's name, which signalled the start of each school day. Parents (although usually it was mothers) were requested to encourage their children with these first steps towards emergent writing: they should help them hold their pencils correctly, focus their attention and give praise as the first stumbling marks are placed upon the paper. The parents were advised that they should only leave their child when they felt he or she was truly settled.

At the start of each school day, the primary classroom was, therefore, a hive of activity, with parents and children coming and going. It was, however, the one time in the day when the staff had a chance to observe the children at a distance and to reflect on their progress while the mothers busied themselves with the children: taking off their coats, hanging them on their pegs and beginning the writing exercise. But it was also a time when the parents too could be observed in their relationships with their children. Thus, the start of the school day served as a moment when the assumed interdependency between home, family and child could once again be considered and the specific relationships could be evaluated by the staff:

6. *'Sally's mother still wants to keep her a baby.'*
7. *'You'd think that her father would think about getting a foster mother for Susie instead of always rushing off to get back to work in the shop – her education is the most important thing.'*
8. *'Paul's first day and she* [his mother] *can't stay.'*
9. *'Kim's mother has not told us her new work number.'*
10. *'Of course, Terry's an only child . . .'.*
11. *'Vicky's parents are very over-protective.'*
12. *'She's very pushy . . . Donna's mother.'*
13. *'At home, she* [Sarah] *is noisy, apparently.'*
14. *'That's the first time . . . the first ones, who have said that they don't want their child* [Ali] *to go all day at first.'*
15. *'She* [Paula] *showed us her pre-reading work!'*

16. *'Her* [Kelly's] *mother is rather stuck-up.'*
17. *'He didn't want his child* [Danny] *to come to nursery . . . said, "I don't want no interference in my child's education".'*
18. *'Her* [Rebecca's] *trouble is her mother.'*

And so it was that the day began.

These conversational snippets image these first days well. Standing together as they welcomed the children into the classroom, the two teachers and the classroom assistants might swap such casual remarks or later, over coffee in the staff room, recall a more significant event or observation. Some comments were approving; many were disapproving; all imaged the potentiality of the child through a consideration of the images of family and home embodied in parental actions.

In the examples cited above, for example, only Ali's parents (14) were spoken of with approval.[10] That they were willing to spend time to ease their son into school to ensure his contentment, and that they were therefore not using the school as a baby-sitting service, was seen as a reflection of their excellent parenting skills. Sally (6), Vicky (11), Terry (10) and Rebecca (18), on the other hand, were imaged as being too dependent upon their mothers. Potentially, they would pose a problem. By contrast, Susie (7), Paul (8) and Kim (9) were thought to be too independent and self-sufficient, a demeanour seen to have been fostered by a lack of parental concern. Donna (12) Kelly (16) and Danny (17), though not yet imaged as problematic children on account of their own actions were, nonetheless, singled out as possessing that potential: staff felt themselves at risk from their parents. Being literally *in loco parentis*, the teachers were at first a little wary of these children, fearful of future confrontations with their parents. Thus, Kelly's expensive clothes were felt not only to be inappropriate for wearing at school, but also a source of danger: who would tell her mother about paint splashed on her dress or a torn shirt?[11]

10. It is noticeable that approval was rarely voiced. The teachers were on the look-out for danger signs, those that would make their job as teachers more difficult, a job that they saw as being integral to the shaping of a child's educational and personal future. Thus, as explored later, explanations for educational failure were more readily sought in the inadequacies of the home, than through the more uncomfortable and possibly disquieting process of reflecting on their own practice as teachers.

11. The staff could scarcely disguise their amusement the day it was discovered that Kelly had nits in her hair. In their view this cast doubt on Kelly's mother's apparent claim for good mothering, evidenced in the material displays of wealth and care through the clothing Kelly wore to school.

For Sarah (13) and Paula (15) home background (families and homes) were cited as explanations of their behaviour for very different reasons. In all her time at nursery school and during these early days at primary school Sarah rarely spoke. A pretty child, intelligent and unobtrusive, she did what she was asked. She was never any trouble except for her silence. This was an enigma. That she came from a clean, well-ordered home, that her family was a caring middle-class family whose mother did not go out to work, and that she had two brothers already at the school, simply compounded the mystery. More puzzling still was the fact that of all the children in the class Sarah's depicted childhood was the image of what *childhood* should be: the experience of a warm and loving home and family. But in her withdrawn social behaviour and self-composed, independent demeanour she herself was not representative of what a *child* should be: happy in an innocent and dependent vulnerability (Ennew 1986). Paula, on the other hand, would seem, by all accounts, to image the exemplary child: articulate, intelligent, helpful, and arriving at school already with a grasp of basic writing and reading skills. Her mother was a teacher, who spent a great deal of time assisting her daughter. But the staff remained cautious and regarded Paula's skills with a good deal of scepticism at first; her educationally centred childhood, organized by a 'pushy' parent, ran contrary to more popular images of a carefree mythical childhood. Without a hint of irony, one member of staff, herself a mother, observed: 'Teachers' children are the worst.'

In these examples, then, can be seen the ways in which the identities of individual children were marked out at the start of their school careers through a set of metaphoric interconnections' being drawn between the role of the family (especially that of mothering) and the home environment. Each was held to image the other and to constitute the child. It was, then, through a set of stereotypical images that a child's identity as a school pupil was initially mapped out: for the staff it provided what Rapport terms a 'cognitive anchor' through which to begin to get to know their pupils, something that might act as a 'bulwark against the unexpected randomness of future events' (1995:280–1). Furthermore, for the children themselves, as I shall next show, these connections, routinely made between home, family and child, served as a discourse within which their 'migrant selves', their becoming-a-pupil, began to be contextualized.

The First Weeks

As the children began to settle into school, so the teachers began to focus more closely on the individual skills and potential that each child demonstrated at school. They were keenly observant of children's changing moods and of possible conflicts emerging between individual children as they began to interact with one another. And as their knowledge of the children increased, so a process of revision and re-evaluation began, with the triadic interconnectedness of home, family and child beginning to be called into question. On arrival at school, Richard (3) defied the teacher's expectations: the slumped child he had been at home had been transformed into a pleasant schoolboy, helpful and eager to please.

But besides getting better acquainted with the children as individuals, the staff had also to begin to categorize them as pupils. In many cases this meant a refining or reclassification of initial judgements made about their abilities. These judgements had been derived from their first encounters with the children: at home, through observations in the first few days or gleaned from conversations with staff in the nursery unit attached to the school. Jenny's home visit, for example, had been regarded as a great success. The home environment had met with staff approval, and her mother had eagerly cooperated with the teachers. In her first few weeks at school, however, Jenny failed to match up to the staff's expectations of her abilities. One of the teachers commented: 'She's not that good, not as good as I would have thought.' On the other hand, noting that Keith had been placed in the second highest ability grouping, another member of staff observed: 'Is he *that* good then? That surprises me.' Keith's academic success was confounding expectations she had founded on the basis of her previous knowledge about his background. Chris, however, remained something of a mystery. His home and family background had provided few early clues for the staff to begin to make some initial judgements about his educational prospects. His family was lower middle class, their home clean and tidy; his mother and father pleasant and seemingly interested in their children. There was, in effect, nothing to note, because the home/family/child were so ordinary; they were literally not noteworthy. In the first weeks at school the staff anxiously sought to locate him on their scales of achievement: 'he looks as if he should know things but doesn't'. Like Toby, another boy about whom the staff remained undecided, Chris was somewhat reluctantly deemed 'a grey area'.

Thus, during their first few weeks at school, the children were moved up and down implicit assessment scales, scales that endeavoured to correlate a child's current performance with previous knowledge about his/her home and family circumstances. An intelligent answer to a question or a good piece of work would be interpreted in relation to earlier observations to see whether it matched up with the teacher's earlier assessment. And if there was a discrepancy, then the child's pupil identity would be adjusted. Speaking of Roy, one member of staff remarked, somewhat critically, and with more than a touch of irritation: 'he can do a lot more than we were led to believe'. Her annoyance, both on her own and Roy's behalf, was at the now seemingly inaccurate judgements about Roy's abilities that had been made earlier on the basis of a particularized reading of his family and his home that had been passed on to her by teachers working in the nursery unit attached to the school. Roy had literally been misplaced; now she had to adjust her views. Similarly, those who showed signs of failing to live up to an earlier promise of success were also reassigned, with a resigned reluctance. With their academic sights lowered, such children would be identified through the phrase, 'lights on, no one at home'. During the first few busy weeks of term, when staff have quickly to get to know the individual idiosyncrasies of the many children in their care, such early and necessary reclassifications were disconcerting; they disrupted the teachers' recently formed assessment of the academic potential of the class as a whole, and the range of individual ability that had been identified for establishing a teaching strategy.

The Future

Through the examples detailed above it is clear, then, that a child's identity as a child-at-school is conceived as being dependent upon its earlier experiences of nurturing within the family home. However, these identities are not fixed. Through their own actions – producing good work, behaving well – children can change a teacher's view of themselves. This suggests that their movement out of the close confines of the home and the family (and into school) is also acknowledged as a point of transition from a dependent to a more independent life. For any child its future as a school-child is no longer a future predicated on simply being a child (imaged as the outcome of the relation between home and family) but one built around the status of becoming a pupil (represented as the outcome of a new dependency between the teacher and the child). This movement out of and away from the home and the family and the changed nature of the child is, however, more readily acknowledged by the staff in relation to a child's achievements and upward mobility; when this trajectory is in doubt, the home and family may often be retained as images through which teachers can find explanations for the child's *lack* of achievement.

In sum, explanations of academic 'success' focus upon the child–teacher relation, while those of failure may still be sought in the child's home and family environment. Only rarely in this first year of schooling do they come to rest, as later, within the child itself, when the process of individualization, which begins with a child's entry into school, finally begins to bite. Thus, through the close monitoring of a child's changing family and home circumstances explanatory frames are sought out and presented as evidence:

19. *'Dad only has access to Michael at weekends.'*
20. *'John's father is in prison.'*
21. *'Oh, her mother is married to her father, then?'*
22. *'It's rather a weird set-up. His mother is in her 40s and the father in his 20s but there are other odd relationships as well . . . The house has no furniture but lots of mattresses.'*
23. *'Susan's mother is now trying to get a new council house . . . she moved out of the old one to live with her boyfriend.'*
24. *'Did you know . . . his father beat up his mother at the weekend.'*
25. *'She has had three childminders in two weeks!'*
26. *'Alex's sister can't sit still either.'*

Unusual family circumstances remain as reminders of potential problems (19, 20), and as news and bits of gossip about the changing circumstances of the home come to the staff's attention they are added piecemeal to the knowledge the staff already have about a child's home background (21, 22, 23, 24, 25). It is against such a changing profile, moreover, that a child's achievements will be monitored and judged; from such knowledge reasons for 'failure' will most often be derived. Only in the final resort is 'failure' located within the child itself; thus, always eager to excuse and to retain some hope in a child's potential for change and betterment, the staff might look instead to inherited family traits (26) as the locus of trouble or discord.

Conclusion

In this chapter I have sought to show how the images of the child, home and family combine in different ways and at different points in a child's early school career to map out a trajectory of change, growth and development for the child. Fluid in this early period of the life-course, as classic studies of the learning process have shown, these relationships may however become increasingly sedimented out as children mature within the school system (Pollard 1985, 1987; Willis 1977). That is, the early flexibility and fluidity of child–home–family identities described here may rapidly decrease; the classification of children as representing particular kinds of pupils may become more stable and fixed. This occurs through the mutual reinforcement of teacher and pupil expectations, itself the outcome of 'routinized teaching in association with pupil drift' (Pollard and Filer 1996:310).[12]

And an important part of this process is, I have suggested, a particular imaging of the changing identity of the child through the twin images of 'home' and 'family'. That the home is popularly regarded as a personal creation (Finch and Hayes 1994) and that the child is also similarly imaged as the creation of its parents (through particular parenting styles and socializing practices) may be central to many teachers' attitudes towards and conceptions of a child's abilities and potential. In this sense, these images of 'home' and 'family' play a central role in the social construction of childhood (James and Prout 1990). For the teachers, they offer a starting-point from which to engage with the children who enter their care, a platform from which to begin to place them within the wider category of children. However, the fact that these twin concepts together work to position the child as passively dependent suggests that a child's potential for future change and development, which the teachers see as their nurturing task at school, may also be at risk from such a presupposition. In the same way that developmental psychology has brought hegemonic control over a child's maturing body through the concept of staged biological development, so, for teachers, and educational policy-makers more broadly, the twin concepts of home and the family constitute a powerful ideological resource with which teachers may unwittingly and unknowingly 'steady' a child's educational progress through the limitation of expectations.

References

Alderson, P. (1993), *Children's Consent to Surgery*, Buckingham: Open University Press.
Allan, G. and Crow, G. (eds) (1989), *Home and Family: Creating the Domestic Space*, Basingstoke: Macmillan.
Apple, M. (1986), *Teachers and Texts*, London: Routledge.
Aries, P. (1979) [1962], *Centuries of Childhood*, London: Cape.
Bernardes, J. (1986), 'Multidimensional Developmental Pathways: A Proposal to Facilitate the Conceptualisation of Family Diversity', *Sociological Review*, 34(3):590–610.

12. The suggestion is that over time teachers and pupils come to an implicit and shared understanding of levels of expectations and achievements. Mutually agreed, they are rarely exceeded.

Clark, A. (1996), 'Policy and Provision for the Schooling of Children Living in Temporary Accommodation', *Children and Society*, 10 (4): 293–305.

Clarke, L. (1996), 'Demographic Change and the Family Situation of Children', in J. Brannen and M. O'Brien (eds), *Children and Families: Research and Policy*, London: Falmer Press.

Edwards, J. and Strathern, M. (1996), 'Including Our Own' (Paper presented at Boundaries and Identities Conference, Edinburgh).

Ennew, J. (1986), *The Sexual Exploitation of Children*, Cambridge: Polity Press.

Featherstone, M. and Wernick, A. (eds) (1995), *Images of Aging*, London: Routledge.

Finch, J. and Hayes, L. (1994), 'Inheritance, Death and the Concept of Home', *Sociology*, 28 (2): 417–35.

Giddens, A. (1979), *The Central Problems of Social Theory*, London: Macmillan.

Hanssen, E. (1996), 'Finding Care on the Street; Processes in the Careers of Sri Lankan Street Boys', *Childhood* 3 (2): 247–61.

Hockey, J. and James, A. (1993), *Growing Up and Growing Old*, London: Sage.

James, A. (1993), *Childhood Identities: Self and Social Relationships in the Experience of the Child*, Edinburgh: Edinburgh University Press.

—— (1995), 'On Being a Child: The Self, the Group and the Category', in A.P. Cohen and N. Rapport (eds), *Questions of Consciousness*, London: Routledge.

—— and Jenks, C. (1996), 'Public Perceptions of Childhood Criminality', *British Journal of Sociology*, 47(2): 315–31.

—— and Prout, A. (eds) (1990), *Constructing and Reconstructing Childhood*, Basingstoke: Falmer Press

—— and Prout, A. (1996), 'Strategies and Structures: Towards a New Perspective on Children's Experiences of Family Life', in J. Brannen and M.O'Brien (eds) *Children and Families: Research and Policy*, London: Falmer Press.

——, Jenks, C. and Prout, A. (1998), *Theorising Childhood*, Oxford:Polity Press.

Jenkins, R. (1996), *Social Identity*, London: Routledge.

Jenks, C. (1996), 'The Postmodern Child', in J. Brannen and M. O'Brien (eds), *Children and Families: Research and Policy*, London: Falmer Press.

Kosonen, M. (1996), 'Siblings as Providers of Support and Care During Middle Childhood: Children's Perceptions', *Children and Society*, 10 (4): 267–80.

Lakoff, G. and Johnson, M. (1980), *Metaphors We Live By*, Chicago: University of Chicago Press.

Parton, N. (1996), 'The New Politics of Child Protection', in J. Pilcher and S. Wagg (eds), *Thatcher's Children: Politics, Childhood and Society in the 1980s and 1990s*, Lewes: Falmer Press.

Pinchbeck, I. and Hewitt, M. (1973), *Children in English Society, Vol.II*, London: Routledge and Kegan Paul.

Pollard, A. (1985), *The Social World of the Primary School*, London: Holt, Rinehart and Winston.

—— (1987) 'Goodies, Jokers and Gangs', in A. Pollard (ed.), *Children and their Primary Schools*, Lewes: Falmer Press.

—— and Filer, A. (1996), *The Social World of Children's Learning*, London: Cassell.

Pollock, L. (1983), *Forgotten Children: Parent–Child Relations 1500–1900*, Cambridge: Cambridge University Press.

Postman, N. (1982), *The Disappearance of Childhood*, New York: Delacotte Press.

Rapport, N. (1993), *Diverse World-Views in an English Village*, Edinburgh: Edinburgh University Press.

—— (1995) 'Migrant Selves and Stereotypes: Personal Context in a Postmodern world', in S. Pile and N. Thrift (eds), *Mapping the Subject*, London: Routledge.

Schwartz, T. (1976), 'Relations among Generations in Time-limited Cultures', in T. Schwartz (ed.), *Socialisation as Cultural Communication*, London: University of Calinfornia Press.

Simpson, R. (1995), 'Bringing the "Unclear" Family into Focus: Divorce and Re-marriage in Contemporary Britain', Man 29(4):831–53.

Stephens, S. (ed.) (1995), *Children and the Politics of Culture*, Princeton: Princeton University Press.

Stone, L. (1979), *The Family, Sex and Marriage in England 1500–1800*, Harmondsworth: Penguin.

Strathern, M. (1992), *After Nature*, Cambridge: Cambridge University Press.

Veevers, J.E. (1980), *Childless by Choice*, Toronto: Butterworth.

Willis, P. (1977), *Learning to Labour*, Farnborough: Saxon House.

Wilson, A. (1980), 'The Infancy of the History of Childhood: An Appraisal of Phillipe Aries', *History and Theory*, 19 (2):132–54.

6

Domestic Appropriations: Multiple Contexts and Relational Limits in the Home-making of Greater Londoners

Eric Hirsch

Home-making, Contexts of Consumption, and Individuality and Its Limits

The Simon family of north London possess a Spectrum computer, which had in the past been a source of tension and conflict within their home.[1] Mrs Simon had initially purchased the second-hand machine so that her children could develop their keyboard skills. The machine was programmed to play games, and in due course numerous arguments and fights emerged around the use of the computer by the children. What was significant about the conflict (aside from the fact that it was not appreciated by the parents) was how it manifested itself among the children.

The Simons have five children: three boys and two adopted girls. The two girls have black parental origins. The Spectrum became the focus of

1. I am grateful for the helpful assistance of Catherine Harvey with the preparation of the ethnographic material of this chapter. I also want to thank Allen Abramson and Nigel Rapport for their insightful comments on a draft of this chapter. The errors that remain are the sole responsibility of the author. An early draft of the chapter was first presented at the 1996 European Association of Social Anthropologists conference, Barcelona, in a session on 'Consumption and the Household' convened by Sophie Chevalier and Daniel Miller. Finally, I thank the families who kindly let me into their homes to conduct the research.

a male-dominated domain, and the girls were eventually excluded from using the machine. As the parents recall:

> *Mr*: 'The children have a Spectrum . . . technically they don't, because it is broken. I have made no effort at all to repair it. It was a disappointment, not a reflection of the types of games . . . It was not the types of games that I disapproved of. It is because of their behaviour.'
> *Mrs*: 'This is the three boys.'
> *Mr*: 'And their relationship to the girls. They behaved differently than we expected them to.'
> *Mrs*: 'It is true . . . caused a lot of trouble and ill feeling. They'd get really angry with each other . . . Someone hadn't the same amount of time as another one, it was somebody's turn and they went out of turn and then someone had come in and interrupted them and someone was playing a game and they got shouted and screamed at. They were pretty nasty to each other.'
> *Mr*: 'The girls were not allowed near it.'
> *Mrs*: 'They did not get any practice so they did not get any quicker.'
> The eldest daughter adds from the kitchen: 'I got sick of it.'

The use of the machine among the boys revealed aggressive, exclusionist forms of interaction that the parents found incompatible with the overall image of family life sustained in both their London and country homes (see Hirsch 1992 for a more extensive description of these interconnected domains). The machine revealed the limits of individuality that the parents as well as the girls were prepared to accept, and as a consequence the machine was left, in a manner of speaking, to die. The Spectrum was purchased to encourage particular forms of sociability and capacities (equitable, keyboard-user skills); but instead an alternative form of relationship manifested itself, which was not one the parents or the other children wanted to see: the use of the computer by the boys led to alienation from the device on the part of their adopted sisters.

The Simon home, like many similar middle-class homes in Britain at the end of the twentieth century, contains a vast array of material objects, rooms given over to different functions and activities, and mutual arrangements of each (objects/rooms), through which family relations are sustained and reproduced. Although the presence of such arrays is not just a feature of middle-class life, it has been the explicit middle-class emphasis on the delights of the home that has become part of the cultural ideal of other classes (cf. Strathern 1992).[2]

Together with this ideal of domesticity goes the speed with which persons and objects move in both time and space. The sense of ever-present change and movement is one that continually throws into relief the home as a resting-place – 'a haven in a heartless world'. Campbell (1987) has traced the emergence of a key dimension of this emphasis on change – in the form of mass-produced novelty and fashion. He refers to this as the 'romantic ethic' of 'modern autonomous imaginative hedonism' (Campbell 1987), the other side of the coin, so to speak, of Weber's 'Protestant ethic'. Campbell's thesis interestingly overlaps with related studies of late eighteenth-century England that trace the emergence of the middle class and their valuing of the home as a domain separate and distinct from that of the market and the workplace (see Davidoff and Hall 1987; cf. Colley 1996).

Historians have labelled this the 'birth of the consumer society' (McKendrick *et al.* 1983). Historical evidence suggests that persons became less the primary producers of their socio-material worlds and more the consumers in an increasingly commercialized society. A pervasive example of this historical transformation is housing in the Euro-American context, the context of our own homes. Within this general category there is the specific case of 'council housing', which came into particular prominence during the late nineteenth century, heralding the growth and expansion of the 'welfare state'. How do persons transform this state-provided entity into a home? This form of housing is an apt example, as its form and many features of its content are provided by state agencies radically divorced from the lives of the ultimate inhabitants.

Miller (1988) has shed light on these processes of transformation through a case study of a council estate in London, which he used simultaneously to exemplify his more general model of consumption (Miller 1987). Miller's specific focus was the kitchen and the differing degrees to which this was transformed from a condition of 'alienation' (produced by 'anonymous' others) to that of an 'inalienable culture' (see Miller 1987:178–217). This occurred through the distinctive work of appropriation, often, as he found, through the introduction of fitted kitchens. The key analytical terms in Miller's account are those of aliena-tion and appropriation (Miller 1988:353).[3] As he notes more generally:

2. I briefly return to the Simons at the end of this chapter, where the relational limits manifested around the computer are compared with another family context.

3. Miller's use of the notion of alienation derives from several 'classic' sources such as Hegel, Marx and Simmel, and his particular reading of Munn's ethnographic studies. A

'The appropriation of the home is not a substitutive or vicarious activity but a material objectification of certain social resources available in the construction of household identity which in turn provides a foundation for the formation of larger networks. . . . [In this particular case study], [n]eighbours became a kind of collective super-ego in which normative order was interiorised and expressed itself internally. Once this was established, there was little need for the assertion of actual external authority' (Miller 1988:369).

There is, then, a competitive, coercive context in which one makes a home, and one not restricted to those provided by the state (cf. Bourdieu 1984). It is this context that informs the way persons, in their differing ways, construe their own perceptions of home and self, as well as how they construe the perceptions of others in relation to their home. Council housing is perhaps an extreme example of provision controlled entirely by the state; but even here, local factors implicated in the perception of such housing are often quite complex (for example local family networks, work and trade relationships, and so on).

Let us consider for a moment the related notions of alienation and appropriation. As noted, one of the central features of modern life is the predominance of mass-produced commodities (with 'council housing' as a particular manifestation of this wider process). Given this wide-ranging, mass produced environment and the bureaucracies for its management, it has been argued that 'we increasingly live with institutions and objects that we do not see ourselves as having created' (Miller 1997:26). It is further argued that we thus work to invest such entities with our own agency and towards our own purposes, largely in the domestic context. I want to suggest, however, that although appropriation appears to have as its focus the domestic setting, it is often about negotiating a complexity of relations and imagery from other contexts, which overlap with the home context itself.

---

precise definition is difficult to find. What emerges is a use of the notion of alienation seen as intrinsic to all societies, such as those of Melanesia, and as an intrinsic element of the process by which persons create for themselves a meaningful – or 'inalienable' – culture (Miller 1987:61–2). Whether in Melanesia or in modern capitalist societies, Miller suggests that 'certain conditions serve to separate the creators from the object of their creative process' (Miller 1987:62). In modern capitalist societies this separation is greater, and there is the potential for wide-ranging degrees of 'impersonality'. This has led numerous cultural critics to condemn consumerism as a quintessential feature of alienation. Miller argues, by contrast, and in terms of his more general theory of culture, that consumption is potentially a key element in the process of empowerment and/or identity formation, as people 'work' or appropriate that which has an initial condition of alienation (Miller 1994:74).

As we shall see in the brief case-studies below, it is often the relation to senses of alienation at work, or in the precarious boundaries between home and work, that informs particular modes of domestic appropriation. Consumption as appropriation is certainly 'the site through which we change and develop our social relations' (Miller 1997:26). Importantly, though, these social relations must be seen to entail particular limits.

The perception of such limits is implicated in the English way of thinking, where 'the individuality of persons may be considered the primary fact of English kinship' (Strathern 1992:14). Social relations entail limits in the sense that men, women and children – as individuals, and as aspects of their distinct individuality – have expectations that this individuality will not be transgressed. Individuals negotiate their relations so as not to over-reach these limits, as they are elaborated in the domestic context, among other contexts, as we saw above with the Simons. Although:

[I]ndividual partners come together to make (unified) relationships . . . as parents they ought at the same time to stand in an initial condition of . . . differentiation from each other [when children result from such a union they are themselves conceived of as distinct individuals – there will of course be different consequences if they arrive through birth or adoption]. In the relationships they build and elaborate upon, it is important that the prior diversity and individuality of the partners remain (Strathern 1992:22).

As an individual, one is seen to be made up of a number of overlapping roles – whether they be kin roles focused on the family and relatives, or roles that overlap with these, such as worker or neighbour. What is true of the individual person is simultaneously the case for the world at large: that it is made up of a plurality of overlapping contexts and domains. This manner of envisioning connections or linkages both of the worlds of things and of persons is what Strathern (1992:73) characterizes for the English as 'merographic': 'that anything may be a part of something else, minimally part of a description in the act of describing it'. Thus we can speak of or describe an 'economic' or 'religious' aspect to English family life; family life is not equal to these other dimensions, but 'one of the places where the effects of both can be seen' (Strathern 1992:84). All these domains partially overlap, but none is conceptually reducible to any other (as is the case, for example, with Melanesian sociality by contrast).

It is in this light, I suggest, that we should rethink the notions of appropriation and alienation. Using an object may involve no alienation intrinsic to the object, but its use may involve attempting *to appropriate other forms of alienation*. This has more to do with the way other social relations overlap with the home, or the way other contexts appear to impinge on the domestic environment. In other words, we are at any given time potentially 'alienated' in several partially connected contexts. The detail of the case-studies highlights the problem of theorizing too strong a connection between appropriation and alienation as involving any one context and/or object domain.

As the reader will also discover, many examples discussed in the case-studies involve information and communication technologies (ICTs) of various kinds. This is only in part an outcome of the original focus of the research (see next section). More significantly, though, it is related to certain distinctive features of ICT which illustrate the arguments just made. ICT (telephone, television, video, satellite, computers, and so on) involves an active engagement of the individual that often works to the exclusion of others (again, as evidenced by the Simon example above). In addition, ICTs are distinctive through their capacity to connect together other contexts in a single medium – such as the way the telephone can be perceived as a 'lifeline' by some, or as a constant intruder by others. These features are obviously present in other objects routinely found in the home, but their articulation is often less visible or less explicitly recognized by those engaged in their use (see Hirsch 1997).

The Fieldwork Context

The ethnographic material presented here was collected over a two-year period during 1988–90 as part of a project focused on the domestic environment of ICT;[4] this represents the 'ethnographic present' (cf. Hirsch 1997, where more recent (1996) work has been conducted). A total of sixteen families formed part of the research, one half each from central London and outer London. Each family had school-age children. In all cases the parents were married, although in one case this was a re-marriage, and in another foster children were present. Fieldwork with each family was conducted over a 6–9 month period. Visits were made to each home at a pre-arranged time, and a variety of ethnographic methods were used, including structured and unstructured interviews and participant observation (see Hirsch 1992 for more details).

The present chapter includes material on seven of these families. As it turned out for this particular text, five are from central London and the remaining two from outer London. It should become clear when reading

4. The research was carried out in collaboration with Roger Silverstone as part of the Economic and Social Research Council programme on Information and Communication Technologies.

the brief case-studies that three are what might be called solidly 'middle class', one is solidly 'working-class' and the other three fall somewhere in between.

Although my work involved all family members in each home, my accounts here largely focus on the parents. This was not explicitly planned, and is probably related to the briefness of each case and the fact that for the most part, but not necessarily always, the parents were the most articulate as regards the matters of concern in this chapter.

In the pages that follow we shall first meet the Greens, where a dynamic between 'high tech' and 'low tech' in the home is explicitly articulated by the husband and wife. This is then contrasted with another version of this dynamic in the very different domestic setting of the Bells. In each, the contexts of home and work connect together in distinctive ways that inform their modes of appropriation.

Technologies in the home continue in the next pair of case-studies, and again the context of work (or the lack thereof) re-surfaces; but here connections to alternative visions of shopping are also articulated. Among the Mitchells this forms a sort of individual and collective rebirth after a period of intensive alienation created by landlords and legal institutions. Meanwhile for the Selbys, particularly the wife, shopping can be an alienating activity, better pursued by computers.

Finally, in the third pair of case-studies, technology, home and work provide a recurring set of connected contexts. Among the Dobbses, work is continually impinging on home. In the wife's specific acts of appropriation, technologies are made to appear invisible so as to create a unity of appearance in the home, continually disrupted by the intrusive work context. In the case of the Williamses, this overlap of contexts makes a new technology appear as a way of enabling their separation.

As a final note, I should add that all the names used here have been changed.

Case Studies

High Tech, Low Tech: Relational Limits and the Partial Connections of Home and Work

Mr Green, also of north London, faces a different dilemma to that of the Simons. He has created for himself a personal technology account to limit the amount of technology he buys for himself. As he puts it: 'I love having all the gadgets.' His grandfather had an electrical valve shop in the North of England, and Mr Green was raised around gadgetry. But his wife does not share his love of machines. Mrs Green says she hates computers and will not use them at work. She does not see the point to them at all: 'children in the past have learnt all they needed to without them'.

Mr and Mrs Green are both doctors. Mr Green is a medical civil servant and Mrs Green works in a group practice three mornings a week. They have three children and live in a three-bedroom maisonette. Mr Green keeps his portable computer in the living-room. 'I'm a workaholic . . . not working when I come in is a sign of weakness . . . if you want to do things you've got to work hard.' Mrs Green wants the computer taken back to work where it should be, because she sees it as taking up too much space: 'He has it everywhere where it shouldn't be.' When he is working Mr Green will keep the TV or cable on on a split screen 'as wallpaper', or listen to the radio to counteract the laborious aspects of his work and to relieve tension. He was even thinking of getting satellite if he thought that necessary.

Mr Green clearly sees himself as a high flyer in the civil service, and the machinery he surrounds himself with at home is part of this personal project of getting on and succeeding. At the same time, he is also disabled by polio he suffered as a young boy, and can only walk with the use of canes or a wheelchair. It would seem that the fast-paced machinery he is so involved in and through which he accesses the whole globe is not unrelated to his own very laboured movement and general lack of mobility.

By contrast, Mrs Green has very limited ambitions for herself. She says she is too lazy to go back to work full-time, which she would find too exhausting. Her fantasy is to work in the Victoria and Albert Museum, with things that do not complain: 'I like looking at pretty things.' Her ideal environment is one devoid of machines and their intrusive effects. She says she would like to go to galleries more often, particularly to view Impressionist and seventeenth-century Dutch painting. Mrs Green reads Jane Austen and autobiographies and often goes to bed early to read while her husband works in the living-room. He does not like (human) distractions.

There are radios all around the Green house. The radio is something both Mr and Mrs Green enjoy. They wake up to the radio every morning. As Mrs Green says: 'I put it on first thing so its a mixture of surfacing to the world and not wanting to surface.' The house then becomes a rush as Mrs Green prepares the children for school and drives them there as part of a complicated daily rota, while Mr Green prepares himself for work.

Mr Green says there is so much that is good on the radio, and regrets not having more time to listen: 'so many good programmes which I miss – like the unloved wife, just have no time to listen, and when you do you're amazed'.

Although Mrs Green has a negative view of the high-tech – computers, video, even disliking the intrusive effects of the telephone – and her husband attempts to limit it through his 'technology account', Mrs Green would not think twice about the need to have a washing-machine. Mrs Bell, who lives in the same general area of London, however, cannot get her husband to buy her one. The Bells live in a two-bedroom flat on a council estate with their two children. Mr Bell works as a cinema projectionist in a west London cinema, and has worked in this profession since leaving school nearly thirty years ago. Mrs Bell is from the Philippines, and has lived in the UK for the last fifteen years. They met while she worked as an usherette in the same west London cinema.

Every day Mrs Bell does hand-washing, and she visits the local launderette on a weekly basis to wash larger items. She speaks of the radio as alleviating the 'hardness' of her work: 'It takes me out of myself.' In a similar way 'talking on the telephone is really just being myself', talking with friends and arranging visits with the children. By contrast, when Mr Bell comes home he then seeks solitude in the local pub reading the *Daily Telegraph* and drinking pints of Guinness. He is preoccupied about his own disempowerment at work. Projectionists have been trans-formed over the years from valued technicians to time-keepers overseeing several films at once. Mr Bell has regrets about not joining the BBC as a cable boy when the opportunity arose many years ago. This would have probably led to his becoming a cameraman early on in his career. But at the time it would have meant a drop in wages and status: 'At the time the cinema was a modern environment . . . I was having a good time that way and didn't want to work with the stuffy BBC, so I just passed it by.'

In many ways Mr Bell seems to feel trapped in the world he once found so exciting and modern. There are, as a result, numerous personally created limits that he finds himself unable to transcend. For example, during that time in the 1960s Mr Bell built up a record collection of what he calls mainly 'middle-of-the-road' artists, Cliff Richards and Cilla Black. There are now over two hundred records, although nothing new has been added for many years. Occasionally Mr Bell will take out an LP and play it, although much of the music on Radio Two, he admits, captures the sound he finds so enjoyable. Mrs Bell does not listen to the records, and they are out of bounds for the children. Mr Bell reflects how his work has had an effect on his taste in music: 'Carousel', 'West

Side Story' and so on. But it is not only the cinema he sees as shaping his sense of musical preference; it was his very upbringing that focused him towards his choice of profession.

His father died when he was six years old, and he was brought up by his grandparents. His grandfather was chief electrician at the Hippodrome, and his grandmother, wardrobe mistress at the Coliseum: 'So I sort of grew up with an atmosphere of theatre on the technical side of it . . . not the performing side, the other side of it.' This led to his choice of a career in the cinema, which he sees as 'partly hereditary'. As he says 'the West End, the glory of it all'. But the glory has all gone, and he says he would be straight out if he won the pools.

Whereas Mrs Bell can be herself when speaking with her Filipino friends on the telephone or when visiting, Mr Bell's individuality emerges most clearly in his interest in cinema organ music and model trams, which both evoke his past and times he clearly feels more attached to. It would seem that the washing-machine is iconic for both Mr and Mrs Bell, each in their own way – iconic of Mr Bell's inability to advance in his work and of a limit he is maintaining in relation to hers.

Love to Shop, hate to shop: multiple forms and contexts of alienation

Not far from the Bells, live the Mitchells in their privately rented two-bedroom flat. Mr and Mrs Mitchell no longer work, and their young son, aged nine, attends a local Catholic school. Unlike the Bells, Mr and Mrs Mitchell feel unable to pursue any individual interests or relationships, as all their time and energy goes into fighting a lengthy and costly court battle with their landlord: a case they are subsequently to lose. The case concerns the disrepair of their flat and their claim that the landlord is legally responsible. In many ways their relationship has collapsed upon itself, as every moment is spent together as part of their pursuit of this court case. They see themselves as having been consumed by a corrupt legal system.

Before they initiated the case Mr Mitchell worked as a car trader, and prior to the birth of their son Mrs Mitchell worked as an unchartered accountant. As an outgrowth of the lengthy and unpredictable court case Mr Mitchell developed arthritis in his back, and now finds it difficult to work. Their savings have been completely depleted by the case. Now one of their preoccupations, aside from the legal battle, is their own self-sufficiency, their ability to get by on very little. As Mr Mitchell reflects: 'We often go to Sainsbury [the supermarket] and you can't help observe what people buy and the rubbish . . . I think a lot of this was inherited . . . when I used to take my mother out shopping years ago . . . she'd only shop in certain places . . . she knew that was the freshest, best buy . . . like my mother buying a piece of meat, she used to drive the butcher mad . . . show me this, show me that; that's still with us, isn't it?'

They contrast their current situation with that before their legal battle and the birth of their son: 'We used to get around a lot more in those days, we used to go to a lot of first nights . . . David Hamilton . . . he used to have a lot of these first-night . . . when he couldn't make it he used to give the tickets to us, you see.' Mr Mitchell, in particular, saw himself as part of a lively London culture, getting by through 'duckin' and divin'' as a car trader.

In effect, the collapse of their legal challenge has been paralleled by what they see as the collapse of the world around them as they previously knew it. Instead of their area consisting of 'nice English-types' it has been transformed into 'yuppiedom' following the property boom of the late 1980s; instead of being Conservative supporters they see themselves as now radicalized. They contrast the remembered sense of one-time 'community' with the debt-ridden property speculators they now perceive all around them. Many of their day-to-day pursuits, such as buying food, clothes, and so on, which they once pursued as part of their workaday lives, have now become magnified and taken on a special significance in the light of their lack of relationships with the world of work or shopping more generally.

At the end of my fieldwork with the Mitchells, after their final appeal in the House of Lords was defeated, they were evicted from their flat and put in a Housing Association property. This was a considerably smaller flat, and unlike their previous accommodation it was not furnished. Their conception of the situation was one of being cast adrift, but also reborn, and this was expressed in their relationship to the purchase of new items for their home, many of which involved the use of credit facilities. In Mrs Mitchell's words: 'Bought the washing-machine because for the money I was paying at the launderette and the inconvenience of going . . . that way you didn't have to pay anything until September and then pay so much and I would have gathered some money together.' Before doing so, they visited all the shops they could not afford (such as Selfridge's, John Lewis, and so on) in order to get ideas and see what was on offer and see where they could get what they wanted at the cheapest price. Part of their release from the recent trauma of their past was to create a new world of objects – a new home – around them and to take pleasure in their ability to do so.

Some miles away, in the borough of Camden, live the Selbys. Unlike the Mitchells, Mrs Selby hates going shopping, and would as soon do it by computer from home. 'I hate shopping . . . communal changing-rooms . . . I hate it . . . I mean, I'm not the most beautiful of shapes to start with . . . it's awful to constantly try things on and you feel you look like a sack of potatoes each time you look at yourself, it's not the most flattering of things to go through.' The Selbys live in a large 1960s council estate of 520 units. They occupy a two-bedroom maisonette with their two sons aged four and eight. Mr and Mrs Selby have very different backgrounds. He comes from an affluent Knightsbridge family and went to boarding-school until he was eighteen; a time he particularly enjoyed for the cricket he used to play. Although he passed seven 'O' levels his sporting interests got in the way of passing any 'A' levels. His father was the chairman of a timber company, but his son did not want to follow in his footsteps: 'It was too much to live up to.' He appears to have received no inheritance from his family, the estate passing to his two elder sisters, with whom he has no contact. His family also did not approve of his marriage. Mrs Selby comes from a Jewish/Welsh background, although her family moved to London when she was young. Her father was a cabinet-maker. Mr and Mrs Selby met while they worked at Harrods and he was playing on the cricket team and she on the netball team. He now works as a travel agent in the local area, while she is a qualified play leader.

The central focus of the Selbys' home life is television, particularly for Mr Selby. He spends his evenings and weekends at home in front of the TV: 'you sit and watch it, which is lazy as you can get . . . its a form of relaxation . . . once the children are in bed then time is irrelevant . . . it's a way of switching off'. But switching off from what? From work and work failures from the past (a failed newsagent business during the 1980s), from the childhood memories of the past and what could have been, from his own family relationships – his wife? Mr and Mrs Selby have very different tastes in programme viewing, and there are battles about who has or thinks they have the upper hand in what they watch. Mrs Selby says '. . . any news programme I'll watch, given the choice, given the chance . . . he just doesn't like the news . . . nearly all the current affairs I like and he just looks at me blankly'. Mr Selby prefers any sports programme while she is not keen on them. He notes that 'She tells me what to watch; but having said that, she'll still watch what I want to watch.' In a sense, Mrs Selby has decided to limit her individual interests so as to sustain the relation between her husband and herself. 'It's not that important, much as I want to watch it as needing my husband's company: we might not say a word to each other, but we're there together.'

During the period of fieldwork the Selbys bought a computer to help their eldest son build up his confidence, as he was suffering from a learning difficulty at school. In due course he has become very confident with the computer but more in the mode encouraged by his father, that of game-playing and as a form of 'switching-off relaxation'. Mrs Selby's interest in the machine as an educational tool has now been transformed into an extension of the television during evening viewing and at the weekend as a form of continual entertainment. Whereas the TV is the central focus of the main room, the computer now stands directly behind Mr Selby's TV chair. Mrs Selby is clearly concerned about the way the computer has been taken over as an aspect of entertainment as opposed to the educational focus she desires. But to achieve this end would entail transgressing a limit in her relationship with her husband that she values: being together with him on his terms.

Time at Work, Time at Home: Multiple Forms and Contexts of Appropriation

Whereas the Selbys have their TV and computer in clear view of all those who enter their home from outside, on the edge of greater London live the Dobbses, and Mrs Dobbs in particular is concerned that all the technologies in her home are as concealed as possible. She does not want exposed computers or VCRs in the sitting room. All technologies should be concealed in matching pieces of furniture (Queen Anne reproductions). Why is Mrs Dobbs so concerned with concealing the technology in the home? Her explicit desire is to create a 'homey' setting, where technology facilitates efficiency and comfort but does not appear intrusive or detract from the domesticity of the home. In many respects this is just the opposite of the situation created by Mr Dobbs's profession as a policeman and his relentless shiftwork, which constantly intrudes on any sort of continuity that can be sustained in their family relationships.

The Dobbses live in a three-bedroom detached home on a newly built development. They have three daughters, who all go to a local school. Mrs Dobbs works as an agency nurse, and both she and her husband left school at sixteen. She is planning to start training as a social worker.

Their current home is very important to both Mr and Mrs Dobbs. Having his own home was especially important to Mr Dobbs, and he says he emphasized this to Mrs Dobbs before they got married; they both worked towards this goal in due course. Having obtained the house, Mr Dobbs is little interested in the way it is decorated or the objects that it contains. Although the kitchen has not yet been redecorated, Mrs Dobbs has firm plans. She would like wooden fitted cupboards throughout, not only as actual cupboard space but also to contain the oven, the fridge, the microwave, and so forth. The effect, she hopes, will be uniformity, so that from the outside all that can be seen will be cupboards.

Her concern with the creation of a particular domesticity is related to the manner she separates home from work. When she leaves work at 5.00 p.m. Mrs Dobbs feels that her job is left entirely behind until she returns the next time. Mr Dobbs, however, has telephone calls from work when he is at home, and at times is called back into work or asked to work at the sports and social club, to which Mrs Dobbs objects. Both admit that they have 'no social life as such' because of Mr Dobbs's shiftwork.

Mr Dobbs's pattern of work varies from day to day and from week to week, so that there is little routine of uniformity in the time the family spends together. As a result the family seldom eat together, watch TV together or spend weekends together. Effort is made to make Sunday dinner a regular ritual; but again, the timing of this meal depends on Mr Dobbs's shifts. These two aspects of the Dobbses home life continually emerged during my fieldwork with them: the inability to achieve a regular pattern of family life owing to Mr Dobbs's shiftwork; and Mrs Dobbs's continual attempts to create a uniform image inside their home, hiding any sign of an intrusive technology that might indicate a relationship with the outside world.

Like the Dobbses, the Williams family, who also live on the edge of Greater London, have a problem with time. It is also connected with the boundary between work and home; but its resolution seems to be less defined around the achievement of a uniform household interior than around the capturing of the weekend as a seemingly alternative time. Mr and Mrs Williams are both pharmacists, and each works at a local hospital: Mr Williams in a full-time capacity, and Mrs Williams more recently on a part-time basis, having spent five years away from work after the birth of their two children, a daughter aged eleven and a son aged eight. The Williamses live in a three-bedroom semi-detached house.

Mrs Williams feels that Mr Williams often comes home from work too tired or too late to do anything in the house with her or the children. Mr Williams's perception is that he often comes home to find no one in. Mrs Williams takes the children swimming every Monday night, and she is also a member of the PTA at their school, is involved in the local church and goes to a keep-fit class once a week. The daughter goes to Guides, music practice and dance lessons, and the son also attends a music group and Cubs. As Mr Williams expresses it: 'I think it's very easy, too, to simplify it and say it's purely down to my job and my coming home late, but you've got to be fair . . . it's not as simple as that. These days life is busy for everybody, not just for me . . . you have commitments because of the children: every evening they've got something on.'

Mr Williams perceived the dilemma caused by his long hours at work and decided to invest in a computer and modem to do some of this work at home. He also found that if he was on call at the hospital and was phoned up about a particular drug he could, in turn, phone into the main computer from home and let them know its current status. But the computer in the home has created its own problems, as it can only be placed in the sitting-room, and it is not at all popular there with him or his wife: 'Well, its not very nice if you are sitting either side of it, you have to look round it to talk to the person sitting there.' The planned solution is to relocate the machine in the conservatory that is currently being built and will act as an office, playroom, and the like.

As with the Simons, with whom I opened this discussion, the computer has also become a site of a competitive and largely male-dominated culture. Mr Williams and his son, in particular, excel at using the various games on the computer. Mrs Williams uses the computer little, and her daughter plays the games but refuses to compete with her brother or father. This situation has clear parallels with the Simon case, the difference being that it has not explicitly been addressed by the family members. This is probably due to the fact that conflict has not emerged, as the daughter does not compete for access. In addition, the same aggravating factors have not become visible around the machine (such as 'natural'-born brothers versus adopted sisters).

The Simons and Williamses also bear comparison in another way. The Simon household oscillates between an urban life of intensely hard work and wide-ranging social relationships and a rural private and cut-off life (when sailing on their boat), where social relationships are at a minimum and where the long-term ideals of the nuclear family are perhaps realized in all their intensity (see Hirsch 1992:221). The Williamses as a family also attempt to achieve this image of unity; but instead of being part of a city/country dynamic they create a sort of alternative time. As Mrs Williams suggests: 'The weekend is a different time . . . because it's a time when we rush around and do different things we don't have to do . . . the weekends are a time when we are actually together.' And Mr Williams emphasizes this image by removing his wristwatch, 'in principle', at the weekend and often not shaving as well. Housework and shopping are also all done before the start of the weekend. If infringed upon by the need of Mr Williams to work on a Saturday, this sense of unity is in his words 'ruined', and can only be recaptured on the next occasion. Both Mr and Mrs Williams, then, gauge their relationship so as secure this alternative time of unity and avoid transgressing what they see as this important limit.

Conclusion: Re-siting Alienation and Appropriation, or Multiple Contexts and Relational Limits in English Home-making

For too long, as Miller (1987) argued, objects, material culture and consumption more generally have been sidelined by mainstream social anthropology. Over the last decade Miller has sought to re-position consumption and the object-form at the centre of social anthropological inquiry. Much of his argument centres on the fact that in the modern world institutions and objects are increasingly divorced from the original creation of those who use them. Given this condition much of our personal action and relations can be theorized to involve consumption as a form of appropriation, which has as its objective the transcendence of potential alienation; transcending the separation of creators from the objects of their creative processes (Miller 1987:62).

The key question, it would seem, is how this abstract formulation works itself out in practice. The 'Council Estate' paper (Miller 1988) argues that the alienating condition of this form of housing, most evident in the kitchen (Miller 1988:356), is subject to various degrees of appropriation. Miller's work drew insights from Strathern's synthetic account of Melanesian sociality, which culminated in *The Gender of the Gift* (Strathern 1988). Then, as also more recently (1997), Miller suggests that we are not really so different from Melanesians in the way we sustain relationships through material forms:

> Despite living in a capitalist, self consciously modern society, we still evolve new and complex forms of exchange and difference that employ objects to construct a changing but widely held sense of how people should act and of the kinds of relationships they should have with each other. As in Melanesia, our choice of goods is most often dominated by a focus upon relationships in the family – that is, kinship (Miller 1997:25).

Kinship certainly has this significance in both contexts; but are we dealing with forms of kinship that are comparable in this regard? One of the evident features of English kinship is the way it can appear and disappear depending on context: 'The person can be thought of both as an individual entity and as an entity enmeshed in social relationships' (Strathern 1993:155, emphasis removed). This is in turn related to the way contexts or domains are viewed as overlapping – as partially connected – and how the person her/himself is perceived as containing a multiplicity of overlapping roles. Melanesian kinship does *not* look like this.

Once we begin to recognize this 'merographic' (Strathern 1992) nature of English kinship we can better recognize the multiple contexts through which alienation and appropriation operate – sometimes in conjunction, but at other moments displaced. There is a difficulty in reconciling a general theory of cultural processes where alienation is an intrinsic feature, based on the writings of Hegel, Marx and Simmel, and detailed empirical studies that document the great variation in what persons actually experience as alienating (cf. Carrier 1990; Forty 1986). Making something one's own (at home) may not entail the overcoming of alienation in that context or with the objects therein. Rather, it may involve alienation in other, partially connected contexts, but displaced to the home context and its specific object domain.

Consider for a moment the Dobbses. Mrs Dobbs clearly found her husband's working life too often overlapping with the stricter division between home and work she maintained. Her 'appropriation' of the technologies in the home, explicitly concerned with creating a particular aesthetic, at the same time appears to be connected to a sense of erasing signs of connections with the outside world that continually interfere in their home life. If anything, it is the negative consequences for their home life of Mr Dobbs's shiftwork that she is attempting to appropriate, through creating a particular 'homey' effect. By contrast, Mr Green's technology account is an attempt to limit the number of technical objects he brings into the home, at once a financial decision and also a way of negotiating his individuality in relation to his wife's. It is she that finds the objects alienating in contrast to the artistic and literary contexts where she can feel at one with herself. Or again, the limits Mr Bell imposes on his wife at home (refusing to purchase a washing-machine) are partially connected to his own felt disempowerment at work.

In each of these examples, and as evidently in all the others, alienation and appropriation involve overlapping or multiple contexts and social relations negotiated within particular limits. ICTs, as I have suggested, both historically and in the present, sustain and elaborate this in explicit fashion (see Hirsch 1997). This may all be glossed as consumption. I would suggest, however, that the model of consumption as making things one's own (appropriation) in the context of alienation (Miller 1997:14–15) is too unidimensional and constricting.

Too great a focus on objects and material culture as the site of appropriation and alienation obscures the multiple contexts and relational limits of modern social life. Home-making and domestic consumption may be the setting where much of this unfolds. At the same time, though, the home is itself a part of an overlapping set of contexts, each context subject to differing degrees of alienation. Forms of appropriation worked out in the home operate in conjunction with the particular relational limits therein negotiated.[5] In short, domestic appropriation may be only partially connected with the home and what appear at first to be the objects of a home domain.

References

Bourdieu, P. (1984), *Distinction. A Social Critique of the Judgement of Taste*, London: Routledge and Kegan Paul.

Campbell, C. (1987), *The Romantic Ethic and the Spirit of Modern Consumerism*, Oxford: Blackwell.

Carrier, J. (1990) 'The Symbolism of Possession in Commodity Advertising', *Man*, 25:693–706.

Colley, L. (1996), *Britons. Forging the Nation 1707–1837*, London: Vintage.

Davidoff, L. and Hall, C. (1987), *Family Fortunes. Men and Women of the English Middle Class, 1780–1850*, London: Hutchinson.

Forty, A. (1986), *Objects of Desire. Design and Society 1750–1980.* London: Thames and Hudson.

Hirsch, E. (1992), 'The Long Term and the Short Term of Domestic Consumption: An Ethnographic Case Study', in R. Silverstone and E. Hirsch (eds), *Consuming Technologies. Media and Information in Domestic Spaces*, London: Routledge.

—— (1997), 'New technologies and domestic consumption', in C. Geraghty and D. Lusted (eds), *The Television Studies Book*, London: Edward Arnold.

McKendrick, N., Brewer, J. and Plumb, J. (1983), *The Birth of a Consumer Society. The Commercialization of Eighteenth-century England*, London: Hutchison.

Miller, D. (1987), *Material Culture and Mass Consumption*, Oxford: Blackwell.

—— (1988), 'Appropriating the State on the Council Estate', *Man*, 23: 353–72.

—— (1994), *Modernity. An Ethnographic Approach. Dualism and Mass Consumption in Trinidad*, Oxford: Berg.

5. And what are now *multiple home* contexts, following divorce, remarriage, and so on, which increasingly form part of the experience of English family life (cf. Simpson 1994).

—— (1997), 'Consumption and its Consequences', in H. Mackay (ed.), *Consumption and Everyday Life*, London: Sage.

Simpson, R. (1994), 'Bringing the "Unclear" Family into Focus: Divorce and Re-marriage in Contemporary Britain', *Man*, 29: 831–51.

Strathern, M. (1988), *The Gender of the Gift. Problems with Women and Problems with Society in Melanesia*, Berkeley: University of California Press.

—— (1992), *After Nature. English Kinship in the Late Twentieth Century*, Cambridge: Cambridge University Press.

—— (1993), 'Regulation, Substitution and Possibility', in J. Edwards, S. Franklin, E. Hirsch, F. Price, and M. Strathern (eds), *Technologies of Procreation. Kinship in the Age of Assisted Conception*, Manchester: Manchester University Press.

New Identities and the Local Factor — or When is Home in Town a Good Move?

Sandra Wallman

Introduction

Beginning with a definition of 'home' as a proxy for 'belonging some-where', this chapter explores conditions of belonging in urban settings and sets out to account for variations in peoples' construction of the urban home. Two questions direct the approach. One is cultural: Is home in the city a good or bad thing ? The other is structural, or better, systematic: Which kind of city-ness do [which] people identify with, feel good about, and make a home in ?

A contrast with not-urban – i.e. rural – places, is implied by these questions, as are blanket all-positive/all-negative evaluations of town or country. At this level the contrasts are very crude, and all we can be sure of is that there is no consistency in the way the preference swings – whether it will be cities good: countryside bad or vice versa.[1] In any case, cultural attitudes of this generality are difficult to pin down in the field and somewhat beside the point: my concern here is not to make good and bad categories, but to map conditions that affect the way living in the city is experienced, and might account for the way a particular

---

1. One example of two 'cultures' applying the good/bad labels quite oppositely is provided by the contrast between traditional English anti-urbanism and traditional Italian contempt for the (literally) uncivilized rural person. It shows in eighteenth- and nineteenth-century portraits of the gentry – the English pose against green countryside, the Italians in ancient stone towns. The point is not that Italian towns are lovelier, but that the setting so rarely matched the subject's real home.

181

home-in-town is evaluated – noticing always that not everyone experiences/ evaluates the 'same' place in the same way.

Since 'home', as I conceive it, is compounded of identities of place and people, my argument depends heavily on assumptions about the relation between them – i.e. between the *identity of people* (as groups or individuals) and the *identity of the urban space* in question. This relationship is such that the identity of a/the city as home has to be double-sided – one side being how it is identified; the other how people identify themselves in or with it. Because these are not once-for-all identifications, it follows that no city setting is a good (or bad) home for everybody; and that the measure of its good (or bad)-ness likewise varies. My interest focuses on these variations – on which differences make a difference to how Londoners feel about where they (and others) live – how they rate the place and feel about moving into or within it; whether they identify themselves with it or by it; on what grounds they consider it a good or bad home.

In some ways London is a very particular example. It has been described as a collection of villages, each with its own style and locus of belonging, and each firmly distinguished from the next. Indeed, some Londoners are less daunted by going to other countries than to other parts of the city, and many never cross the river between north and south. These habits of movement underwrite the city's famous 'manor orientations'. No doubt the Local Government Act of 1965, which expanded the scope and altered the character of the town halls responsible for the city's residents, also affected its village-y identities;[2] but it is crucial to my argument that different parts of the metropolis vary as much as they ever did in their capacity to adapt to change and to absorb newcomers.

Unique as London is in some respects, these variations say something about 'home' in other cities too. My assumption is that the logic of identity is nowhere haphazard and (so) that the explanation of anomalies emerging out of research in London will have wider relevance. One thing to be explained is the fact that local identity may be publicly more salient than ethnicity, even in a markedly polyglot area. Another is the gap between outsider and insider, official and personal views of the same geographical home.

2. With the Local Government Act (1965), units of London that had served as administrative centres, each with its own Mayor and Town Hall, were amalgamated into nine much larger new boroughs: Battersea became part of London Borough of Wandsworth, Bow of the London Borough of Tower Hamlets, and so on. There is no space here to explore the effect of this on local efficacy and the qualities of the urban home, but the prescience of Jacobs (1961) is striking.

Two separate studies provide the case material for this argument. They are developments of the same research trajectory, but are different in scope, objective and method. The first study was a situation analysis of events sparked by official threat to the community life and continuity of a small polyglot street – Pearman Street – in the south London borough of Lambeth. The history of this short period in its long life is especially rich in evidence for the many factors affecting the symbolic construction of a particular place as home or worthy-to-be-home, and it nicely illustrates the epidemic yearning to belong felt by those outside the idealized home that Pearman Street, with all its material shortcomings, came to represent. Notably, it provides a sharp example of global preoccupations being imposed on localized concepts of home.

This study raised issues for a much larger project, which provides the basis for the second case. The focus here is on variations in the structural (i.e. infrastructural) conditions of belonging set by different kinds of urban place, and constituting different kinds of urban home. It makes a systematic comparison of livelihood in two old style[3] inner London boroughs – namely Battersea, in south London, and Bow in the East End. They were then[4] similar in being dominantly working-class,[5] low-income areas with a sprinkling of 'gentry' and a visible ethnic mix, but with different economic and identity styles – i.e. they were identified in official and unofficial classifications as different kinds of places, and different kinds of people found/felt themselves at home in each.

Following a short statement of the general approach in the second section of the chapter, the case-studies are presented in turn in the third section – first Pearman Street, and then Battersea/Bow. A framework for their combined discussion is provided in the fourth section by four 'Signposts', each signalling an analytic proposition that one or the other case demonstrates – viz: *boundaries* (and the logic of exclusion and belonging in urban places); *localism* (in the sense of identification with or by area of residence); *betterment* (as a measure of whether 'this place' is safer, richer, more home-like, 'more me' in relation to the last place I was in and to my expectations of this one); and *compression* (which refers to the experience or the outcome of cultures' being 'brought up against each other' in variegated settings). The conclusion in the fifth section brings the issues and the evidence back to the starting-point.

3. That is, pre-1965. See Note 2.
4. The period referred to is 1975–85.
5. And in the extent to which the class 'boxes' were coming unstuck! See Boundaries below.

Identity Options and the Choice of 'Home'

The classic distinction between structure and organization[6] underpins the perspective of this chapter in two ways. The first is that each city setting provides a framework of options that put at least an outer limit on how individuals or groups can make a livelihood in it. They may 'choose' in some sense among the options offered, but they cannot take up options that are not there. Of course not everybody uses the same geographic setting in the same way, but inevitably the 'conditions of possibility' of each person or group (as in Bourdieu 1977) are both enhanced and limited by the 'capability' of the place itself (Wallman 1997). The ice-cream parlour offers a ready metaphor for option and choice in this sense: you may want strawberry flavour, and have prepared yourself to eat only strawberry, but if strawberry is not on offer, it is not an option.

This constraint applies very obviously to the economic aspects of livelihood, but 'getting by' in the city, especially in the city, depends also on the skilful management of non-material resources – identity among them. And just as you cannot choose to use job skills in a local system that has no market for them, so ethnicity (or any other locus of belonging) is not utilizable in every city setting, or for every purpose in it.

Notice that this observation refers to *kinds* of, or *loci* of, identity – not to its presence or absence. It would be hard for any long-standing city-dweller to have no sense of being local at all. The regular residents of ordinary urban neighbourhoods get to know each other by sight. They meet shopping, standing at the bus stop or walking in the street, and over time they learn the public habits and timetables of people they do not know by name and probably never visit where they live. Recognizing and being recognized by others create a sense of belonging in inner-city areas just as much as they do in a rural village,[7] although the potential for turning 'traffic relations' into action sets or sources of support may be more crucial to survival in town (Hannerz 1980).[8]

My second angle on city settings is that they are also social systems, made up of arenas of interaction and opportunity that operate as sub-

6. Structure being the framework of social, economic or conceptual options available; organization the pattern of choices taken among them (Firth 1951; Barth 1966). Note thatthe model does not depend on this selection's being made consciously or deliberately. We are talking social process here, and individual human purpose is a small part of it. Among the constraints on it are the definitions and purposes of other groups or individuals.

7. This is why difference in the density and reach of networks, as between Battersea-and Bow-type systems (below) , is significant to styles of local identity.

8. The Pearman Street example is prototypical of the 'conversion' that Hannerz describes.

systems of the whole, and that combine to make up its social style. Systems are by definition in movement, and/but controlled by some logical principle. Social and/or urban systems likewise are perpetually in process, and/but we believe the flux to be intelligible. In anthropology specifically, the logic of systems: sub-systems transformations is covered by the credo of context – viz : the meaning of an action, relationship or resource depends on other-things-happening; and (therefore) its value, effect, etc., is dependent on a particular context and will change when it changes. Thus the home-ness (homeliness? hominess?) of any cityscape is determined as much by the urban system that provides its context as by the original cultures and motivations of the people living in it; and it may be fundamentally altered, whether for good or ill, by changes happening at any level in the system of which it is a part.

The next section summarizes the ethnographic materials: first the story of 'Housing Action' in Pearman Street, in the densely urban area around Waterloo Station;[9] then the comparison of Battersea and Bow, also rundown parts of inner London, and used here to represent opposite ideal types of urban structure. I have already indicated that the case- studies, though intellectually linked, were unlike in methodology, scope and method. But nevertheless the cases complement each other, in that they demonstrate different ways of evaluating urban places, and different dimensions of the appeal of those places as 'home'.

It is also important that the ethnographic events of Pearman Street, Battersea and Bow, summarized in the next section, all happened in the same handful of years and share a single historical-political context. In that period, English media discourse about 'home' was dominated by race and recession (see Wallman 1981), and although these were also facts of livelihood for many Londoners, their significance was inevitably not the same at both levels.

Case Studies

Pearman Street

The Pearman Street residents' defence of 'home' was sparked by the threat of the compulsory purchase and demolition of their houses and fuelled by the 1974 Housing Act. Parliament's intention, with this

---

9. The story was first told in Wallman 1975 . The fact that Waterloo Station is now the terminus for Eurostar trains to the Continent has again changed values and evaluations of Pearman Street.

legislation, was to prevent the indiscriminate application of sledgehammer solutions to inner-city problems: '. . . local authorities should place at the centre of their policy a commitment to flexible, co-ordinated and continuous renewal, . . . in ways which avoid the disruption of, indeed provide for the enhancement of, established communities' (Circular 13/75, para. 5). On the face of it, central government was showing a proper sense of the times: by 1974 the generalized destruction and redevelopment of inner-city 'homes', so common in industrial cities in the 1960s, began to be outmoded through the knowledge that it was too often of greater social and economic cost than benefit. The same round of legislation provided for funds to be set aside so that local government Housing Action Areas might be established in 'strong communities' needing 'only' rehabilitation of their housing stock. For reasons that are not relevant to this argument, these intentions were quite quickly contradicted by the halving of central government funds for the rehabilitation of housing in London. The fact that funds for demolition and redevelopment were not similarly cut was justification for even the most conservationist of local government councils to deal with its inner city by razing it to the ground and starting again: where conditions are bad and resources are allocated to improve them, it is doing nothing that is unacceptable. In any case, the notion that the case for demolition is made by a simple preponderance of technically unfit dwellings is most likely to achieve the rapid and visible results that an elected government body thrives on – unless and until protest from parts of its constituency begins to be heard.

Pearman Street, in the period of these events, comprised eighty-eight households[10] distributed over thirty-four three-storey Victorian houses standing in two short terraces in north Lambeth. The residents are[11] of many racial, ethnic and language backgrounds (Table 7.1) and cover the full age range: more than half are in the 'economically active' years (eighteen to sixty); close to a fifth are over sixty; and over a quarter are under the age of seventeen – this last item giving it a demographic structure more reminiscent of a developing country than of 'normal' urban Europe. Many residents have 'always' lived there; a few moved in last year (Table 7.2). The very high proportion of family households (Table 7.3) is a factor in the general hominess of the street: in classic urban sociology, 'high familism' has long been recognized to make for 'good' urban environments (Jacobs 1961). In terms of familism, length of residence and commitment to the place (Table 7.4 – discussed below) it

---

10. Six households could not be contacted. Some tables therefore show N=82.
11. This is again the ethnographic present: it does not indicate the time of writing.

Table 7.1 Origins of Residents (self-defined)

Austria	1	Greek Cyprus	2	Latvia	4	South	1
Barbados	1	Guyana	1	Nigeria	3	St Lucia	1
Colombia	1	Hong Kong	1	Northern	1	Spain	1
				Ireland			
Cuba	1	India	1			Turkish	2
						Cyprus	
Eire	3	Italy	1	Pakistan	1	Trinidad	1
England	24	Kenya	1	Portugal	1	Uganda	1
Ghana	1	Lambeth	35	Russia	3	Wales	1

Base 88   Mixed 7   Total count 95   Households

Table 7.2 Length of Residence by Tenure

Time in Years	Owner-Occupiers	Unfurnished	Unfurnished Controlled	Furnished	All	
Less than 1	–	–	–	8	8	
1–5	3	10	–	14	27	
6–10	5	4	–	4	13	
11–20	6	2	6	3	17	
21–30	4	–	6	–	10	
31–40	–	–	7	–	7 ⎫	15
41–50	–	–	2	–	2 ⎬	per
Over 50	1	–	3	–	4 ⎭	cent
Totals	19	16	24	29	88	

(Base 88)

does not seem to matter whether people own their properties or the furniture in them.[12]

In 1975 this polyglot collection of householders got together to defend their home street against the 'compulsory purchase order' (CPO) served on it by Lambeth Council two years earlier. Some of the better-informed residents communicated the implications of the CPO to their neighbours: once (compulsorily) bought up in the way the law provided, the street's buildings would be pulled down and its residents dispersed, perhaps to

12. This came as a surprise to some observers who expected only owner-occupiers would be seriously concerned with maintaining the buildings and the fabric of the community.

Table 7.3 Familism by Tenure

Persons in Household	Owner-Occupiers	Unfurnished	Unfurnished Controlled	Furnished	All (per cent)
Singles	8	0	9	15	32 (39)
Couples	3	8	8	9	28 (34)
Small Family	3	7	4	2	16 (20)
Large or Extended Family	5	0	0	1	6 (7)
Totals	19	15	21	27	82 (100)

(Base 82)

better accommodation, in other places. Their opposition was timely because the new Housing Act had just come into being.[13] The Act gave them the option of a Public Enquiry, during which the case caught the eyes of local press and national media and brought little Pearman Street the kind of attention no one had anticipated.[14]

Its 'Housing Action' was ultimately successful: Lambeth Council (the local government authority) changed its plans for the place. The CPO was revoked, the bulldozers deflected and the community maintained. But the public imagination was largely unmoved by the David and Goliath dimensions of the story, and focused instead on the 'polyglot harmony' of 'Lambeth's United Nations' (*South London Press*, 18 March 1975). One high-circulation national paper (*The Daily Mail*), under the photograph sub-caption 'like one big happy family', quoted an owner-occupier, the father of nine children, who described it as 'unique . . . something really special'; and an elderly tenant who had lived in the same house for seventeen years 'and never dreamed of moving. . . . People are so friendly, so tolerant – it's a street full of good neighbours.' The item identified the speakers as Nigerian and Italian – as though national origin were the key to their views.

13. Also by the fact that two other CPOs had recently been revoked by the Minister.
14. The local Residents' Association, with input from this author, made a survey to prepare for the Public Enquiry. Some of its results are used here. The process of designing and doing the survey communicated the issues to residents and focused their opposition to the CPO.

Table 7.4 Number of Households wishing to Stay or Leave according to Tenure

	Owner-Occupiers	Unfurnished	Unfurnished Controlled	Furnished	All	
Stay IN ANY EVENT	18	5	5	18	46	83 per cent
Stay CONDITIONAL upon repairs, improvements, etc.	–	7	9	6	22	
LEAVE for new Council Accommodation	1	2	6	2	11	17 per cent
UNDECIDED	–	1	1	1	3	
TOTALS	19 (23%)	15 (18%)	21 (26%)	27 (33%)	82 (100%)	
No Contact		(1)	(3)	(2)	(6)	

The last man's affirmation that in long years of residence he had 'never dreamed of moving' is a nice proxy for identification with 'this place' as a good or good enough home environment in London. The Residents' Association survey extended the question to all households in the street. It is important that it was designed in a way that allowed people to complain about the material state of their flats or houses without compromising what they felt about the street.[15]

Table 7.5 Amenity Available and Tenure

Amenity	Owner-occupied (per cent)	Unfurnished (per cent)	Furnished
Sole use of bath in bathroom	80	5	13
Sole use of bath elsewhere	10	7	3
Shared use of bath	–	2	30
No bath	10	86	54
	100	100	100
Shared WC	–	18	33
Shared kitchen	–	–	33
No hot water	–	49	7

(Base: 88)

The results confirmed *that from the point of view of people who live in it* , the desirability of Pearman Street as a place to call home was not measured by grades of housing amenity (compare Tables 7.4 & 7.5). Given the state of housing in the street at that time it is unlikely that all the 46 per cent of residents who said they would prefer to *stay in any event* had nothing in the physical fabric of their homes that they would have wished to improve. In effect, the majority of those who elected to stay made their choice irrespective of, or at least without reference to, material conditions.

Similarly for cultural diversity: here the contrast between insiders' and outsiders' views is profound. Public interest in Pearman Street focused only around the fact that it has *both* a strong sense of community and an

15. This was in contrast to the logic of Lambeth Council's pre-CPO opinion check, which allowed for one Yes/No response to a question like – Would you rather move to a nice dry house somewhere else, or continue living here with conditions as bad as they now are?

unusually mixed population. And because this is[16] a combination that some of us would wish, others cannot countenance, and still others consider impossible outside the educated middle class, all outside interests fastened on diversity as the crucial feature of Pearman Street.

For the residents it never was. In the context of liking or disliking the street and specifying reasons for staying or leaving (*Why I want to stay . . . Why I want to leave . . .* as free responses in the survey), diversity/ homogeneity was not the issue either way. No one so much as mentioned the class, colour or strange habits of their neighbours. We may note that some of the householders wanting to leave were remembered as making anti-black statements *at some time* (one held immigrants responsible for her long wait for a council flat), and that those wanting to stay tended to use unifying phrases – *very friendly; of one mind; a real neighbourhood; community feeling; like a family* – in describing their commitment to it. But since we know neither the context nor the weight of each statement (nor, indeed, how much it was influenced by outsiders' narratives) it would be wrong to impute consistently opposite sentiments to Leavers and Stayers.

As is confirmed by comparing Battersea and Bow (below), the style of any urban system appeals to some more than to others; and there are more than racist explanations for not feeling at home with diversity. Not being used to it is one. More simply, it is possible that those who are socially comfortable – who feel at home – will perceive their neighbours to be like themselves, whatever their ethnic (etc.) attributes, while those who wish to leave – who do not *for whatever reason* feel at home – will look for the cause of their frustration and will perceive 'otherness'. By this logic diversity *as such* cannot account for the presence or absence of community feeling, the strength or weakness of the pull towards home.

Battersea vs Bow

The second case compares Battersea, another area of inner south London (and not, as it happens, very far from Pearman Street) with Bow, a slice of the so-called East End. The initial Battersea research, provoked in some part by the conundrum of Pearman Street, set out to identify contexts in which ethnicity counts or does not count in the management of urban livelihood. Our finding was that it counted very little. Since the next aim was to find out which factors accounted for this demonstrably a-ethnic ethos, specific parameters of the Bow area, among those parts of London

16. Sc. then was . . .

widely acknowledged to 'notice' ethnic difference and to value ethnic organization, were set against their counterparts in Battersea. The idea was to see what might be learned from experiment-by-comparison.

The population of Battersea is[17] mixed in a way that leaves plenty of scope for ethnic solidarity or discrimination; but exclusivity has never had much bearing on the business of livelihood. No immigrant population has ever been narrowly associated with one industry or industrial role, and there is no evidence of ethnic niches or ethnic-specific patterns of employment. While it has 'always' been polyglot by London standards, equally Battersea has 'always' measured outsider status by newness to or non-involvement in the area rather than by colour or foreign origin. On the one side, in-migrants assimiliate with an enthusiasm that indicates that the practical or affective value of local belonging outweighs the resource potential of their ethnic or regional origins. On the other, the pre-resident hosts, whether native-born or earlier immigrants, seem ready to share their urban home with newcomers. In boundary terms, the local system is open to anyone who chooses to make a home in it, and in-migration is limited only by the preferences of the incomer. And since this gives it a relatively a-ethnic style,[18] a Battersea-type system will appeal most to home-seekers who do not have or do not choose to maximize ethnic-specific resources.[19]

Now by comparison: a (relatively) closed system would constitute a more exclusionist and more ethnicity-enhancing home. Belonging to it is more likely to be ascribed than achieved, and entry will be less negotiable.

The East End of London qualifies on all these counts. In it, Bow is especially appropriate to our purposes.[20] Again, the local style is of long standing. In the nineteenth century and for some part of the twentieth, it was the centre of London's dockland, clothing and furniture industries.

17. Use of the present tense in this section should be read as 1975–85. (see Note 3 above). Ethnographic and other details about Battersea are set out at length in Wallman 1982, 1984a.

18. The term a-ethnic, in place of the more common 'non-ethnic' or 'anti-ethnic' formulations, underlines the fact that ethnicity, in this kind of context, is beside the point – not that people deny, oppose or are committed to trying to set it aside.

19. The point here is that there can be different kinds of ethnics in the ethnic mix. Some build their economic and social organization on their origins, others around individual or narrowly familistic interests. By this token Jews and Asians, who more often fit the former type, are less 'modern' (post-modern?) than West Indians, who usually fit the latter. These different types are (were) demographically dominant in Bow and Battersea respectively. The point is not taken up in this chapter, but it is substantiated by census data and implied in other studies.

20. For the reasoning behind its selection over other East End areas, see Wallman 1984b.

These made it an important locus of employment opportunity and dominated its industrial structure, even beyond its economic heyday. But while, over the years, new people of many races, religions and nationalities came to make their homes in it, no Battersea-like mix ever occurred in Bow. Newcomers have 'always' tended to settle in homogeneous population blocks, and ethnic boundaries to coincide with geographic lines – one side of a road, one housing block, one unit being almost entirely white, the other no less dominantly black. Here the local 'home' style is exclusivist.

What makes it so different?

Local dependence on a single industry means that, when the single industry dies, the families of people defined by it move out, blocks at a time, leaving space for replacement blocks of in-migrants, who take it up because their resources or preferences are different. However limited the choice, these local options are better *for them* than for the out-migrants, and presumably better also, in some way, than the options they left behind.

Where the natives and earlier settlers are largely white and the new immigrants largely black, colour, work culture and length of residence vary together. But because only colour difference is visible, the pattern strikes the eye as a version of racial or even racist segregation. By the logic of the argument I am exploring, however, the apparent ethnic exclusivity of home and housing might 'just' be evidence of structural homogeneity – in turn explained by overlap of the components of the urban system. Whatever the case, the effect is that this style of urban system is hard to penetrate and hard to change.

The contrast between the two areas as urban systems is schematic, and the figures imply the opposite styles of home that are entailed. In the matter of *boundary styles*, Figure 7.1 suggests that the Battersea (Type A) structure is relatively open because there is no neat overlap of the rings representing various resource domains. The A-type incomer arrow demonstrates that entry into the local system can be achieved by crossing only one of its constituent boundaries. In practice, access to, say, housing confers the right to local status – largely without reference to the ethnic origin, etc., of the in-migrant. Residents do not live and work and play in one ghetto-like area or identify with a set of peers defined by any fixed set of 'tribal' characteristics.

On the same figure, the Bow (Type B) version shows the various domains overlaid. Local residents are likely to work in closely bounded groups, and the people who control, say, information about jobs will tend also to control access to other resources. The incomer arrow here shows that belonging is achieved only by breaching all the boundaries together.

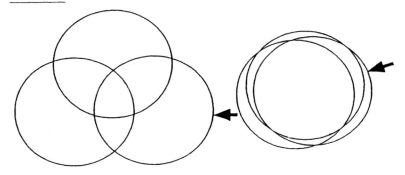

Figure 7.1 Local systems, with boundary overlap, showing implications for entry by arrow.

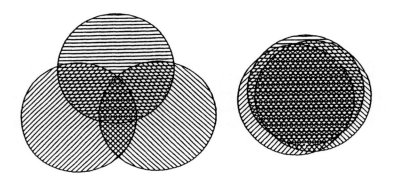

Figure 7.2 Local systems, network effect, showing more and less density and reach of local connections.

Figure 7.2 spells out the *network effect* of these boundary patterns and brings the contrast down to the level of interaction. At the heart of the more open Type A (Battersea) system, there is a core of many-stranded relationships[21] providing the focus of localist identity, but wider and more diffuse connections are included in the constellation of the system. In the Type B (Bow) version, local resources are nested in one overlapping system. This tighter localism is probably cosier overall, but imples also the constraints of a (relatively) closed system: both the possibility of its

21. This contrast echoes the classic distinction between uniplex and multiplex relationships. It is noteworthy, however, that the latter have been considered characteristic of *rural* settings.

adapting to economic or demographic change, and the scope for incomers to determine their own style of being at home are much more limited.

Signposts

Old Boundaries, New Identities

Since a traditional concern of anthropology has been the identification of social-cultural places, the fluidity of local-ness has always been at odds with our professional aspirations. Societies were identified with whole and integrated cultures, each a bounded universe of meanings. This image may have been useful for politicians and for social research, but probably never matched the way things were. (It is never easy to distinguish models from facts.) Either way, traditional classifications fail to convey the degree to which identity of places, cultures or individuals is compromised by movement across time and space. Increasingly, identity – as we see it, study it and experience it – is better understood as a search than as a quality of places or persons; and as the editors of this volume put it, migration becomes the essence of the age.

The migrations at stake are not 'just' population movements. They are cognitive as well as physical. Along with high rates of movement between and within countries, into and inside towns, there is an increasing awareness of the *possibility* of movement. Alongside this, mass media images, no doubt reflecting the mixture of people in many cities, sharpen ordinary citizens' 'awareness of cultural forms which are not primarily theirs' (Paine 1992) and bring increasing numbers of people up against the realities of difference and flux (see *Compression* below).

At every level, boundaries and identities are not what they were. Not only do these trends make us re-examine the image of individuals as members of fixed and separate societies, cultures, social classes, ethnic groups – or, indeed, of a single identified city. They also provoke new ways of thinking about 'home' – and about good and bad city-ness.[22]

Start with class. In the past, the realities of socio-economic life were such that class categories had the quality of boxes determining what people would do, and where, on the ground and in aspiration, they could go (Figure 7.3). Now even the non-affluent are, in both these senses, more mobile and less likely to define themselves by the old constraints (Figure 7.4). To position a new acquaintance it is no longer useful to ask

---

22. The future best city will be the one that gives individuals most scope to express selves which cannot be – will not be – boxed in by any one of the old identity categories. See Wallman 1993.

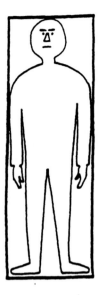

Figure 7.3 The past: boxed in by class categories. ('What do you do?')

Figure 7.4 The present, up side: removal of the old constraints. ('What are you into?')

'What are you?' or even 'What do you do?'. The crucial question is more often some version of the old hippie query 'What are you into?' Loosely translated, the question asks which of the many contexts of your life defines you best. Existentially as well as physically, identity is becoming something that has to be achieved – sought and found – in activities and places that may only be recognized as appropriate by being there. The down side of options is the need to make choices, and the preoccupation (at least in Euro-American discourse) with identity issues, the search for roots and new definitions of 'home' suggest that we are uneasy – lost? – as well as joyful outside the old boxes (Figure 7.5).

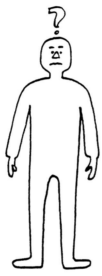

Figure 7.5 The present, down side: preoccupation with identity issues. ('Where are my roots?')

As for socio-economic status, so for ethnic groups. Ethnicity has never been about culture difference as such. We know it as the sense of difference occurring when members of a cultural, tribal, racial or national group interact with non-members. Each needs a 'them' to feel like part of an 'us'. And to exercise the urban theme, the facts of migration are such that an encounter with 'not-us' is many times more likely to happen in a city.[23]

23. Since demographic mix is common in urban places, this has, on one level, 'always' been the case. But the new intensity of 'globalization' and 'compression' processes entails that, at the cultural level, the city experience involves increasingly more encounters than it used to.

The essential point is that *real* differences between people are no more (and no less) than *potential* identity-markers which will be mobilized only where *that* particular difference suits the purpose and fits the context of the occasion. This is as it has always been. But now we are struck by how often that purpose is individually focused, and by how far the separate self will go to negotiate being 'at home'.

Some commentators read this as undermining the fundamental groupness of ethnicity. Tambiah considers it to have superseded the value of class and nation as bases for the mobilization of political action (1989: 336), but in a modern (post-modern?) form. This entails that ethnic boundaries may no longer be as Barth (1969) described them – maintained 'through structured and stable interactions . . . guided by a "systematic set of rules". Instead [Tambiah] sees (and foresees) flux; and [sometimes] violence in the flux' (Paine 1992: 195). It is the flux, not the diversification, which is at issue. Along similar lines, Hannerz's (1985, 1992) sense is that the world system, rather than creating cultural homogeneity on a global scale – the much-vaunted global home – can only replace one diversity with another. More to our point, he sees the new diversity as being based more on interrelations and less on distinctiveness than the old.

All of us agree that neither the experience nor the expression of identity is uniform. The sense of belonging/being at home/having 'arrived', here specifically in an urban place (and no matter from which starting-point) depends heavily on the role of local differences within the global whole: on local sub-systems within the global system. Again Hannerz: starting with 'the premise that the world is one [we then must] . . . proceed to examine the flow and management of meaning' across the global whole (1985: 3). And: 'Much of the density and complexity of meaning systems as we encounter them today is the product of the interplay between local cultures and the expansive influences of the world system' (1985: 15).

This quotation gives the impression that the concept of local culture is unproblematic. In categorical opposition to 'the global', its meaning is clear. But (again) for other than ideal-typical purposes, there is much to be said about the variability of concepts of localness – how far the local extends, how much it shifts, who is and is not qualified to be 'a local' at all. A short detour on localism makes the point for our present purposes.

Localism

Most simply, localism can be defined as identity with a localized space. It implies both the sense of belonging and the right to belong, and is both cause and effect of the relation between people and place. Consistent with the kind of people:place dynamic signalled at the start, we can add that localism works in both directions: i.e. the local at once defines/ identifies its adherents and is defined/identified by them.

Three other observations of the local make a sequence which is germane to this discussion of home. Viz: ethnicity, work and locality are common alternative foci of group identity in the present world; they seem to operate in zero sum relation – more of one, less of the other; there is something in each local system that inclines it towards one or the other. In the Battersea:Bow contrast (above), the inclination towards or away from identity with origin and locality begins to be intelligible.

One aspect of localism is the matter of how much people simply spend time in, do things in, their area of residence as opposed to anywhere else. There could be maps made of movement in and out of a district or an urban neighbourhood. These patterns depend on infrastructure to some extent, and to some extent on the siting and organization of work: some areas have more people in them in the daytime than at night; others are 'dormitory suburbs' for workers employed away from the place they live.

But the mere fact that belonging cannot be read off any of these demographic patterns *as such* makes it plain that localism is not the same as just being there. It is a function of how much local people identify themselves by the area, how they visualize it, how loyal they are to its needs or peculiarities. And these identifications vary to the extent that they are sensitive to other things happening in each person's life – the distribution of their kin, the support of friends – as much as on the qualities and structures of the area itself.

Betterment?

Once the emphasis has shifted from absolute to relative perceptions of a city's good-ness there is room to enter the logic of personal circumstances into the equation. The way a move to, or a home in, town is evaluated depends (also) on the availability and recognition of alternatives to going/ being there, and on the actual consequences, intended and unintended, of arrival. Only if a migration[24] constituted progress towards the better meeting of material needs *and* a greater sense of autonomy and self-esteem could it be counted wholly successful.[25] These are not necessarily

24. Throughout this section, the terms *migration, migrant,* etc. refer to migrants/ migrations of identity as well as geographic movement. Similarly *home* is about both identity and place.

25. This observation, and the discussion following, comes from the *Introduction* to Wallman 1977.

complementary processes. Commonly, and not just in cities, both objectives are compromised and neither is achieved: with any move the home-seeker stands to lose as well as gain.

There are different kinds of loss involved, each with implications for the way people feel about where they and others are. The first is loss relative to aspiration: What did the migrant hope to achieve by changing home? The intensity of this version will vary with the closeness of fit between aspirations, the migrant's resource endowment, and how well his/her resources suit the new 'place' – although the ability to refocus aspiration on to more attainable goals might ease it. A second refraction of loss is relative to the gain of others. This one is politically very salient: the fact that I am materially better off than I was in my previous home is plain gain, but it could still be soured by the greater wealth of people I now live with – by migrants who have made it better, say, whose very success is evidence of my (relative) failure. The third knot in the migrant's double bind is the most insoluble. It is the one in which gain of one sort *directly* entails loss of another. Thus, most of us want to keep up with the Joneses *and* to distinguish ourselves from them; to give our children more options than we have had *and* to see them choose as we would have chosen. And most of all we want to enjoy material home improvements *and* to remain independent, authentic – i.e. to feel at home.

At the level of experience, it is said, all change is loss, and all loss can be understood as a kind of grief (Marris 1974). Thus it is probably inevitable that losses in other-than-material dimensions should be felt by any group enjoying better or worse material standards of life than they were brought up to expect: it is enough that the authentic way of doing things has been breached by change. It is in this sense that the established residents of an urban area suffer the changes brought by migration no less than the migrants themselves.

But the perceived effect of such change depends on the extent to which it can be incorporated into the identities and meanings of the past – on what Marris calls 'the balance between continuity, growth and loss' (1974:20). It is difficult to know what this balance will be before it happens, but Marris distinguishes the three kinds of change that make it up. The first offers no threat to continuity: the new is 'better but like' the old. The second requires adaptation and (so) growth, but still maintains continuity since 'the familiar . . . is incorporated within a broader understanding or range of interests . . . [and does not] threaten the integrity of what has already been learned' – or, indeed, of previous identity or identities. The third constitutes 'a crisis of discontinuity' and the 'discrediting of familiar assumptions' – a loss so fundamental that it must provoke either radical innovation or despair.

These many elements are integral to the search for home, both as a material place and a non-material goal. They go some way towards explaining gain/loss ratios of the migration experience, and positive/ negative evaluations of arrival points along the way. At one level it is all about 'push' and 'pull': *How wanting was the previous home? How attractive is the new one?* At another level it is a question of fit: *How well do the migrant's economic and identity resources, carried as baggage down the road or across the world, match the options offered by the new place?* The earlier short detour on localism set out identity implications of the scope and structure of an urban setting. Moving gradually closer to the local arena in which these influences and fluidities are acted out, the next section uses the concept of cultural *compression* to round out the logic of situations in which people and place interact.

Compression[26]

Like localism, cultural compression has both demographic and experiential dimensions. On the demographic side, whether the modern migrants are 'pulled' by better economic prospects, 'pushed' by persecution, or involved in the quest for a self, they are rarely moving to vacant homes. Quite the contrary: the likelihood nowadays is that they fetch up in cities with an already high density of population. Inevitably, those in search of new homes press up against 'locals' of that place who already have homes to defend. In physical terms, the supply of homes is finite: what you take, I lose. But on the experiential side, once matters of symbolism and culture come into play, the crude laws of material competition do not apply. Nor, indeed, is it necessary for material people to interact: even homogeneous populations now come up against otherness as soon as they have access to modern media of communication, and can be altered by it at one remove.

In Paine's words:

'. . . each culture is compressed against others, and compressed as well against global trends . . . Talk about how one can travel further and further and have it make less and less difference misses the important point. Even refugees who endure danger and deprivation in their journeys across the globe, on reaching their geographical destinations likely find other taxing and longer-run "journeys" begin after they reach the geographical destination. These are journeys of incorporation'.

26. This section leans on Paine's references as well as his formulations. Where these are not quoted from the 1992 publication, they are taken, with his permission, from working drafts of it.

Paine offers the Saami:Norwegian compression as a template:

'When I say that Saami culture is compressed against the Norwegian I aver that a version or versions of Saami culture is/are maintained. That's the first point: a compressed culture is not one withering on the vine . . . Rather, compression indicates selection from a rich treasury of cultural emblems. There is a trimming of the vine [and therefore a] possibility of cultural intensification, even in situations we are used to calling acculturation . . . The second point is that the compression is relational . . . and may be emphatically unequal . . . [but anyway] implies the likelihood of [a] combination of idioms or emblems which were previously incommensurable, even mutually hostile. A third point is that these processes . . . are volatile. What is selected, combined or suppressed is open to change and is even reversible . . .' (Paine 1992: 199).

His conclusion harks back to the dilemma of our lost boxes, lost 'homes':

'While these processes have clear bonuses – the reinvention of the individual qua Saami for instance – they also exact a heavy price. Namely a lack of coevalness among persons who are ascriptively of the same 'culture' but . . . have made different selections and combinations' (1992:200).

Because conditions of cultural compression are new as well as global, the implications are still speculative. Certainly it becomes difficult to sustain exclusivist notions, whether of 'their' culture or 'ours'. But more significant to the present theme, *'Cultures may* [now] *be represented as zones of control or of abandonment, of recollection and of forgetting, of force or of dependence, of exclusiveness or of sharing . . .'* and increasingly, exile, immigration and the crossing of boundaries are what the world is about (Said 1989: 225).

Likewise, of course, the urban home. For boundary crossing/breaching/defending, read 'seeking and maintaining home space'. For recollecting and forgetting culture, read 'creating new localisms'. And to understand the balance between exclusiveness and sharing, consider the style of localism that each urban system sustains.

Conclusion

This chapter is a step towards a modest general theory that might account for different responses to change, to intervention, and to outsiders in different city settings, and by different groups in the same setting.[27] The

27. Because the theory is cumulative it lifts a lot from my previous work. I beg indulgence for so much self-reference, but must note Wallman 1978 and1979 as well as the citations in the text.

city settings in question are not whole towns as urban types, but parts of cities as urban systems, each with its own style of livelihood and framework of identity options. My working and therefore provisional definition of an urban system has two elements: it is driven by a particular relation between people and place (as was set out in the introductory statement); and that relation is compounded of the styles of localism and compression that characterize it (and were set out among the *signposts* to the analysis in the preceding section).

The Battersea:Bow comparison illustrates two distinct styles of localism and begins to suggest the kinds of difference between city settings that suit or do not suit particular kinds of migrant. Each system offers a distinct set of economic and identity options that, according to who is defining it, make it a better or worse place to call home. Variation in the dynamics of cultural compression also makes a difference. Both areas are polyglot and close to the centre of the same metropolitan city: residents of either would be hard put to it to avoid knowledge of/contact with/selecting from the repertoire of one or more other cultures as they go about their livelihood. But the boundary and network effects described suggest more *group*-ness of the cultural encounter in the more closed system, here represented by Bow, and a more exposed *individual* encounter with/compression by otherness in the relatively open Battersea-type case. And both group and individual perspectives resonate along Pearman Street.

These observations put a different gloss on other signposts to the discussion. For example, it is not only identity of the self that is altered when the framework of ascribed status falls away, equally identification of and with 'the other' takes new turns. Secondly, the cosiness of a 'boxed' or tightly bounded circumstance does not by any means preclude the compression experience: in this era even a (material or conceptual) fortress of a home suffers or enjoys the global condition. Finally, an ideal type model of this A:B sort cannot do justice to the volatility of the compression process. A real life home-in-the-city is situated somewhere along the continuum between them, and the cultural options are 'selected, combined or suppressed' to match the logic of the situation to hand.

A number of issues germane to understanding the home-potential of inner city areas are represented, not to say confused, in this account. Most fundamental is the distinction between *dwelling* (as a material place) and *home* (as a conceptual place that I identify myself by and with). It is a distinction that the outsider may not appreciate: even housing authorities committed to making things 'better' for clients in their constituency can only measure progress by material increment.

The same distinction harks back to the definition of localism as a sense of belonging that is both more than and other than just 'being there'. The fact that residents may have been made (more) conscious of identifying with Pearman Street by the threat of dispersal and demolition does not deny the reality of their emotional investment in it. The street could not have pulled itself together to contest the CPO except with the ties forged by years of continuous and viable neighbouring.

Nonetheless, the CPO threat probably altered both the strength and the style of localism characteristic of Pearman Street as an urban system. The analytic stasis of the Battersea:Bow comparison notwithstanding, localism, identity and certainly cultural compression are *processes* in real life, not categorical states. Ideal types are used as notional still points in social process, providing opposite ends of the (also notional) continuum between them and a frame for tracking change within the system in view (cf. Leach 1961). In this discussion, Bow and Battersea are frozen in snapshot contrast to highlight variation in the scope offered to ethnicity as a locus of home in the city; and Pearman Street appears in mid-situation, a moving picture that emphasizes the volatility of home and of home-maker/home-seeker identifications.

For this reason alone it has to follow that Pearman Street as an *urban system* fits neither A-type or B-type specifications entirely. The tally of its characteristics adds to the sense of its bridging the gap between them. It is more open than closed to outsiders; and culturally heterogenous rather than homogenous in its residents' origins. But by the end of the story told here, all those cultures are *explicitly* compressed into a local system that is at once tightly bounded and a-ethnic in its identity style.

This is exactly the combination of characteristics that was bound to appeal to the public's 'global' need. With a little help from the media, Pearman Street came to be idealized as the past and future of the good urban home. In the way it was seen to cherish children, the family, neighbourliness ... it represented the once safe, now lost home of the childhood perhaps nobody had ever had. And in the way the original cultures of people migrating into it were integrated – compressed – first by being there, and then around the definition and protection of their common home, Pearman Street – at least from a distance – became the place to which the late twentieth-century person was longing to belong.

References

Barth, Fredrik (1966), *Models of Social Organisation* (Occasional Paper No. 23), London: Royal Anthropological Institute.

—— (ed.) (1969), *Ethnic Groups and Boundaries*, Boston: Little Brown.

Bourdieu, Pierre (1977), *Outline of a Theory of Practice*, Cambridge University Press.

Firth, Raymond (1951), *Elements of Social Organisation*, London: Watts.

Hannerz, Ulf (1980), *Exploring the City*, New York: Columbia University Press.

—— (1985), 'The World System of Culture. The International Flow of Meaning and its Local Management' (xerox).

—— (1992), *Cultural Complexity: Studies on the Social Organization of Meaning*, New York: Columbia University Press.

Jacobs, Jane (1961),The Death and Life of Great American Cities. New York: Random House.

Leach, E. R. (1961), *Political Systems of Highland Burma*, London: Athlone.

Marris, Peter (1974), *Loss and Change*, London: Routledge & Kegan Paul.

Paine, Robert (1992), 'The Marabar Caves, 1920–2020', in S. Wallman (ed.), *Contemporary Futures* (ASA Monographs 30), London: Routledge.

Said, E. W. (1989), 'Representing the Colonized: Anthropology's Interlocutors', *Critical Inquiry*, 15 (Winter).

Tambiah, S. J. (1989), 'Ethnic Conflict in the World Today', *American Ethnology*, 16: 2.

Wallman, S. (1975), 'A Street in Waterloo', *New Community*, Vol.V, No. 4.

—— (ed.) (1977), *Perceptions of Development*, Cambridge University Press.

—— (1978), 'The Boundaries of "Race": Processes of Ethnicity in England', Man Vol.13, No. 2.

—— (ed.) (1979), *Ethnicity at Work*, London: Macmillan & Co.

—— (1981), 'Refractions of Rhetoric: Evidence for the Meaning of "Race" in England', in R. Paine (ed.), *Politically Speaking*, Institute for the Study of Human Issues for Memorial University of Newfoundland, Institute of Social and Economic Research.

—— (1982), *Living in South London*. London: Gower Press/L. S. E.

—— (1984a), *Eight London Households*, London: Tavistock.

—— (1984b), 'Structures of Informality: The Scope for Unofficial Economic Organisation', in R. Finnegan, A. Gallie and A. Roberts (eds), *New Approaches to Economic Life*, Manchester University Press.

—— (1993), 'Reframing Context: Pointers to the Post-industrial City', in A. P. Cohen and K. Fukui (eds), Humanising the City? Social Contexts of Urban Life at the Time of the Millennium, Edinburgh University Press.

—— (1997), 'Appropriate Anthropology and the Risky Inspiration of "Capability" Brown', in A. James, J. Hockey and A. Dawson (eds), *After Writing Culture: Epistemology and Praxis in Contemporary Anthropology*, (ASA Monographs 34), London: Routledge.

The Dislocation of Identity: Contestations of 'Home Community' in Northern England

Andrew Dawson

Background and Introduction

This chapter explores the construction, use and contestation of community by the participants in a club for the elderly residents of a former coal-mining town. It addresses several aspects or issues of home, in this case the community as home, some of which are identified in the opening passages of this volume. First, home community as an idea that usually refers (though we do not see this as a precondition of home) to a place, in this case the town of Hirst in North-East England.[1] Secondly, home community as an idea that people write. In this case the writing is literal, for beyond conversation, the creation and performance of poetry and song constitutes the principal activity within the club. This represents part of the continuity of a local tradition of artistic creativity that was established in the miners' welfare associations and championed by a 'modernist' urban intellectual élite in the early part of this century (see Fever 1988). Authors and audience alike credit the poetry and songs with a special significance. They convey ideas about reality in a manner that one is not given the licence to articulate in everyday talk. One of their major concerns is the issue of community. Thirdly, in speaking of the uses of community the chapter demonstrates how its identity is situationally and

---

1. Hirst's real name has been concealed to preserve the confidentiality of specific people in this study.

strategically constructed and deployed. In this context the ideas of the homogeneity and solidarity of community (though often not explicitly expressed in these terms) relate specifically to the social divisions and potential conflicts that participants must negotiate when they come together. Fourthly, the chapter explores the contestation of home community. It has long been an axiom of interpretative anthropological practice to conceptualize community as a multivocal symbol. This chapter demonstrates how, when co-opted into conflict over material or other resources, in this case consultative positions in a local heritage museum, the idiosyncratic meanings of community that people hold become more loudly articulated and, as a result, the senses of community that people share begin to fragment. Having listed these concerns, the chapter's key framing theme is, however, that of the relationship between home and movement.

Throughout the 1950s, 1960s and 1970s coal-mining communities came to constitute a major obsession of scholars concerned with the study of the British working class (Crow and Allan 1994:2). This was perhaps unsurprising. The history of British coal-mining is a history of industrial action (Allen 1981). Uncovering the roots of miners' militancy became a particular focus of concern in sociological writing. Several accounts identified as central the relative social and cultural homogeneity and the solidarity of mining communities (see, for example Dennis et al. 1969). Running alongside this tradition of thought an equally powerful set of critiques replaced visions of homogeneity with visions of diversity, of religion (Moore 1975) and of class (Crow and Allan 1994:37) for example. Also, solidarity was replaced by conflict, between classes, between micro-localities (communities within communities), and between the increasingly home-centred and 'privatized' individuals who inhabited them. In an era characterized by the omnipresence of Marxian ideas and a consequent periodic politicization of academic departments, the ideas of these divergent writers were often co-opted into political debate, with their subtleties set aside and replaced by polarizing polemic. For many, mining communities were 'working-class communities' *per se* and their class-conscious members were the quintessential representatives of an industrial proletariat capable of instigating rapid social change. Others dismissed such ideas as the wishful thinking of intellectual or political communards.

Having said this, there is one key set of points that transcend the intellectual and political divide and that almost all accounts of mining communities agree upon. They are physically isolated. Their members are notoriously geographically immobile; even when mining people do travel, usually as part of wage migration, they almost invariably are drawn back by an unbreakable attachment to kin, familiar tradition, or place (R. Taylor 1979). Finally, it is argued, this geographical mobility engenders a deep sense of localism. In his ideal-typical depiction of the mining community Bulmer summarizes the picture as follows: 'The social ties of work, leisure, neighbourhood and friendship overlap to form close-knit and interlocking locally based collectivities of actors. The solidarity of the community is strengthened . . . by a shared history of living and working in one place over a long period of time' (1975:87–8).

The vision of mining people in sociological debate is, then, one of ultimate homebodies. Many are socially fixed, working-class with little opportunity for social mobility. Unquestionably they are spatially fixed (isolated, geographically immobile and localistic in outlook). We might add to this another dimension of fixity in the case of elderly mining people. On most weeks the club I worked in is visited by a concert party from one of the many other local clubs for elderly people. One of the most popular acts is a karaoke-style performance of a song of the moment. The performance is usually an instant cue for laughter, and not just because of the apparent absurdity of old folk dabbling in youth culture. The songs are carefully chosen to enable a performance that, mockingly and even cruelly perhaps, makes light of the predicaments faced by participants. Thus, for example, the performance of Madonna's 'Like a Virgin' and Eddie Cochrane's 'Shaking All Over' were references, not even thinly veiled, to loss of sexuality and Parkinson's disease respectively. One week the participants were treated to a particularly experientially apt song, Talking Heads' 'We're on a Road to Nowhere'. The references were clearly understood. For these elderly mining people at least their social and spatial fixity is added to and compounded by their fixity in time; time is running out – death is up ahead. It is in this triple-faceted fixity that I find the central rationale for this chapter, for what better (more adverse) context in which to test out our iterological thesis that identity should be treated as a search. This chapter asks, then, 'In the construction, use and contestation of their community identity what role does social, spatial and temporal movement have for people who are socially, spatially and temporally fixed in the extreme?'

The Construction of a 'Northern Working-class Mining Community'

The central components of the idea of community constructed within the clubs are the linked ideas of homogeneity and solidarity. At one level these are animated by ideas about dependency. Homogeneity is represented as born of common dependency on the mining industry. At another level they are animated by ideas about class and occupation. Solidarity is represented simultaneously as a response to the results of exploitation, a response to the danger and horror of working conditions and an inevitable outcome of living conditions. Finally, and most importantly, they are animated by ideas about space, where a sense of community is cultivated by contrast with the social worlds beyond its boundaries. In what amounts to a highly segmented image of community four key spatial referents are contrasted: Northern England to Southern England, mining to non-mining areas, home community to other local communities and colliery to non-colliery housing. Participants view themselves as northerners and mining people of a specific micro-locality and of specific living conditions. The contrasting of these spatial referents generates a series of oppositions, many of which refer to social and cultural life. Prevalent amongst these is a contrasting of the homogeneity and solidarity of the home community with the diversity, individualism, social atomism and privatism of the south, non-mining areas and, to a lesser extent, other local communities, especially those that lack colliery housing. Thus, through such contrast, as Brow comments, differences and conflicts, 'amongst those who are incorporated within a community are often muted or obscured' (1990:3).

The interrelationship between ideas of dependency and, to a greater extent, class, occupation and space can best be demonstrated through extended discussions of the idea of solidarity that emerges in the clubs, and of the participants' concern with putative images. Solidarity and its social and institutional manifestations are explained largely in terms of the relationships between these spatial referents and in terms of the working and living conditions generated through these relationships. Talk about community resonates with a socialist discourse that has developed through years of political domination in the area by the Labour Party and the National Union of Mineworkers and, to a lesser extent, other more radical left-wing groups. This emphasizes the idea that areas such as Hirst have been produced, then marginalized and, ultimately, destroyed as part of the capitalist development process. Club participants give this a highly regionalist slant. The nation is seen as suffering from the disease of regional state favouritism, where southerners are the main beneficiaries of government policy. Southern wealth is fuelled by northern endeavour, and regional economic slumps and underdevelopment are more than crises of capital. They are the result of *ad hoc* exploitation of north by south. Importantly, regional state neglect has led out of necessity to the development of locally specific forms of behaviour and organization, such as unusually high levels of cooperation, mutuality and sociability, systems of informal obligation and roles whereby people acted as unpaid community midwives, morticians, mourners and so on, and an alternative institutional infrastructure, incorporating the cooperative movement and the information networks embedded within working men's clubs.

The working conditions formerly encountered by participants, in particular the threat of mining death, are seen to have necessitated solidarity. Anthropologists and social historians have commented extensively on the effects upon women's social relationships of living under this threat (see, for example, Szurek 1985 and Williamson 1982). Local descriptions highlight the cooperative element in men's social relationships that is rooted in safe working practices. The inherent and unpredictable possibility of death in the pit and an inextricable association of the pit and death pervades local culture. It is implicit within the myriad of avoidance practices intended to stave off the threat of death. Miners refrained from uttering the word 'pig', avoided seeing women on their way to the night shift and refrained from washing their backs throughout the course of the working week. It is also implicit in the very language of the area. Entry to the pit and burial share the same words: to go 'doon bye' and the 'last doon bye'. Death is to have 'your chocks draan'. Chocks are drawn, or pit props are removed, to terminate the productive life of a seam. Drawing on this deeply embedded theme of association, poetry, song and conversation represent men as apart from normal life and its inherent divisions in a state where they are equal and united by the common condition of suspension between life and death (Dawson 1990:120).

The design and usage of the colliery home is a no less powerful referent of solidarity and community in general. Images within poetry, song and conversation depict cramped living conditions, the denial of privacy, collective domestic work and the home as a symbol of community. Here a distinction is made between the house's front and back. The difference is apparently that between decorative and functional. However, according to the ideal, front and back doors were used differently. The back door was for everyday usage, and was permanently unlocked for ease of access to neighbours. The front door was kept locked and opened only for strangers, higher-status groups, the exit of the dead, and the entry of a new child and on wedding days. The front doorstep, an object of copious cleaning with a small clay 'holy stone', is a threshold in the fullest sense of the word, between inside and outside, family and non-family, life and death and community and non-community (Dawson 1990:152–6).

The relating of spatial referents provides one further key component within the construction of community: putative images. These tend to concern drinking habits, language and the association of local people with the dirt of the mining industry. For participants, images of the heavy-drinking, linguistically incomprehensible and dirt-besmirched local are a matter for celebration rather than rejection. This celebration involves a highlighting of the perceived non-locals' misrepresentation of the beer, the language and the dirt, and a transformation of their significance. This transformation is underscored by a linguistic and symbolic distinction between coal dust and ordinary dirt.

Drinking is represented as therapeutic; it washes dust from the body. It is solidarity-making; its local name is 'discourse oil'. It is also a compensation for intolerable working lives.

> 'Then buzzer blaas, and man to man
> They queue infront o' the cage
> For ten lang ooers belaa they'll gan
> To mek a livin wage.
>
> Then who wad dare that man to judge
> If Sat'day neet he boozes?
> Aye who amang ye wad begrudge
> That comfort if he chooses?'

Similarly, as one would expect, the impenetrability of local language is not seen as an indication of ignorance or low intelligence. It is celebrated self-consciously as complex and clever. This is implicit within the descriptive titles given to it. For example, the 'Pitmatic' refers to a dynamic and inventive process where pit terminology is taken and generated into nouns, verbs, adjectives, adverbs and phrases for metaphorical usage in the description of everyday reality (Dawson 1990:132).

Finally, the area and its people's association with dirt is a particularly significant element of community identity. One eminent Northumbrian historian comments on Hirst's newness, and compares it with a neighbouring town: 'where Morpeth stems from antiquity, [Hirst] is red raw beneath its grime' (Chaplin 1975:2). Again, however, the dirt is an object of celebration. Coal is imbued with a heavy symbolic load. It is endowed with human qualities and is gendered: one poem speaks of 'Black Queen Coal'. It is credited with powers of protection. Even in this area, where pneumoconiosis is common, it is represented as safe and therapeutic. This is made possible by the linguistic and symbolic distinction between coal dust and ordinary dirt. The former is referred to as 'duff', and the latter as 'muck'. Duff is clean and muck is dirty. One poem typifies the distinction:

> 'There's sum folk wad say that Aa'm dorty
> For me table's the back of me shuvell,
> But coal dust's not dorty like muck is,
> Aal pitmen, for heartborn suck coal.'

The distinction informs systems of animal classification (Dawson 1990), and alternative status hierarchies. The elevated position of the 'stone men', who clear seams for ordinary miners to work in, is explained by their inhalation of what are perceived to be more dangerous substances than coal dust. More importantly, the distinction transforms a deprecating association with dirt into a cherished mark of identity.

> 'His pit claes has that special tang,
> Of oil, and duff and smoke
> That to colliery hooses aal belang,
> And singles out pit folk.'

The Uses of Community: Conflict and its Resolution

Club meetings always begin and end with the simplest of songs,

> 'Here we are again
> Happy as can be
> All good friends
> And jolly good company.'

And . . .

> 'Just like Darby and Joan
> In a world of our own
> We'll build a nest
> Way in the west
> Be it so humble
> We'll never grumble.

Though the grey locks are showing
And the dark clouds are drawing
Fear won't betide us
Our love will guide us
Just like Darby and Joan.'

In combination with a range of formal institutional practices the celebration of community serves to promote the kind of harmonious social relations expressed as an ideal within these songs. Homogeneity and the suppression of diversity is at their core. For example, in an 'everyone contributes – everyone wins a prize' draw prizes were always concealed in anonymous brown paper bags. The practice disguised disparities in the value of gifts donated and received. It disguised differences in the wealth of participants. And it made impossible potentially humiliating acts of charity by the wealthy toward the poor. So, too, was solidarity. For example, images of the dependency, exploitation and working and living conditions at the heart of community life are constantly used to rationalize the kind of mutualistic and cooperative organization that characterizes the clubs. Through their ability to obscure differences, mute conflict and promote ideas of homogeneity and solidarity the institutional practices and the idea of community served, in effect, to nurture a form of institutionalized liminality. Indeed, the use of songs in the clubs bears the typical hallmarks of much ritual. They speak of a 'world of our own', a world of 'good company' and 'love', and of a world whose entry and exit they clearly demarcate.

Having said this, the success of this combination was uneven to say the least. The ambience in the clubs was often characterized by barely suppressed antagonism, which on occasions erupted into conflict. In recent years the potential for such conflict has intensified dramatically with the clubs' increasing politicization. Reflecting the contemporary and entirely laudable vogues in Labour Party culture for 'minority' and 'communitarian' politics, the elderly are given a greater role in local governmental participatory development strategies. To exclude them would be ageist. To include them is to provide a means by which to visit the disappearing community upon which, in part, the community of the future will be built.[2] The clubs are now to act as conduits for the input of elderly people within these participatory development strategies.

2. For an exposition of the idea of revisiting the communities of the past and making the communities of the future in communitarian thought see Waltzer (1984). For a critique of the romanticism of communitarianism see C. Taylor (1994). For an analysis of the role of communitarian thought in Labour Party culture see Kenny (1995).

At the time of research several clubs were approached by local govern-ment, who sought the involvement of elderly people in the running and construction of a museum of mining. Participants from each club were asked to choose one from amongst them who with others would act as voluntary curator, record local poems, songs and passages of dialect for broadcast in the museum and serve on an advisory body concerned with the design of the museum's displays.

Initially, in the club, it had been thought that one candidate would emerge through polite agreement and that he/she would receive the backing of all participants. In the event two fairly resolute candidates and groups of backers emerged. A ballot was called by the club leaders, and in the days leading up to it a fairly vociferous and often conflictual debate took place. The conflictual nature of the debate was hardly surprising. First, in the eyes of participants the advisory body that the successful candidate would serve on was responsible for nothing less than playing a leading role in the construction of a visual and oral representation of the community. This kind of activity is the very *raison d'être* of the clubs. Secondly, the debate focused on the issue of the ownership of rights to community definition. Thirdly, the divergent biographies of the respective candidates lent the debate a particularly polarizing set of substantive issues around which claims to ownership of definitional rights were contested. One of the candidates was a former school head teacher, an activist in the local historical movement and a lifelong resident of the town. The other was a former miner who in the economic depression of the 1930s had temporarily moved for work to the coalfields of Kent, Canada and the United States of America. In terms of class at least, the social profiles of the two groups of supporters reflected broadly those of the two candidates.

The first set of issues were, then, those of class and occupation. The right of community definition accorded to the former miner was represented as stemming from his direct erstwhile involvement in mining. The second key issue was residency. The right of community definition accorded to the former headmaster was represented as stemming from his unbroken residency in the town.

The Contestation of Community

In conflict, particularly that surrounding the issue of ownership of rights to community definition, community is a symbol to be contested and appropriated. Not quite a full process of inclusion and exclusion, this consists of the representation of location and dislocation between community identity and the identity of certain of its members, such that some people are represented as more 'of' the community than others. A series of representational strategies are deployed.

First, in relation to their objective referents, community identity and the identity of its members are dislocated and relocated. At one level, personal identity is dislocated from its objective referents and relocated in line with the objective referents of community. In this way, the former head teacher and his cohorts were able to contest both the right of community definition accorded to the former miner by virtue of his direct erstwhile involvement in mining and the right of community definition denied to himself by virtue of the apparent contrast between his middle-class status and the working-classness of the community. In real terms this was achieved by highlighting the fact that, as an activist within local historical circles, he had become an expert in the histories, songs, poetry and dialect of the local mining working class. With change, wrought largely by the demise of mining, the referents of community are steadily disappearing. As such, a sense of community is increasingly obtained at a second remove, through learning rather than direct experience. More-over, the central images of community represent increasingly part of a cultural fiction that becomes ever more elaborated as they are celebrated in the burgeoning local history societies, writing groups and, since the former head teacher went on to secure his election alongside others of his cohorts from other clubs, the local museum. It is clear that community is, reflecting processes extant in other parts of the United Kingdom (see, for example, Gilbert 1992 and Young 1988) and elsewhere (see, for example, Hroch 1985), being refined as a discourse by a middle class that manipulate images and symbols that have only a condensed historical meaning for them, rather than a more personal historic link. What is important to note is that through his mastery of apparently mining and working-class specific cultural forms, the middle-class former head teacher was able to represent himself as more working-class than the working class. Here, then, personal identity is dislocated from the objective referent of class.

At another level, community identity is dislocated from its objective referents and relocated in line with personal identity. In this way, the former miner and his cohorts were able to contest both the right to community definition accorded to the former head teacher by virtue of his unbroken residency and the right to community definition denied to himself by virtue of his itinerancy. In real terms this was achieved by critical reappraisal of the idea of the 'local' community and deployment of the argument that the community of central positive significance in the lives of these people is that of the international working class. Poetically, the critique and argument were rooted in the representation of locally specific forms and manifestations of solidarity as more part of a submissive, albeit understandable, culture of compensation than of a culture reactive to exploitation. As one poem states,

'Better than aall is the closeness of friends
Aroond us to help us to bear
The many great comforts which poverty sends
For of these nearly aall have their share.

There are also the gud things in life, be it said
Forbye its mare unpleasant labours
Consarn for your welfare, material aid
Are the riches enjoyed b' gud neighbours'.

The critique and argument resonates with a series of strands of socialist thinking that have historically played a major role in British mining communities. In some thinking the 'local' community was an idea too intimately connected with the paternalistically oppressive objectives of pre-nationalization mining companies, whose strategies of control involved the discursive construction of communities (Dawson 1990:30–8). Indeed, with respect to community, it is almost impossible, Williamson writes, 'to disentangle cleanly that which reflected the action of the coal company and that which evolved from the men' (1982:62). In other similar thinking, such as that of the internationalism of the Communist Party of Great Britain in the 1930s (a politically formative era for many of the club participants), local community identity is represented as a form of ideological epiphenomenon that militates against the development of class consciousness. What is important to note is that through deployment of the discourse of the international community of the working class the former itinerant miner who had spent much of his life out of the local community could represent himself as more of the community than others with histories of permanent residency. Here, then, community identity is effectively dislocated from the objective referent of place; community is represented as beyond the place one calls home.

A second strategy consists of the relocation of identities through their re-presentation. Again, this strategy was utilized by the former miner and his cohorts to contest both the right to community definition accorded to the former head teacher by virtue of his unbroken residency and the right denied to himself by virtue of his itinerancy. Personal identity is re-presented as commensurate with community identity and vice versa. In real terms this consisted of a re-presentation of travel as a rite of passage to belonging and community membership. Three, often explicitly stated, reasons were given for why this should be so. First, travel was claimed as an origin(al) experience of belonging. Much was made of the newness of Hirst, a town that simply did not exist before the onset of the mining industry in the eighteenth century. The argument was embellished with some considerable subtlety. For example, in commenting on the complexity and cleverness of local language, one supporter of the former miner was able to add the descriptive term 'Polyglottal Buzz' to that of the 'Pitmatic'. The term refers to the multifarious inputs to the language, from the migrant settlers who were the area's first significant population. Secondly, mirroring the emphasis on spatial segmentation in the way that community is constructed, travel was represented as heightening through lived contrast consciousness of a community whose distinctiveness derives from juxtaposition with the world beyond its boundaries. As one participant told me, 'When I went away as a youngster, I got to know who I was by looking at who I wasn't.' Thirdly, mirroring socialist internationalism, travel was represented as enabling consciousness of a community of the working class which, because locally suppressed, is realized principally in its international aspect (see also Olwig 1993). Conversely, and somewhat paradoxically given the use of socialist inter-nationalist ideas, through localizing these three discourses, of origins, hybridity and internationalism, travel was represented as a quintessential characteristic of local community and culture. In essence, apart from the fact that it is a working-class coal-mining town, what distinguishes Hirst from the isolated agricultural communities that surround it is that it is a migrant town *per se*, it has a kind of 'been-to' culture and, in at least some cases, its people are conscious of its international locatedness.

Home and Movement

We began this volume by pointing to some of the critiques directed at the traditional anthropological depiction of socio-cultural 'places': fixities of social relations and cultural routines localized in space and time. The depiction has elicited a somewhat extreme response in calls to study, for example, 'non-places' (Auge 1992), transience (Clifford 1992) and deterritorialization (Appadurai 1991:194). Though studies of this variety would constitute an invaluable contribution to the inventory of con-temporary issues we must tackle, as a recipe for the transformation of anthropology's substantive foci it is absurd in the extreme, a call for nomadology rather than anthropology (Clifford 1992:108). Our aim should instead be to capture the ambivalence that is at the heart of most people's existences, of lives characterized simultaneously by fixity, an intense orientation to the here and now, and movement, spatial and temporal transience. Doreen Massey captures evocatively at least some of this reality when she states,

> most people actually still live in places like Harlesden or West Brom. Much of life for many people, even in the heart of the first world, still consists of waiting at a bus-shelter with your shopping for a bus that never comes. . . . [but] even as you wait, in a bus-shelter in Harlesden or West Brom, for a bus that never comes, your shopping bag is likely to contain at least some products of the global raiding party which is constantly conducted to supply the consumer demands of the world's relatively comfortably-off (1992:8–9).

Several approaches have been developed to capture this ambivalence. For example, moving in focus from the global to the local, Massey offers a 'geography of social relations' where, according to the argument, it is the presence of the outside within which helps to construct the specificity of local places (1992). Moving in focus from the local to the global, Olwig offers the concepts 'cultural sites' and 'translocal networks', where the global and local ties between people are firmly identified with particular places (1997:35). Finally, Clifford's depiction of 'cultures as sites of traveling' conveys a sense of the global world of intercultural import–export in which local communities are enmeshed (1992). In these and in many others amongst the myriad of valuable contributions to the understanding of a diminishingly space- and time-bound world is an emphasis on the physicality of movement to, from, between and through places, an emphasis on the movement of the products of international capitalism (see above), remittances, people (bodies), televisual imagery, and so on. However, not all movement consists of the physical.

I began this chapter, with reference to sociological literature on the mining community, by depicting the people in this study as the ultimate homebodies, who face extreme conditions of social, spatial and temporal fixity. However, it is clear that their competing definitions of community, their homes that are constructed through a process of identity location and dislocation, are also engineered through engagement in a kind of movement. At one level people move socially, to working class from the objectively perceived social status of middle class, for example. At another level they move spatially, to the southern locus of their exploitation and

depreciation,[3] and from local community to international community to
internationally located local community. Finally, they move temporally
to defining moments of community: to Hirst's moment of inception, to
its depression years era of intermittent wage migration and the rise of
socialist internationalism, and to its golden age of artistic creativity.[4] In
essence, whilst these people face conditions of fixity, like many others, I
suspect, they engage cognitively in movement. Furthermore, we may be
able to describe fixity and movement as interdependent modalities. I have
described a situation where the imagination of other places and times
informs images of community constructed in the here and now that people
seek to still in perpetuity, in this case in the bricks, mortar, display cabinets
and cassette tapes of a heritage museum, perhaps so as to overcome the
crisis of discontinuity that impending death threatens: movement gives
on to fixity gives on to movement. Here then are Home Bodies and
Migrant Minds.[5]

References

Allen, V. L. (1981), *The Militancy of British Miners*, Shipley: The Moor Press.
Appadurai, A. (1991), 'Global Ethnoscapes: Notes and Queries for a Transnational
    Anthropology', in R. G. Fox (ed.), *Recapturing Anthropology: Working in
    the Present,* Santa Fé: School of American Research Press.
Auge, M. (1992), *Non-lieux: Introduction à Une Anthropologie de la Surmod-
    ernité*, Paris: Seuil.
Brow, J. (1990), 'Notes on Community and Hegemony and the Uses of the Past',
    Anthropological Quarterly, 63(1):12–35.
Bulmer, M. (1975), 'Sociological Models of the Mining Community', *Sociological
    Review,* 23:61–92.
Chaplin, S. (1975), 'Introduction', in F. Reed, *The Sense On't*, pp. 1–7 Newcastle:
    Northern House.
—— (1992), 'Traveling Cultures', in L. Grossberg, C. Nelson, and P. Treichler
    (eds), *Cultural Studies,* pp. 96–116, New York: Routledge.
Crow, G. and Allan, G. (1994), *Community Life: An Introduction to Local Social
    Relations*, London: Harvester Wheatsheaf.

3. The kind of historic internal colonialism depicted by these people gives the lie to the
suggestion that space compression is new, a phenomenon of the postmodern age.
    4. Contestation of identity of place almost always involves groups' laying claims to
moments in time when the definition of the area and the social relations dominant within it
were advantageous to the particular group (Massey 1992:13).
    5. For their help with this chapter, my thanks to Colin Creighton, Mark Johnson, Maurice
Mullard, Norman O'Neill and members of the Hull Sociology and Anthropology 'kitchen
table workshop'.

Dawson, A. (1990), 'Ageing and Change in Pit Villages of North East England', Unpublished Ph.D. thesis, University of Essex.

Dennis, N., Henriques, F. and Slaughter, C. (1969), *Coal is Our Life: An Analysis of a Yorkshire Mining Community*, London: Tavistock.

Fever, W. (1988), *The Pitmen Painters: The Ashington Group, 1934–84*, London: Chatto and Windus.

Gilbert, D. (1992), *Class, Community and Collective Action: Social Change in Two British Coalfields, 1850–1926*, Oxford: Clarendon Press.

Hroch, M. (1985), *Social Conditions of National Revival in Europe*, Cambridge: Cambridge University Press.

Kenny, M. (1995), *First New Left: British Intellectuals After Stalin*, London: Lawrence and Wishart.

Massey, D. (1992), 'A Place Called Home?', *New Formations: A Journal of Culture/Theory? Politics*, 17: The Question of 'Home', pp. 3–15.

Moore, R. (1975), 'Religion as a Source of Variation in Working Class Images of Society', in M. Bulmer (ed.), *Working-Class Images of Society*, pp. 35–54, London: Routledge and Kegan Paul.

Olwig, K. F. (1993), *Global Culture, Island Identity: Continuity and Change in the Afro-Caribbean Community of Nevis*, Reading: Harwood Academic Press.

—— (1997), 'Cultural Sites: Sustaining a Home in a Deterritorialized World', in K. Hastrup and K. F. Olwig (eds), pp. 17–38, *Siting Culture: The Shifting Anthropological Object*, London: Routledge.

Szurek, J. (1985), 'I'll Have a Collier for My Sweetheart: Work and Gender in a British Coal Mining Town', Unpublished Ph.D. thesis, Brown University.

Taylor, C. (1994), *Sources of Self: The Making of the Modern Identity*, Cambridge: Cambridge University Press.

Taylor, R. (1979), 'Migration and the Residual Community', *Sociological Review* 27(3):475–89.

Waltzer, M. (1984), 'Welfare, Membership and Need', in M. Sandel (ed.), *Liberalism and its Critics*, pp. 200–17, Oxford: Basil Blackwell.

Williamson, B. (1982), *Class, Culture and Community: A Biographical Study of Social Change in Mining*, London: Routledge and Kegan Paul.

Young, E. (1988), 'Rhetoric, Division and Constraint: Elements in Local Social Mobilization', *Sociological Review*, 61(2):92–109.

Part III
Initiating a
Response

Epilogue: Contested Homes: Home-making and the Making of Anthropology

Karen Fog Olwig

During one of his recent visits to Denmark the Danish American entertainer Victor Borge was asked by a Danish journalist whether he had considered movieng back home from the United States. 'Home?' the octogenarian asked, and added, 'But I am in my home all the time, its walls are just very far apart!' With this play on the dual meaning of 'home' as both a concrete physical place and a personal space of identification, Victor Borge projected himself as a man of the world who has not allowed himself to be constrained by ties to his original homeland or the particular locality of his everyday life. His life rather has taken place in the home of his personal space of relations and identification, which spans the Atlantic – and probably several other oceans and continents as well.

This verbal exchange between the cosmopolitan artist and the parochial reporter may serve as an apt illustration of the complexity of the notion of home. It is this complexity that, according to the editors of this book, makes 'home' an appropriate focal point for the study of identity.[1] In the introductory chapter, Rapport and Dawson suggest that home is a useful analytical construct because it refers to a conceptual space of considerable importance in the modern-day world of fluidity and movement. 'Home' is 'where one best knows oneself' (p. 9), and it thereby constitutes an important basis for developing and maintaining personal identities. The search for identity, to follow Rapport and Dawson, involves movement, in body and mind, within and between spaces of varying scales that are identified as home. This edited volume on 'migrants of identity' has

---

1. I would like to thank Nigel Rapport, Vered Amit-Talai and Kenneth Olwig for their useful comments on this epilogue.

therefore proposed to 'discuss and analyse the search for identity in terms of conceptualizations of "home"' (p. 4), and to explore 'physical and cognitive movement within and between homes, and the relation between the two' which takes place in the course of this search (p. 4).

The Diversity of Home Sites

At first glance the differing homes identified in the ethnographic case-studies represent a bewildering array of seemingly incongruous 'physical and conceptual spaces where identities are worked on', to use Allison James's expression. The studies range from personal narratives and life routines to family homes, to local communities in rural and urban areas, to national homelands and political federations. The sort of self-knowledge, and identity, that individuals can generate in these very different 'home sites' appears to vary a great deal. Upon closer examination, however, it becomes apparent that these various ideas of home share a common denominator. This is the manifestation of home as something quite different from the common conception of home as a place of harmony providing a homogeneous haven of refuge from external conflict. These essays show that home is rather a contested domain: an arena where differing interests struggle to define their own spaces within which to localize and cultivate their identity. The sort of self-knowledge, and identity, that individuals can generate within the varied home sites differs considerably. Within the physical bounds of a given home site there may thus be space for many homes, between which a given person may migrate in the process of developing and maintaining personal identities. Individuals, furthermore, may perceive the same homes in rather different ways, depending on their particular position in society.

Stef Jansen's essay on narrations of Post-Yugoslav identities illustrates the contested meaning of home by taking its point of departure in differing perceptions of the larger home of one's nation as conditioned by social position. The narrations examined are published accounts by female authors whom he terms 'privileged refugees' who have remained in place, but lost their homes. They represent a minority of educated urban intellectuals, many of them of mixed ethnic background, who are not willing (or able) to find a home in the separate, homogenizing national cultures that have arisen in the former Yugoslavia. Refusing to forget their former home in the republics of ex-Yugoslavia, and the multiple identities that it allowed, they become 'Yugozombies', living dead for whom there is no future in the present-day scenario of exclusive, nationalistic identities. They can only find a home in the space of identification provided by their narratives of resistance against the delegitimization of their former identities that they have suffered.

Jansen notes that the displacement from their former home that these narrators have experienced is not voluntary, but enforced, and that this is generally the case with dramatic movements of people. This leads him to call into question the 'overly rosy tone' of much of the literature on nomadism and cosmopolitanism (p. 106). Though the reflexivity and articulateness of these narrators may be admired, the situation that produced this creativity is highly problematic. The universality of the cosmopolitan perception of home is thrown into question when it is confronted by particularistic national constructions, just as the nationalistic construction is thrown into question by cosmopolitanism. Here there is no objective middle ground or postmodern freedom to construct one's own virtual home space. Identity, here, must be constructed in the narratives that enable these authors to withdraw from the national homes that have replaced the home they once knew as Yugoslavia.

The difficulty of reconciling different conceptualizations of a good home is also an important topic in Allison James's analysis of the way in which childhood is constructed through dominant images of the 'home' and 'family'. She shows how schoolteachers, on the basis of home visits prior to the children's entrance into the school, pigeonhole many of their future pupils into an assortment of potential social problem areas corresponding to the ways in which the family homes matched up to the teachers' notions of a proper home environment. This categorization, in turn, enables teachers to explain academic failure among children in terms of a problematic home and family background, even while they may still see the teacher–student relationship as the main axis of the students' academic success. For many of the children academic success therefore depends not only on their scholarly achievements, but just as significantly on their ability to dismantle the teachers' pre-categorization of them. James bases her analysis primarily on the teachers' internal discussions on the children, and it therefore becomes mainly a critique of ways in which 'home' and 'family' are used as 'important symbolic markers of the child's identity' (p. 147). James's study suggests that a next step in the deconstruction of Western perceptions of childhood would be that of identifying what other kinds of homes or spaces of identity the children attempt to develop both inside and outside the institutional setting of the family and school, which is normally defined as their proper place. Eric Hirsch's ethnography of home life in Greater London sheds some light on this issue.

On the basis of an analysis of the use of information and communication technologies in a number of London homes, Hirsch explores questions of agency as this relates to issues of appropriation and alienation. Electronic equipment purchased by parents for educational purposes is seen to turn boys, in particular, into computer games addicts who will do anything to satisfy their cravings for virtual satisfaction. Game addiction causes aggressive relations of dominance to emerge among the boys as they struggle to gain personal access to the computer's domain. Frightened by this disruption of the harmonious, happy family home, some parents interviewed by Hirsch explained that they decided to ban the technology from the home.

One may wonder whether the children in Hirsch's study necessarily experienced the computer as an agent that had seized them and turned them into disruptive semi-monsters. Hirsch does not present many data on what the children themselves thought about their computer experience. Is it possible that they perceived this technology as providing an alternative home where they might develop skills and assert forms of identity that were contradictory to those defined by the confining space of the family home as defined by adults? The home, after all, is here portrayed as part of a shifting conceptual space made up of a plurality of partially-connected social contexts. For the children, it would seem, home is not just where the heart is, but also (or more so) the place of the flickering screen.

In several cases, according to Hirsch, the conflicts generated by electronic equipment in the home did not just pit adults and (some of the) children against each other, but also women against men. Some women resented men's preoccupation with sports programmes on television and their temptation to bring office work into the home on their portable laptop computers. An alternative interpretation of Hirsch's argument might therefore be that these two forms of electronic equipment did not so much capture their users as create a space within the home that was captured by the males of the household. These technologies thus essentially constituted the introduction into the home of male spheres of activity that had formerly taken place outside the home. The television set and laptop computer in the home thereby provided a space in the home where males might pursue forms of activity and identity that might not previously have been allowed into the home. The conflicts that this introduction brought about might thus have been due less to the properties of the electronic machines than to conflicts generated by this intrusion of male domains into a home traditionally defined by female home-makers, whether as mothers, wives or educators. These conflicts suggest that the English home, with its wars fought in cyber blood, may be in its own way as much a contested domain as the embattled national homes of former Yugoslavia. The narratives written in the macho scripts of computer war games and the high-tech language of the computer literati provide a means of migrating from the enclosed and mothering home encapsulated by the dining-room and the parlour into a realm of identity constructed in the male animal's 'den'.

In Sandra Wallman's discussion of the Pearman Street community in London we seem to find a happier correspondence of opinions concerning what constitutes a good home. Everybody — local residents as well as the general public — all agree that Pearman Street is just the sort of community that one would like to call home. This agreement turns out to be more apparent than real, however, when the reasons for liking this community are scrutinized. The residents explained that they liked the area because it was characterized by a general feeling of friendliness, neighbourliness, community and family spirit. This neighbourhood was a home for a community manifesting a common human spirit. This common spirit, by nature, sought to ignore the racial and ethnic differences between neighbouring people, many of whom must have migrated to the community from far-distant corners of the earth. The general public, however, emphasized that it was the mixed character and community spirit of this neigbourhood that made it desirable. Regardless of these differing perceptions, Wallman shows, the shared image of Pearman Street as an ideal community allowed local residents to muster widespread public support for the preservation of the area in the face of an urban renewal plan that would have demolished much of the neighbourhood's sub-standard housing and forced many inhabitants to leave the area. The various notions of an ideal community had little impact on social life in Pearman Street, because the differences of opinion were divided between outsiders and insiders. For the outsiders, the community was not a concrete place of social and economic relations, but a model of an ideal place to live: 'the now lost home of the childhood perhaps nobody had had'. A 'working misunderstanding' (Sahlins 1985) could therefore be generated among outsiders and insiders that functioned to preserve the neighbourhood. Two differing narratives involving both movement and community allowed differing groups to use Pearman Street as a symbol of home identity.

The dividing lines are not always drawn in such a serendipitous fashion between residents and outsiders, as Andrew Dawson shows in his discussion on the contestation of home community in Northern England. Here, a local heritage centre is the nucleus of a conflict where two social groups vie for the control over the representations of belonging to be projected from this centre. The first representation is associated largely with the middle class, whereas the second is mainly of working-class origin. The conflicting claims revolve partly around what kind of prominence the heritage centre should be allowed to give to the area's history of mining, and partly around the validity to be conferred by the centre on differing forms of attachment to the area. Was belonging an outcome of unbroken residence through time, as maintained by representatives of the middle class? Or was it created through attachment to a defunct mining industry that had involved intermittent wage migration to destinations outside the community, as maintained by representatives of the working class? In the latter case belonging involved external attachments that helped to create wider, non-local ties of class-based solidarity. The heritage centre provides here a locus around which differing groups weave antithetical narratives of belonging that are all based upon movement. The one involves the need for socially mobile middle-class people to establish a home that exudes an identity of permanent attachment, whereas the other involves the need of a redundant and socially constricted industrial workforce to enlarge its sense of horizon.

The conceptualization of a home site, these case-studies show, is thus not just a matter of identifying a place where one may learn to know oneself best. Indeed, the homes traversed by people in these case-studies are more than important spaces where travellers may search for self-knowledge and establish sources of belonging. These homes also demarcate relations of inclusion and exclusion, which reflect structures of power beyond the domain of those searching for identity. Though these relations may be phrased in terms of uplifting moral discourse on family values and the home, they concern, and conceal, other forms of categorization. Categorizations based upon ethnicity, class, gender (cf. Ortner 1991) are not as open to discussion, because they are a potential source of conflict. We should therefore not always expect homes to be ideal sites for the generation of individual self-knowledge. Nor should we necessarily expect them to be happy places. They may rather be sites where the knowledge and understanding of less socially desirable forms of self and identity are effectively excluded. A pressing issue therefore becomes that of examining why some home sites, in certain socio-cultural contexts, are of greater salience than others, and why such homes become accepted as 'proper'.

The Politics of Home

Migrants of identity are not only involved in a personal, social psychological journey between various personal home sites that they choose, within a fragmented world, for the purpose of developing private identities. The project of getting to know oneself may involve a deeply personal process of reflection and self-awareness; but this process also necessarily engages migrants of identity in a dialogue with significant others. Individuals are therefore not entirely free to conceptualize home sites according to individualized needs. They must somehow deal with homes that are also credible to others. The problems that this may create are vividly brought out in the chapters by Jansen and James, in which they make it clear that not everybody is equally well equipped to find such shared homes amidst the struggle for personal identity. Young children, as James shows, are expected to develop their identity within a specific kind of family home. This means that if children seek to develop forms of self-understanding that do not correspond to the dominant family home ideal their efforts will be suppressed or tend to go unrecognized. The same holds true for those children who may attempt to develop identities in spaces outside the family home, for example, on the street – where children are perceived to be 'matter out of place' (personal communication Olga Nieuwenhuys, in reference to Douglas 1966). Much of the current anthropological research on children and childhood is premised on the idea that children are not passive recipients of the various measures of socialization to which they are exposed during their upbringing, but rather active co-creators of their own childhood (Prout and James 1990). If this is so, anthropologists must also be attuned to the possible existence of other kinds of home, cherished by children, that do not conform to those designated for them by adults. These homes, be they found on the street or in cyberspace, may be sources of migrant identities that confound adult socialization.

Adults are in a better position than children to refuse imposed forms of identity and give vent to their aversion from such forms. This is certainly the case in Jansen's study of ex-Yugoslavian women who preferred to become socially marginalized rather than embrace an unacceptable home. When these women began to experience strong condemnation of their particular concept of a home, and hence of their personal identities, they consequently reacted by becoming even more conscious of their self-knowledge and by engaging in a vehement public assertion of this identity through an outpouring of highly articulate and reflexive writings. Here they were speaking from the point of view of a critical stance towards the national project, which they had developed through their position as 'privileged refugees': cosmopolitan and well-educated persons who were able to see beyond the confines of the local national projects of the new nation-states in post-Yugoslavia. The fact that only a small number of women have articulated a non-nationalistic identity publicly does not necessarily mean that their numbers are small. It may rather indicate that only a small minority is in a position to give voice to this 'other' identity. A study of Bosnian refugees in Denmark thus shows that a fair number of these refugees choose to identify themselves as Yugoslavian, rather than as nationals of Bosnia. They prefer not to make a public issue of this, however, owing to the political conflicts that it may create among Bosnian refugees in Denmark as well as in their relations with family and friends living in the new nation-state of Bosnia (Grünenberg 1997). The ability to define and assert a home therefore requires a certain amount of personal resources.

The political significance of mastering the art of home-making is brought out in Ladislav Holy's analysis of the way in which images of place were created and sustained in the course of the eighteenth century to establish a particular Czech discourse of patriotism. Through a process of 'sacralization' of the natural scenery, language and folk culture of Bohemia this area became a homeland for the entire Czech people. This does not mean that Bohemian folk communities, as actual collectivities of social and economic relations and cultural values, were upheld as a model for the Czech nation. The patriotic movement was spearheaded by the Bohemian nobility, who feared that their political and economic privileges were being undermined by political and administrative measures undertaken by the Austrian Monarchy that then ruled the Czech people. This nobility had no intention of creating a Czech nation according to a Bohemian folk community model. Rather the nobility, and the urban elite who followed them in the Czech national project, used elements of Bohemian folk communities as props to create the imagery of and sentiments toward a homeland that could form the basis of a Czech national entity under their leadership. This staging of Bohemia as a homeland for Czechs was most apparent in the building and decorating of the national theatre, where various aspects of the Bohemian homeland figured prominently. By presenting the nation as a homeland, Holy argues, it became possible to imagine the national community as one big home rather than as shared 'blood and soil or as a community of people linked together through common ancestry' (p. 129). In this way, the national revivalists created a strong, positive image of belonging and a more subtle, but equally effective, image of exclusion in relation to this homeland. Since this homeland was identified largely through Bohemian folk icons with little bearing on the actual relations of everyday life, these mechanisms of inclusion and exclusion were not challenged.

In Nigel Rapport's study of North American 'Anglo-Saxon' Jews we find another example of an influential group of people who have succeeded in defining and sustaining a homeland for themselves. This chapter, which focuses on those Jews who give up their diasporic life to come home to Israel, provides an interesting analysis of some of the problems that arise when this imagined homeland is turned into the site of one's everyday life. In their diasporic situation the Anglo-Saxon Jews have maintained an alienated critical distance from their physical North American or British homeland, which they expect to abandon when they enter their 'real' home; but they do not find this imagined home when they actually immigrate. Rather, they experience Israel primarily in the form of 'centralist and essentialist institutions' (p. 81) that make it increasingly difficult for them to identify Israel as home. In some ways their situation resembles that of the cosmopolitan Yugoslavian women writers who are alienated by the nationalistic climate of the homelands that have been imposed upon them. The immigrants to Israel, however, soon discover that they belong to a large and well-consolidated group of compatriot 'privileged refugees' who are 'equally intent upon individual negotiations and individual settlements' with the Israeli nation-state (ibid.). The critical distancing that they formerly directed against their North American or British home is now redirected toward their new Israeli home. Former diasporic discourses are hereby resurrected as 'immigrant discourses', which then shape the 'routinized homes' that they develop in their new environment.

The fact that immigrants to Israel from widely different places do not have similar socio-cultural backgrounds or interests is of little conse-quence in an individualistic society, where the fact of sharing a 'common opposition' and a desire to stay 'cognitively apart' helps create a familiar 'home-from-home'. Israel is a sufficiently roomy and convenient place for these individuals, who wish to search for and assert their personal identity – at least as long as they qualify for membership in the national community! Indeed, since there may be some disagreement over the specifics of the over-riding national identity of Israel, it may be more convenient for members of this community to find a home for their identity in personal narratives with individual, like-minded fellow citizens than to engage in collective manifestations of cultural identity at the national level. The Israeli project therefore seems to rest comfortably on such personal narratives, related by 'privileged refugees' of alienation.

The great variety of homes examined in the ethnographic cases makes it clear that anthropologists play an important role in the foregrounding of certain identity spaces. The homes selected for anthropological scrutiny do not necessarily represent the only identity spaces of the people under study, or even the most important of these spaces. The children examined by James also live in local communities where they might find various other homes for themselves, just as the inhabitants of Pearman Street belong to differing family homes as well as to the local community examined by Wallman. The particular home chosen by the anthropologist as a focal point of analysis will have important implications for the conclusions that the anthropologist will draw concerning the kind of self-knowledge and identity-making that takes place among the people studied. This is quite apparent in Vered Amit-Talai's study of middle-class expatriates working in offshore branches of multinational firms located in the Cayman Islands.

The expatriates interviewed by Amit-Talai explain that they have left their former homes in North America or Europe in order to pursue their professional careers and the economic possibilities offered by the offshore paradise of the Cayman Islands. They soon find that they have become part of a large international workforce that is expected to remain mobile and is only allowed to touch ground temporarily wherever its skills are needed. This leaves them in a form of limbo, Amit-Talai argues, because they have few or no ties to their former place of residence, yet at the same time they do not tend to develop ties of home to the Caymans. Island policy, in fact, actively hinders this by reserving citizen rights to the native-born population. The expatriates therefore remain in an eternal situation of transience in the Cayman Islands, and find themselves in a situation of longing for, yet fearing their return to the 'real world' outside the liminal space where some of them have lived for many years and raised their families. For Amit-Talai, this study of expatriates provides an opportunity to critique the notion of 'cultural site', which I have used in an analysis of the significance of place in West Indian family networks (Olwig 1997). Since this abstract concept was not intended to be taken literally as applying to all social groups it would, indeed, have been misapplied if used in this way in treating the subjects of Amit-Talai's study. Her study thus exemplifies the way that the anthropologist's choice of home sites in the analyses of ethnographic case-studies has important implications for the understanding of identity-making.

The Social Life of Homes

Home – where you know yourself best – is hardly primarily an abstract discursive space for most people. It is a much more broadly based place of identification generated through what Rapport and Dawson describe as 'a routine set of practices, in a repetition of habitual social interactions, in the ritual of a regularly used personal name' (p. 27). Home, in other words, is created through social relations as they unfold in the give-and-take of ordinary everyday life. Whereas home may become a fairly abstract space of self-knowledge in narratives, it is a very concrete place of mutual relations of exchange, usually involving concrete rights and obligations, in the social life of the narrators.

Closer scrutiny of the social routines of the ordinary life that is associated with home as lived space might help develop a more nuanced conceptualization of this important space of identification. I would here suggest that whereas home necessarily involves a set of social inter-relationships that are attributed with cultural meaning, for example through discourse, the social relationships that are generated through discourse constitute only one form that these interrelationships may take. Thus it may be useful to distinguish between home as a locus involving specific relations of social and economic rights and obligations, and home as a more abstract entity that is primarily expressed through various types of narratives and other forms of symbolic interchange. These two aspects of home mutually reinforce and implicate one another, so that 'home' will not exist in the form of a concrete set of socio-economic rights and obligations if it does not receive some sort of recognition and validation through narratives and other kinds of symbolic expression among inter-acting individuals. Similarly, the social and economic practices of home will have an important bearing on the kinds of narratives of home that will be related by the individuals involved. The expatriates on the Cayman Islands associate their feeling of homelessness with their 'unreal' life in the Cayman Islands, where they are not allowed to establish a permanent home, and they contrast this with the 'reality' of the world from where they come, and where they had a home. According to Amit-Talai, reality would consist of a life of 'real settlement' where these people could find a home for themselves in 'permanence and stability for both work and residence' (p. 53). This reality, one might add, is more than likely also one of routine jobs, lower wages, high taxes and a modest standard of living – all aspects of life that these expatriates are not keen to face again. It is therefore tempting to conclude that these expatriates, like the Anglo-Saxon Jews in Israel, chose not to locate their home in 'reality', but rather in their shared narratives of homelessness. This illustrates the importance of examining processes of identification both at the discursive level and within the wider context of social relations (where discourse is merely one of many forms of social practice), if the anthropologist is to capture the complex tensions between differing ideas and practices of home that become manifest through movement.

It may be argued that discourse and narratives of home have come to constitute the most salient forms of expressing places of belonging in a world in movement, where many social relations are not localized, and therefore within easy reach. I would suggest that this may be a particularly middle-class, Western point of view. It is possible that it is because a number of the authors unconsciously share the middle-class values depicted by Andrew Dawson in the conflict over the North England heritage centre that they tend to choose to examine home as a space of self-knowledge and identity rather than as the space of social relations and awareness emphasized by the working-class miners. By emptying a home of its social content it can be erected as a generalized icon of social collectictivities of various kinds, such as a nation or homeland for those of the right ethnic, religious or economic background, or as an ideal community that reminds one of a long-lost childhood. The upholding of an idealized, harmonious home, associated with specific values and social relations, may create a perfect place of identification for some, a prison for others. The interrelationship between home as a conceptual space of identification and home as a nodal point in social relations is of great importance, and it presents a significant topic for follow-up work within this pioneering approach to identity and movement.

References

Douglas, Mary (1966), *Purity and Danger*, London: Routledge & Kegan Paul.

Grünenberg, Kristina (1997), *"Det Tomme Rum?" Midlertidighed, flygtningelandsbyer og bosniske krigsflygtninge i Danmark*. University of Copenhagen, Institute of Anthropology, Kandidatspeciale.

Olwig, Karen Fog (1997), 'Cultural Sites: Sustaining a Home in a Deterritorialized World', pp.17–38 in Karen Fog Olwig and Kirsten Hastrup (eds), *Siting Culture. The Shifting Anthropological Object*, London: Routledge.

Ortner, Sherry (1991), 'Reading America: Preliminary Notes on Class and Culture,' pp. 163–89 in Richard G. Fox*Recapturing Anthropology*, (ed.), Santa Fé: School of American Research Press.

Prout, Alan and James, Allison (1990), 'A new Paradigm for the Sociology of Childhood? Provenance, Promise and Problems', in *Constructing and Reconstructing Childhood: Contemporary Issues in the Sociological Study of Childhood*, pp 7–34, London: The Falmer Press.

Sahlins, Marshall (1985), *Islands of History*, Chicago: University of Chicago Press.

List of Contributors

Vered Amit-Talai: Associate Professor of Anthropology, Concordia University of Montreal.

Andrew Dawson: Lecturer in Social Anthropology, University of Hull.

Eric Hirsch: Lecturer in Social Anthropology, Brunel University.

Ladislav Holy (deceased): Professor of Social Anthropology University of St. Andrews.

Allison James: Reader in Applied Anthropology, University of Hull.

Stef Jansen: Researcher in Sociology and Anthropology, University of Hull.

Karen Fog Olwig: Senior Lecturer in Anthropology, University of Copenhagen.

Nigel Rapport: Professor of Anthropological and Philosophical Studies, University of St. Andrews.

Sandra Wallman: Professor of Urban Change, University College London.

Index

Alderson, P. 145
alienation, 162–7, 176–8, 228, 233
Allan, G. & Crow, G. 143, 208
Allen, V. 208
americans, 3, 13, 55, 63–81 *passim*, 232
Amit-Talai, V. 10–12, 234–5
Anderson, B. 123
Appadurai, A. 11, 26, 42, 91, 218
Apple, M. 151
appropriation, 163–7, 176–8, 228
Aries, P. 144
Aronoff, M. 64
Aronowitz, S. 56
Arshi, S. 28
Atwood, M. 85
Auge, M. 6, 7, 22, 107, 218
Avruch, K. 64, 66, 78

Bachelard, G. 80
Balbin, B. 118
Bammer, A. 7, 86
Bar-Tal, D. 113
Barth, F. 183, 197
Basch, L. 43, 52, 56
Bateson, G. 9, 19–21, 26, 33
Bauman, Z. 88, 100–1
Beaverstock, J. 44
belonging, 16–17, 22, 53–5, 91–4, 111, 130, 144, 146, 151, 181–4, 191–3, 198, 203–4, 218, 229, 232, 236 *see also* community
Bennett, C. 98
Berger, J. 5–7, 23–4, 27–8, 30, 34, 80

Berger, P. & B. 10, 31–2
Bernardes, J. 143
Bhabha, H. 42, 88, 101
Bhachu, P. 45
Billig, M. 113, 122–3
Bourdieu, P. 20, 164
Brooks, P. 34
Brow, J. 210
Bulmer, M. 209
Butor, M. 19, 34

Campbell, C. 163
Campbell, D. 51
Carrier, J. 10, 177
Carter, P. 22
Castells, M. 42
Cayman Islands, 10, 12–13, 41–56 *passim*, 234–5
Certeau, M. de 105, 107
Chambers, I. 9, 23–4, 27–8, 33, 55, 85, 105–6
Chaplin, S. 220
children and childhood, 10–11, 14–16, 139–58, 161–2, 166, 168, 172, 174–5, 204, 227–31, 234, 236 *see also* youth
Clark, A. 146
Clarke, L. 146
Clifford, J. 5, 23, 32–3, 88, 106, 218–19
Cohen, E. 64
Cohen, L. 93
Colley, L. 163
community, 6–7, 10–11, 13, 16–17, 23, 29–32, 42, 55, 63, 75, 81, 111–4, 123, 128–9, 134, 151, 171, 182, 185–91,